TYCHO BRAHE AND THE MEASURE OF THE HEAVENS

☞ Books in the RENAISSANCE LIVES series explore and illustrate the life histories and achievements of significant artists, intellectuals and scientists in the early modern world. They delve into literature, philosophy, the history of art, science and natural history and cover narratives of exploration, statecraft and technology.

Series Editor: François Quiviger

TYCHO BRAHE

and the Measure of the Heavens

JOHN ROBERT CHRISTIANSON

REAKTION BOOKS

In Memory of Mentors
Copenhagen & Minneapolis 1956—64

Lawrence D. Steefel (1894—1976)
Sven Henningsen (1910—1982)
David Harris Willson (1901—1973)
John B. Wolf (1907—1996)
Ralph E. Giesey (1923—2011)
Marion John Nelson (1924—2000)

Published by Reaktion Books Ltd
Unit 32, Waterside
44—48 Wharf Road
London N1 7UX, UK
www.reaktionbooks.co.uk

First published 2020

Printed and bound in China by 1010 Printing International Ltd

A catalogue record for this book is available from the British Library

ISBN 978 1 78914 234 1

COVER: From Tycho Brahe: *Astronomiae instaurate mechanica*,
(Wandsbeck, 1598), original woodcut or engraving later coloured
at unknown date; Open access courtesy of LMU Munich.

CONTENTS

The heavens declare the glory of God,
And the firmament sheweth his handywork.
Day unto day uttereth speech,
And night unto night sheweth knowledge.
PSALM 19:1–2

Where wast thou when I laid the foundations of the earth?
declare, if thou hast understanding. Who hath laid the meas-
ures thereof, if thou knowest? or who hath stretched the line
upon it? Whereupon are the foundations thereof fastened? or
who laid the corner stone thereof; When the morning stars
sang together, and all the sons of God shouted for joy?
JOB 38:4–7

Daten sind der Rohstoff der Zukunft.
'Data are the raw material of the future.'
ANGELA MERKEL, 11 JUNE 2015

Preface: Denmark and the Renaissance

 AS THERE EVER A Renaissance in Scandinavia? Danish museums and other cultural institutions clearly thought so when they decided to celebrate 'the Year of the Renaissance' (*Renæssanceåret*) in 2006. During that year, art historians dived with full force into an international conference on *Reframing the Danish Renaissance*.[1] Thomas DaCosta Kaufmann brought the discouraging news that the Renaissance came to Denmark 'only belatedly, and in late or Mannerist forms . . . not just at second but at third hand'. He dated the Danish Renaissance, such as it was, to 1559–1650, and said it began when artists and architects from the Low Countries arrived 'as intermediaries or indeed surrogates for Italians or for the Italian art which the Danes could not get'. Kaufmann thought it would be better to give up on the concept of a 'Danish Renaissance' and try to view Denmark more positively as a cultural 'frontier', where productive interaction took place between Central Europe, Scandinavia and the Baltic and North Sea regions. Birgitte Bøggild Johannsen disagreed and said that 'cultural traffic . . . of basically classical origin and Italian transmission' was not so belated after all, since it began to arrive in Denmark three-quarters of a century earlier than 1559 with a Saxon queen of Denmark who mediated contacts with the art of Dürer and Cranach and patronized art that used perspectival space and classical decorations. Bøggild Johannsen wanted to 'decentre' the whole concept of the Renaissance, to see it as a cultural movement in which every region had its own Renaissance (*cujus regio, ejus renovatio*), including often a Gothic Renaissance that glorified *patriae mores* ('native ways'), as in Denmark. Tycho Brahe was barely mentioned in the course of this debate among art historians.

A book published in 2006 entitled *Danmark og renæssancen, 1500–1650* (Denmark and the Renaissance, 1500–1650), however, did have a chapter on Tycho Brahe – it showed him to be a humanist who cultivated the Muses and Hermes Trismegistus and who was influenced by Renaissance authors such as Ficino, Pico, Paracelsus and Copernicus.[2] A third book, edited by Håkan Håkansson, published in the same year, focused directly on Tycho Brahe and his relationship to the Renaissance.[3] It described Tycho as a humanist who aspired to revive ancient wisdom and whose drive *ad fontes* led him to the empirical method of the ancients, which inspired his innovative discoveries. The authors of this collective work saw Tycho as an aristocrat and talented Latin poet who emulated Ovid and built his observatory-residence in the tradition of an Italian Renaissance villa, and as an astronomer of epochal achievement whose extensive Latin correspondence 'consolidated and maintained the international community of science that existed in Europe of the Renaissance'.[4] From the periphery, these authors wanted to move Tycho Brahe to the centre of the Renaissance in Denmark.

And there he was, at the heart of the most ambitious public event of Denmark's 'Year of the Renaissance', a major exhibit at the National Museum in Copenhagen entitled 'The World of Tycho Brahe: Denmark in Europe, 1550–1600'. This large exhibit included 450 artefacts ranging from tapestries, paintings, altarpieces, scientific instruments and a mounted knight in armour, to extensive use of film and interactive materials, supplemented by scholarly lectures, performances and curricular materials, as well as twenty scholarly studies by established Danish experts who saw Tycho Brahe not simply as Danish but as a world-class figure of the late Renaissance.[5]

This activity and scholarship in the Scandinavian languages reached out to deal with a wide range of Tycho Brahe's cultural activities, while scholarship in the major languages continued to see him primarily as an astronomer.[6] As this book searches to find his place in Renaissance life, it will be necessary to draw on this extensive Nordic literature and integrate it in some way with the research and writing on Tycho Brahe's astronomy by researchers in many lands.

Victor E. Thoren's monumental 1990 biography was a milestone in scholarship on Tycho Brahe's astronomy, just as Peter Zeeberg's 1994 study of his long Latin poem, *Urania Titani*, was a turning point in the study of Tycho's cultural achievement.[7] My own *On Tycho's Island* (2000) examined the organization and staffing of Tycho's research centre at Uraniborg and pointed to the impact of his former assistants upon seventeenth-century science.[8] Poul Grinder-Hansen's recent biography of King Frederick II and his history of Kronborg Castle threw new light on the Danish cultural context, as works by Eliška Fučiková and others have done on Emperor Rudolf II's Prague.[9] Dreyer's edition of Tycho's collected works in fifteen volumes continues to provide a foundation for studies of Tycho Brahe, as it has done for the past century, even though its editorial principles have been seriously challenged in recent years.[10]

It now appears that Denmark's connection with the Renaissance began with the Italian journey of King Christian I in 1475, which was led by a court marshal who was an ancestor of Tycho Brahe. This 'pilgrimage' to Rome was commemorated in works of art in Castello di Malpaga near Bergamo, Mantegna's Camera degli Sposi in Mantua, and the Ospedale Santo Spirito in Sassia in Rome, where Pope Sixtus IV received King Christian with enormous pomp. In the next generation, Renaissance artists influenced the court of Queen Christine in Odense; in the third generation, King Christian II and his Habsburg Queen, Elizabeth of Austria, welcomed Erasmus of Rotterdam to their court, patronized Albrecht Dürer, Lucas Cranach, Jan Gossaert, Jacob Binck and Quentin Metsys, and began to reform Danish education along Erasmian lines. The Lutheran Reformation of 1536 established a solid humanist curriculum in Danish grammar schools and the University of Copenhagen. The following generation of Danish noblemen and theologians went on long academic tours to Wittenberg and other universities in Germany, Switzerland, France and Italy. This in turn fuelled the blossoming of Late Renaissance and Mannerist art and culture under King Frederick II in the prosperous years after 1570, when Tycho Brahe occupied a central place in Danish cultural life.

This book will argue that Tycho Brahe's Uraniborg was established as a satellite to Kronborg Castle and functioned as the royal chamber of arts and wonders (*Kunst- und Wunderkammer*), an integral part of Danish royal power and prestige.

Kronborg and Uraniborg together formed a site of courtly Renaissance culture comparable to Castiglione's Urbino, Lorenzo the Magnificent's Florence, Emperor Rudolf II's Prague, and the England of Bacon and Shakespeare under Queen Elizabeth I. In two of these brilliant places, Uraniborg and Prague, Tycho Brahe established and promoted principles of scientific research that helped to shape the mainstream of modern science. Previous research has focused on Tycho's observational data and theoretical models. This book focuses on his empirical methods and shows that they had a more profound and enduring effect on the history of science.

ONE

Birthright Challenged, 1546–70

CRIES OF CHILDBIRTH at daybreak, and 'then was my son Tyge born during the day between nine and ten at Knutstorp [Castle]', wrote Otto Brahe.[1] It was 14 December 1546, just after the shortest day of the year in the Julian calendar, when the sun rose at half past nine and set at half past four in the Danish province of Skåne. Following Nordic custom, the infant received his paternal grandfather's given name and a patronymic, as well as his noble surname: Tyge Brahe Ottesen. At university, he Latinized Tyge to Tycho. 'Man is the measure of all things,' Pythagoras said. This child would measure the stars and find ways to take the measure of all things.

Beate Bille and Otto Brahe had been married two years, and she had borne a daughter named Lisbeth before Tycho.[2] One year after Tycho's birth, on 21 December 1547, came a second son, Steen, born at Gladsaxehus Castle in eastern Skåne. Now, Otto and Beate had two healthy sons, and 'it happened by a particular decree of Fate' that Tycho was taken away 'without the knowledge of my parents' by 'my beloved paternal uncle Jørgen Brahe, who . . . brought me up, and thereafter he supported me generously during his lifetime until my eighteenth year, and he always treated me as his own

1, 2 Marcus Jordan's map of Denmark (engraving 1585). *Detail*: Skåne (SCHA-NI-A) and the Sound (*Œrs Sunt*) with its name divided by the island of Hven; Knutstorp was just below 'SCHA' on the insert, Herrevad Abbey (*Heratzcloster*) just above.

son . . . For his own marriage was childless.'[3] Jørgen Brahe of Tosterup was married to 'the noble and wise Mistress Inger Oxe, a sister of the great Peter Oxe, who later became [Steward of the Realm] of the Danish royal court [and who] as long as she lived regarded me with exceptional love, as if I were her own son'.[4] Tycho was five when Jørgen Brahe became governor (*lensmand*) of Vordingborg Castle, one of the largest commands in Denmark. Three years later, the Dowager Queen Sophie of Pomerania put him in charge of Nykøbing Castle while he remained the king's governor at Vordingborg.

Tycho's 'particular decree of Fate' meant that he was sent to grammar school at seven, 'for my father, Otto Brahe, whom I recollect with deference, was not particularly anxious that his five sons, of whom I am the eldest, should learn Latin'.[5] Jørgen Brahe and Inger Oxe wanted Tycho to become a cosmopolitan Renaissance courtier like his uncle Peter Oxe, and to be trained in Latin, Greek, the humanities and the law to serve as a diplomat, administrator and councillor.

A ten-year-old boy could hardly grasp the speed with which Peter Oxe fell from high favour in 1556 when he withdrew from court, resigned all his offices and then in June 1558 fled for his life.[6] All of Peter Oxe's brothers-in-law lost their major commands, but the Dowager Queen saw no reason to deprive Jørgen Brahe of Nykøbing Castle.

As these events transpired, Tycho was learning to read, write, speak and understand Latin with remarkable speed and was ready to enter university at the age of twelve. He came to Copenhagen and lived in the household of a professor who supervised his studies.[7] When his brother Steen turned twelve one year later, however, he was not sent to school but placed in service at Vordingborg Castle as a page to Councillor Steen Rosensparre of Skarhult and Mette Rosenkrantz.[8]

Denmark was an elective monarchy governed by a narrow elite of interrelated families whose members occupied the Council of the Realm (*Rigsråd*). This body held the power to elect kings and to negotiate a *håndfæstning* or charter that bound the monarch to obey the law and guaranteed the privileges of all estates, and they required each king to sign such a charter before his coronation. The Council advised the king, held major commands and court offices, sat annually at Whitsuntide with the king as the supreme Court of King in Council (*Retterting*), and could depose a monarch who did not abide by his *håndfæstning*. Five senior Councillors held the high administrative offices of Steward of the Realm, Royal Chancellor, Marshal of the Realm, Admiral of the Realm and Chancellor of the Realm.[9] Tycho's father, both grandfathers and all four of his great-grandfathers sat in the Council of the Realm, and many of his ancestors held these high offices.

Councillors bore no title of nobility beyond the 'honourable and wellborn' (*ærlig og velbyrdig*) of all Danish nobles.[10] Every member of a Danish noble family was noble and displayed the same coat of arms. The Brahe arms was 'sable, a pale argent' and the crest 'a peacock feather upright between two urochs horns sable, a fess argent, each bearing four peacock feathers fesswise'. Patents of nobility were extremely rare, which meant that the nobility was essentially a closed caste that traced noble descent in all paternal and maternal lines.

Intermarriage between the royal houses of Denmark, Norway and Sweden in the late middle ages had left a single heiress, Queen Margaret, as ruler of all three kingdoms. In

1397 her three Councils elected Erik of Pomerania as her successor but deposed him in 1439 and elected Christopher of Bavaria. When King Christopher III died without issue in 1448, the three Councils in turn elected a duke of Oldenburg as King Christian I, whose direct descendants rule Denmark and Norway to this day.[11] When Christian I's grandson, Christian II, tried to break the power of the aristocracy, all three Councils deposed him. Sweden broke away from the union, and Gustavus Vasa, Tycho's kinsman, founded a new dynasty to rule Sweden, while Denmark and

3 *Peter Oxe*, 1574, oil on wood.

Norway elected Christian's uncle as King Frederick I.[12]
Christian fled to Brabant with his Habsburg queen in 1523,
and when he later tried to return in force, he was taken
prisoner.

Two years earlier in Worms, Frederick I's eighteen-
year-old son, Duke Christian, witnessed Martin Luther's
stalwart defence before Emperor Charles and became a
fervent Lutheran. He implemented a Lutheran Reformation in Schleswig-Holstein by 1529 as his father's Viceroy
(*Statthalter, Statholder*).[13] When Frederick died in 1533, aristocratic Catholic prelates persuaded the Council of the Realm

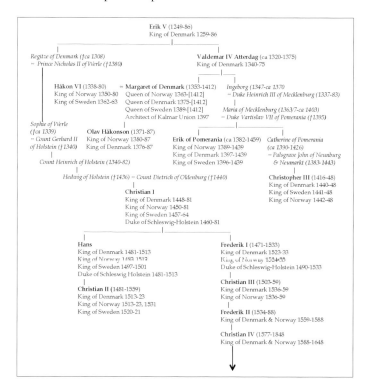

4 Kings of Denmark, 1249–1648.

to postpone the election rather than elect Duke Christian, whereupon he raised an army and conquered his father's kingdom by force of arms.[14] As King Christian III of Denmark and Norway by 1536, he deposed the bishops, proclaimed a Lutheran Reformation, and merged the Norwegian Council into the Danish Council. All Church property – around one-third of the entire Kingdom of Denmark – was confiscated and added to the royal domain. The monarch was more powerful than ever before in a vast realm that reached from the Elbe to North Cape and from Iceland to Gotland. His Council of the Realm now consisted entirely of Danish

5 Matthäus Merian the Elder, *Following in the Footsteps of Nature*, 1618, engraving.

and a few Norwegian landed aristocrats, including all the families of Tycho's kinship. Crown and Council in 'strategic alliance' established a highly centralized Lutheran 'diarchy' led by a patriarchal monarch whose court was characterized by order, piety and moderation.[15] The immense royal domain was administered by councillors and their kinsmen at the pleasure of the king.

In the wake of Christian III's Reformation, Copenhagen University was reorganized on the model of Wittenberg with Philip Melanchthon's *studia humanitatis* as the entry to all further studies. Just as Martin Luther had pushed aside centuries of commentary and returned to the original sources of Christian theology in the New Testament and Church Fathers, his friend Philip had returned the seven liberal arts to the sources of wisdom – *ad fontes* – of classical Latin, Greek and Hebrew. Asserting that Cicero and Seneca were more enjoyable than medieval commentaries, Melanchthon immersed students in classical literature and instilled in them the humanist virtues of eloquence, erudition and prudence as well as Lutheran theology and morals.[16] Tycho thrived on these studies and soon discovered Ovid to be his favourite poet.

In his second year at university, a partial eclipse of the Sun occurred on 21 August 1560.[17] Astronomy was not part of preparation for the law, so Tycho was not allowed to attend lectures in the subject. He responded by buying books and studying astronomy on his own.[18] His edition of Johannes de Sacrobosco's *De sphaera* (On the Spheres) contained a preface by Melanchthon that linked astronomy with astrology, which in turn connected the stars to the human microcosm. Melanchthon asserted that astronomy was ultimately a search for the divine mathematical laws that both governed celestial motion and were the 'manifest footprints of God in nature'.[19] Luther taught that Divine Law was written into the laws of Nature as well as Holy Scripture. His theology distinguished between Law and Gospel and asserted that the two forms of Law led us towards faith in the Gospel, the 'good news' that Christ died for our salvation.[20] Tycho's understanding of astronomy-astrology was shaped by these 'Philippist' and Lutheran ideas.

Sacrobosco explained the 'doctrine of the spheres' as the first part of astronomy. The annual path of the Sun circled a plane called the 'ecliptic' that ran through the centre of the 'zodiac', divided at 30° intervals into 'houses', and it crossed the celestial equator (*equinoctial*) twice a year at the 'equinoxes'. The 'zenith' was directly above an observer, and the 'horizon' surrounded him. Every celestial body reached daily 'culminations' at its highest and lowest points on the observer's 'meridian', a great circle through the poles.[21] Sacrobosco also explained Earth's seven climate zones, how eclipses were caused, and how the Sun, Moon and five planets were carried around the zodiac on combinations of circles.

The second part of astronomy was the 'theory of the planets', which had been in dispute ever since Nicolaus Copernicus' Sun-centred cosmology appeared three years before Tycho was born. Sacrobosco followed an alternative system based on the physics of Aristotle's ancient, Earth-centred universe and the astronomy of Claudius Ptolemy.

The third part of astronomy was how to *observe* the stars. Tycho wanted to teach himself this part, even though it was not included in the university curriculum. In 1561, when he

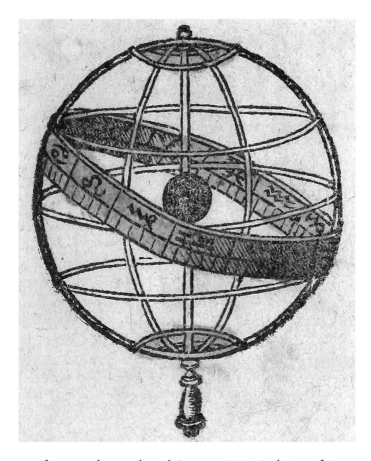

was fourteen, he purchased Gemma Frisius' edition of Peter Apian's *Cosmographia*, which told how to measure angles and locate objects in the skies and on Earth.[22] He also purchased Johannes Regiomontanus' *On Triangles*, which explained how to use trigonometry to calculate the relative positions of celestial bodies for casting horoscopes.[23] Tycho and his student friend Jens Nilssøn acquired the ephemerides of Giovanni Battista Carelli around 1561, which contained

6 Tycho's copy of Sacrobosco's *De sphaera* showed the zodiac on the sphere of the heavens encircling Earth.

tables showing the positions of the Sun, Moon and planets at future times. The 'ecliptical coordinates' used in the tables were *latitude* measured north or south of the ecliptic and *longitude* measured eastwards from the point of the vernal equinox. In observing, Tycho used the 'horizontal coordinates' of *altitude* measured from the true horizon and *azimuth* measured clockwise around the horizon from the point of south, and he learned how to transform these observed 'horizontal coordinates' into the 'ecliptical coordinates' of the ephemerides.

Carelli based his tables of future celestial positions on the fourteenth-century *Alfonsine Tables*. Over the centuries, a slow movement of the Earth's axis had caused a gradual shift in the apparent positions of stars called the 'precession of the equinoxes'. Copernicus had calculated new tables to account for this shift, and Erasmus Reinhold of Wittenberg used Copernicus' tables and theories to calculate the *Prutenic Tables*, from which Johannes Stadius had calculated Copernican ephemerides. Tycho also acquired the ephemerides of Stadius and began to compare its predictions with those of Carelli. In doing so, he was comparing the accuracy of Copernicus' models with those of Ptolemy.

By the time he turned fifteen, Tycho had spent three years studying the Philippist *trivium* of classical languages, literature and logic, and his mentors considered him ready to begin the study of law abroad. Jørgen Brahe engaged an older student, Anders Sørensen Vedel, to serve as his tutor, and in February 1562 they set off to Germany's best law school at Leipzig University, where they lodged in the household of a law professor.[24]

Steen Brahe also went abroad in 1562, when Frederick II arranged his appointment as squire to Count Günther of Schwarzburg-Arnstadt, the Danish envoy to the court of the dowager Duchess Christina of Lorraine. She was Christian II's daughter and was on dangerously good terms with her powerful Habsburg cousins. Moreover, Peter Oxe had entered her service, fomenting wild schemes to gain the throne of Denmark-Norway.[25] Count Günther's mission was to still her wrath by proposing marriage between King Frederick and Christina's daughter, Renata of Lorraine, but Count Günther was also a fiery man, and negotiations soon broke off with bellicose threats.[26]

Although not always diplomatic, Count Günther was eminently suited to train Steen Brahe in the new style of mounted combat. His 'black knights' wore light blue-black plate armour and were armed with swords and a pair of wheel lock pistols. Steen learned how black knights advanced at a trot and executed complex manoeuvres en masse, which demanded discipline, courage and keen horsemanship.

Far from fields of war, Tycho attended lectures in law at Leipzig and secretly studied the astronomy books that Vedel forbade him to use. With a celestial globe 'the size of a fist', he learned the names of all the stars. 'I learned this by myself, without any guidance,' he wrote, 'in fact I never had the benefit of a teacher in mathematics, otherwise I might have made quicker and better progress in these subjects'.[27] This was not actually true. A professor of astronomy-astrology would have taught him that observing stars was a waste of time when it was quicker to look them up in the ephemerides or an almanac. But observation was what he loved, and he

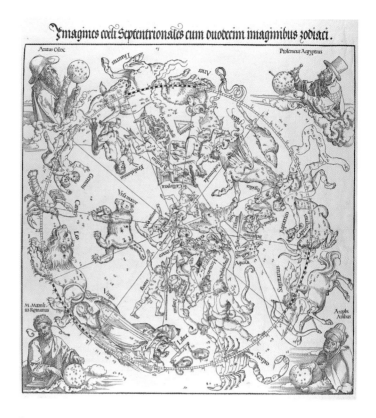

7 Albrecht Dürer's star map of the northern hemisphere, 1515, woodcut.

kept at it. 'Untrammelled by authority, he was free to think creatively.'[28]

These were dangerous times. By 1563 the plots of Peter Oxe, Duchess Christina and their violent confederate Wilhelm von Grumbach raged unabated in Germany and Denmark veered into war with Sweden. Count Günther took command of the Danish army.[29] Steen and most Danish noblemen strapped on armour, but Tycho Brahe was reading law and secretly watching the heavens to observe Saturn and Jupiter approaching conjunction, as they did once every twenty years. The conjunction of 1563 would be followed by another in 1583, which would conclude a 240-year sequence of conjunctions in the three houses of the Watery Trigon. The astrological consequences would be profound.[30]

Tycho had no observational instrument in 1563, but he invented a new tool: the observational notebook. This was not another book full of columns of numbers, but a journal that combined narrative, data and occasional illustrations to describe observations as they took place. Tycho's notebook, one of the great icons of modern science, is preserved today in the Royal Library in Copenhagen. Its first page is headed, 'Anno 1563, seventeen years of age, Leipzig'. After a brief morning observation of Mars, Tycho began at 1:34 a.m. on 18 August 1563 to record his observations of Jupiter and Saturn as they approached conjunction, visually comparing the narrowing distance between them with the gap between various pairs of fixed stars. On 23 August, he observed the planets so close together that they appeared like one immense celestial light. The conjunction was taking place before his very eyes.

The exhilaration of these observations was dashed when he turned to his ephemerides. According to Carelli, the conjunction was not due until 17 September, while Stadius had it on 24 August. How could they be so different, and so wrong? 'I no longer trusted the ephemerides,' he wrote, because they 'suffered from intolerable errors'.[31] Tycho was discovering that the true source of astronomical wisdom was not in books but in the stars themselves. He began to redefine what it meant to return to the ultimate sources, *ad fontes*, of astronomy. Classical and modern literature could provide a conceptual or philosophical framework for astronomy, a system of coordinates, an awareness of God's footprints in the stars, and even instructions for making an instrument, but Tycho now realized that to be an astronomer meant to be an observer. Still short of his seventeenth birthday, without a teacher to guide his practices, Tycho Brahe continued to go his own way and began to acquire 'confidence that what one is already inclined to do is not trivial'.[32]

Tycho plotted the changing positions of Saturn and Jupiter against Albrecht Dürer's star map, compared these positions with the *Alfonsine Tables*, and entered them in his observational notebook.[33] He also began to cast horoscopes of famous individuals using methods described in a book by Melanchthon's friend Johannes Garcaeus, which he entered into a second notebook. Like other perambulating students, Tycho carried a third notebook, an autograph book or *album amicorum* (*stambog, Stammbuch*) in which friends, famous professors and others wrote their names and comments.[34] He kept these three notebooks, each with a purpose of its own.

Keeping a notebook led him to realize that to observe did not simply mean to look: it meant to look, measure and record. In order to measure, instruments were essential. He began to measure celestial angles by using 'a rather large pair of compasses as well as I could, placing the vertex close to my eye and directing one of the legs towards the planet to be observed and the other towards some fixed star near it'.[35] In the spring of 1564, he followed Gemma's instructions and made his first real instrument, a cross-staff, sometimes called a radius or Jacob's staff. It consisted of a calibrated wooden staff around 1 metre (40 in.) in length with a shorter,

sliding staff attached at right angles. An older student and avid cartographer named Bartholomaeus Scultetus showed Tycho how his teacher, Johannes Homelius, had improved subdivision of the scale by placing dots at regular intervals along transversal lines behind the calibration, and Tycho did this on his cross-staff.[36]

Tycho recorded his first cross-staff observations at nine in the evening on 1 May 1564, when he measured angular

8 Tycho Brahe in 1563 drew a sketch of compasses used to observe angles between stars.

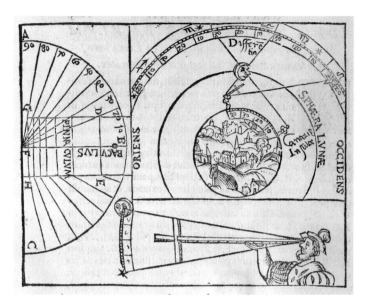

distances between four visible planets and compared his observed positions with the ephemerides of Stadius and Carelli.[37]

> When I had got this radius, I eagerly set about making stellar observations whenever I enjoyed the benefit of a clear sky, and often I stayed awake the whole night through, watching them from a window of one floor, while my [tutor] slept and knew nothing about it.[38]

Observatio generally referred to a 'normative observance' like a monastic rule, but in astronomy and medicine it was beginning to take on the new meaning of 'empirical study of phenomena'.[39] Georg Peurbach had introduced *observatio* to Renaissance astronomy-astrology in the 1450s, and his

9 Apian's illustration of a cross-staff, 1564.

student Johannes Regiomontanus had observed with Bernhard Walther from a balcony in Nuremberg in the years 1471–1500. Now, young Tycho also began to develop what historian Katharine Park describes as 'the habitus of an observer: consistent, disciplined, highly attuned to sources of error, and constantly seeking to improve the quality of his records'.[40]

In his self-taught enthusiasm, Tycho began to discover anomalies that needed to be explained, like the fact that angular distances measured with the cross-staff did not always agree with each other. He searched for the cause of error, found it, and made a table of corrections.[41] His nineteenth-century biographer considered this treatment of 'instrumental error' to be an epochal discovery that guided 'the art of observing into the paths in which modern observers have followed'.[42]

In late May 1565, after three years in Leipzig, Tycho and Vedel came home to a Denmark locked in war.[43] Count Günther had failed to conquer Sweden and had departed to fight the Ottomans in Hungary with Steen Brahe at his side. Tycho's younger brothers, Axel and Jørgen, were also abroad, learning the ways of courtly black knights. Soon after Tycho's return, King Frederick's horse stumbled on the drawbridge to Copenhagen Castle and threw him into the water. Jørgen Brahe plunged in and saved his life, but then took ill and died on 21 June 1565.[44] Because he died intestate, Jørgen Brahe's large estate did not go to Tycho, as he had intended, but to Otto Brahe and his sisters, who turned over lifetime possession to Inger Oxe.

Consequently, Tycho came to live with his birth parents at Aalborghus Castle, where Otto Brahe was governor and also a Councillor of the Realm. Tycho did not observe the stars that entire year but gradually persuaded his father to support his studies of the law abroad.[45] Hans Aalborg, son of an Aalborg alderman, was engaged as his tutor, and in the spring of 1566, they departed for Wittenberg. When a pestilence temporarily closed Wittenberg University, they left in September for Rostock.[46]

Rostock was a Philippist university like Copenhagen, Leipzig and Wittenberg. Tycho lived in the household of Lucas Bacmeister, a professor of theology. Tycho's problems began when he read a lunar eclipse on 28 October 1566 to foretell the death of Suleiman the Magnificent and posted a Latin poem to that effect in the university. Soon after, news arrived that the sultan had died almost six weeks before the eclipse.[47] This was a humiliating but useful lesson on the perils of astrology.

An even greater blow came during a betrothal celebration at Yuletide, when Tycho argued with a 'hot-headed gentleman', a fellow Danish student named Manderup Parsberg.[48] They clashed again at a party on 27 December, and a third time over supper two days later, when they shouted in Danish and stormed outside with rapiers and daggers drawn. Professor Bacmeister's wife urged the others to follow, but it was too late. In midwinter darkness, Tycho's face was covered in blood, and half of his nose was hacked away.[49] Two weeks after turning twenty, he was terribly scarred for life.

The renowned Rostock medical faculty was sadly depleted. There were only two professors, one of whom was young Levinus Battus, full of the new *chymical* therapies of Theophrastus Paracelsus. His colleague, Heinrich Brucaeus, was grounded in the *observatio* of empirical pathology. As Tycho's wounds healed, he learned to wear a flesh-coloured nasal

prosthesis and rub on adhesive ointment from time to time.[50] The healing process gave him time to think and consider his future path in life.

He returned home during the summer holiday of 1567 and announced that he was abandoning the study of law to become a 'natural philosopher'. What must his family have thought when they saw their elegant, grey-eyed and reddish blond-haired lad with these terrible scars clawing across his face, and heard him make such an outrageous proposal? The Bille and Oxe family trees included learned bishops, archbishops and royal chancellors but no 'natural philosophers'. Tycho's brothers were still abroad, doing the right thing in training to be courtly warriors, while Otto Brahe had just led a harrowing winter foray into Sweden. In times like these, what was Tycho thinking?

Perhaps his learned uncle, Steen Bille, would have understood, but he was in command of troops on the Swedish

10 Tobias Stimmer, woodcut of a duelling stance with rapier and dagger, 1570.

border. Peter Oxe would have understood, for he had recently returned from abroad. Through an elaborate series of diplomatic manoeuvres, he had made his peace with Frederick II, returned to a seat in the Council of the Realm, and was now serving as Statholder of Copenhagen. In August 1567, this brilliant financial manager was named Steward of the Realm and took complete charge of the depleted royal finances.[51]

What happened next is unknown. Tycho stayed home until the end of the year and did not observe the stars, then dashed off to Rostock without a tutor. He arrived on 1 January 1568, stayed with Levinus Battus and immediately resumed observing the heavens.[52] On 14 January 1568 he wrote to Hans Aalborg that he planned to await the future in Rostock, 'But my dear Hans, you must bury in deep silence the cause of my departure.'[53] Clearly, something was up. He was in trouble with Rostock's university authorities for getting into the duel, but Peter Oxe intervened to bail him out.[54]

That spring, royal letters patent were issued at Copenhagen Castle, promising Tycho Brahe the next vacant canonry in the collegiate chapter of Roskilde and its endowed prebend.[55] This was what he had been waiting for, and Peter Oxe must have arranged it. With a sinecure like a canonry in the Lutheran cathedral and his eventual inheritance, Tycho could maintain the honourable lifestyle of an aristocrat and spend the rest of his life studying whatever interested him. When he received this news, he ended his years of lukewarm legal studies and headed south, possibly through Wittenberg and Leipzig. He may have been at Castle Neideck when Count Günther of Schwarzburg dubbed Steen Brahe a knight, presented him with spurs, a warhorse and a suit of armour, and

11 Unknown artist, *Urania instructing Ptolemy in the Use of a Quadrant, c.* 1508, woodcut.

saw him off with three black knights under his command to join the personal entourage of Prince William of Orange.[56]

In Nuremberg, Tycho purchased a fine cross-staff and a set of astronomical rings made by Walter Arscenius, a nephew of Gemma Frisius.[57] In Ingolstadt, he visited Peter Apian's son, Philip, a keen observer of heavens and earth, whose huge, triangulated map of Bavaria was one of the cartographic marvels of the age.[58] Eventually, he came to Basel, the city of Paracelsus and Erasmus, where he matriculated in the university with several other Danes and began to prepare for a future career as an aristocratic canon and natural philosopher.[59]

Tycho wanted a more accurate instrument and began to experiment with quadrants, assisted by a young scholar named Hugo Blotius. Quadrants were usually small, hand-held instruments, but Tycho designed one that was 1–1.5 metres (4–5 ft) in radius and precisely graduated, which was so big it proved to be unstable in the wind.[60] In solving one problem, he had created another.

Tycho continued to seek out authorities on astronomy-astrology. He visited Erasmus Oswald Schreckenfuchs in Freiburg im Breisgau near Basel and admired his collection of instruments.[61] Early in the spring of 1569, he left Basel, followed the Danube to Lauingen near Augsburg, and called on Cyprianus Leovitius, a former student of Philip Melanchthon whose astrological prophecies were famous.[62] Tycho knew that Abu Ma'shar of Baghdad (Albumasar), centuries earlier, had discovered patterns of universal history marked by conjunctions of Saturn and Jupiter, and he knew that Leovitius was a renowned authority. These conjunctions remained within a 'trigon' of the same three zodiacal houses for 240 years and then advanced to a new trigon, passing in turn through the four Trigons of Fire, Earth, Air and Water before returning to the first point of Aries, the site of the vernal equinox, every eight hundred years.[63]

Major changes in human affairs occurred with the Great Conjunction that came at the end of each trigon, and even greater changes with the Maximum Conjunction at the start of the whole eight-hundred-year cycle.[64] Both Martin Luther, who rejected astrology, and his friend Melanchthon, an avid astrologer, agreed that God revealed His plans for the world through comets, eclipses and conjunctions. Leovitius had described six Maximum Conjunctions since the time of Adam: the fifth marked the birth of Jesus of Nazareth; the sixth marked the time of Charlemagne's Christian empire; and the seventh soon to come had been preceded by Martin Luther's revival of the 'clearest light of the Gospel'.[65] The Great Conjunction of 1583 would be the last in the Watery Trigon, and the Maximum Conjunction of 1603 would begin a new eight-hundred-year cycle in the Fiery house of Aries. Leovitius predicted that 'new worlds will follow and will begin suddenly with violent changes, for this has happened before'.[66]

Tycho spent some time discussing conjunctions with Leovitius. When the conversation turned to ephemerides, he asked whether Leovitius ever made astronomical observations, and if he had, whether he was surprised to see that the ephemerides he calculated with great effort from the Alfonsine Tables did not agree with the heavens. Leovitius must have been taken aback. He replied that he had no instruments, but that he had observed solar and lunar eclipses using the clocks of friends. This answer must have astonished Tycho. Here

he was, conversing with a leading astronomer-astrologer of
his day, and the man never observed the stars! Leovitius did
not even know the difference between looking at stars and
observing them. Because he was self-taught, Tycho had not
realized that his own obsession with observation was not the
way that sixteenth-century astronomers worked.[67] He and
Leovitius parted on friendly terms, but Tycho came away
with a heightened awareness of the importance of his own
approach, strengthened in his determination to continue
along his chosen path.

In April 1569 Tycho arrived in the great imperial city of
Augsburg, where he contacted the philologist Hieronymus
Wolf and the patrician brothers Burgomaster Paul Hainzel
and Privy Councillor Johann Baptist Hainzel. These learned
Protestants welcomed him into a circle of humanist friends
who gathered as an informal 'academy', holding symposia
enlivened by witty, cultivated conversation. He lodged with a
goldsmith named Lorenz Thenn, who was an avid Paracelsian.
'I was born in chymical fumes and educated among spagyric
ovens and furnaces,' Thenn's grandson later wrote.[68] Tycho
breathed these same fumes and began for the first time to
practise what he called 'chymical exercises' (*chymicis exercitijs*),
the 'spagyric art' or 'pyronomic art' of preparing chemical
medicaments developed by Paracelsus. Tycho set out to reconcile what Hugh Trevor-Roper called the 'metaphysics' and
'ideology' of Paracelsus with the astronomy-astrology of
Philippist humanism.[69] Augsburg also opened Tycho's eyes
to precise, beautiful instruments and automata made for
wealthy connoisseurs like the Hainzels by highly skilled artisans.[70] He commissioned the first of his own revolutionary

new instruments: *Globus Magnus Orichalcicus*, the Great Brass Globe, a scientific instrument of artisanal splendour and intellectual virtuosity by an unknown maker.[71]

Tycho began to observe more regularly than ever before and designed a new instrument he called a 'sextant'. It was rather like a large pair of compasses and was lighter, easier to use and less resistant to the wind than his 1.5-metre (5-ft) quadrant.[72] He wanted to increase the size of instruments to achieve greater accuracy of calibration and hoped eventually to reduce and perhaps even eliminate instrumental error. One day, in his lodgings, he was sketching with compasses and paper to determine the size of an instrument that could be calibrated to a single minute of arc, one-sixtieth of a degree. Paul Hainzel came by, and they discussed the problem at some length. If I ever settle long enough in one place, Tycho said, I intend to build an instrument to accommodate such calibration. Why not here and now? asked Paul Hainzel in his enthusiasm. They could build it in the park of his estate in Gögginen, just outside the city.[73]

Tycho agreed, and the skills of Augsburg's artisans and labourers came into play. A sturdy post was erected in a buried frame, and from it a crew of twenty men hung a gargantuan oaken version of the little hand-held quadrant with a radius of nearly 5.5 metres (18 ft) and a brass scale calibrated to single minutes of arc at tiny intervals of around 1.6 mm.[74] Altitudes of stars were observed through pinhole sights mounted on one edge, and solar altitudes by directing a beam of sunlight through the upper pinhole to the lower sight (D, E). A weighted brass plumb-wire hung from the top to mark angles against the brass scale. This colossal *Quadrans*

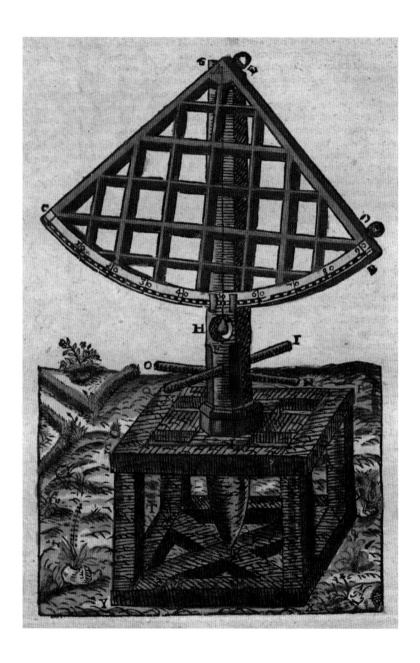

12 Tycho's *Quadrans Maximus* showing the buried supporting frame.

Maximus (great quadrant), as it was called, was cumbersome
but extremely accurate: 'within one-sixth of a minute,' Tycho
wrote, 'provided the observer exercised the necessary care'.[75]
Tycho recorded his first observation on 1 April 1570.[76]

Soon after, the renowned French philosopher Petrus
Ramus (Pierre de la Ramée) passed through Augsburg and
later extolled 'Tycho Bracheus, a young Danish nobleman,
with whom we went to the suburban villa of Hainzel after
dinner to observe the stars by means of a great machine he
has invented'.[77] Standing below the huge quadrant, Ramus
said that the ancient Egyptians once possessed an astronomy
without hypotheses, based entirely on logic and observational
evidence. Perhaps Tycho would be the person to restore this
ancient wisdom in a new form. Tycho replied that the very
axioms of geometry were hypotheses, and hypotheses such
as the axiom of uniform motion expressed in circles or the
use of epicycles were simply ways to give geometrical expres-
sion to apparent motions for the purpose of mathematical
calculation. Hypotheses could change in time, but without
them, Tycho feared that astronomy might simply soar off
into ethereal realms of supramundane, incorporeal intellects,
beyond the angels and all human understanding.[78] Nonethe-
less, his conversations with a first-rate thinker like Ramus,
who acknowledged the importance of his work, helped Tycho
to bring into focus his goals in life.

Tycho and Paul Hainzel observed the Sun together with
the *Quadrans Maximus* for the last time on 16 May 1570.[79] Soon
after, Tycho took his leave of Augsburg and gave the sextant
to Hainzel. Now, at last, he had found his vocation. It was to
be an astronomer and natural philosopher.

TWO

Cloister into Observatory: The New Star, 1570–73

YCHO BRAHE AND HIS BROTHERS had been summoned home to the deathbed of their father. Axel Brahe came from the court of Count John of Nassau-Dillenburg in the Rhineland, Steen Brahe from the court of Electoral Saxony. Their father's seat was now at Helsingborg Castle, where Tycho, at the solstice on the eve of his 24th birthday, observed the Moon with one of his cross-staffs, the only instruments he still possessed.[1] That same day, a peace treaty was signed to end the Northern Seven Years War between Denmark-Norway and Sweden-Finland.

Otto Brahe had put his private affairs in order and drawn up a precise cadastre of his estate.[2] He bore his pain with dignity until his life ebbed away on 9 May 1571.[3] In the following months, his heirs began the process of settling an estate consisting of Knutstorp Castle, Elvedgaard and Tange manors, five hundred farms in Denmark and Norway, fourteen mills and several urban mansions.[4] Terms were reached with Inger Oxe and Otto Brahe's two sisters that allowed Tosterup Castle and the late Jørgen Brahe's estate to be included in the settlement. Danish law recognized no right of primogeniture.[5] Beate Bille kept her dower rights and took over four royal properties (*len*) that Otto Brahe had held as surety for loans, thus becoming an administrator of crown lands in her own right.[6] Eventually, Tycho and Steen were granted Knutstorp Castle; Axel was given Elvedgaard manor, and Jørgen and Knud got Tosterup Castle. Their sister Margrete had already brought Markie manor into her marriage; the deceased sister Lisbeth's inheritance went to her daughter, Lisbeth Gyldenstierne, and an equivalent inheritance was set aside for Sophie.

The return of peace to Scandinavia in 1570 ushered in a period of unprecedented prosperity. Baltic trade soared, royal revenue from the Sound Dues trebled, the vast royal domain was reorganized to provide increased revenue, and King Frederick II repaid his war debts with remarkable speed.[7] The splendours of Renaissance life poured into Denmark. Steward of the Realm Peter Oxe headed the administration in Copenhagen Castle with an able staff of young officials including Anders Sørensen Vedel, the Castle Chaplain since 1568.[8] King Frederick II preferred to hold court in hunting castles outside Copenhagen.[9]

Half-hearted negotiations had produced no suitable candidate for the king's hand until November 1571, when he caught a glimpse of his young cousin Sophie of Mecklenburg and fell in love. Marriage contracts were quickly sealed and the royal wedding was celebrated on 20 July 1572 at Copenhagen Castle. Peter Oxe planned the celebration and escorted the queen to her coronation in Our Lady's Cathedral on 21 July. Inger Oxe took over as Stewardess (*Hofmesterinde*) of the fourteen-year-old Queen's court and summoned nine aristocratic maids of honour to assist.[10] Tycho Brahe was enrolled as a noble courtier during the week of the marriage celebration,

which included feasting, fireworks, mock battles on land and sea, and lavish public entertainment in Copenhagen, followed by courtly celebrations at Frederiksborg Castle and elsewhere for much of the summer.[11]

That same summer, another royal wedding in Paris touched off the massacre of St Bartholomew's Eve, when

13 Hans Knieper, *Sophie of Mecklenburg, Queen of Denmark, c.* 1572, oil on canvas.

Catholic mobs, enraged by the marriage of the king's sister to a Protestant, set out to slaughter every single Protestant in France. Danish students later told lurid tales of butchery and narrow escapes while the French ambassador, Charles de Danzay, tried to blame the Duke of Guise and not his royal masters for the bloodshed.[12] Petrus Ramus was among thousands of murdered Protestants.

Although he became a courtier, Tycho did not always reside at court like Inger Oxe or his friend Petrus Severinus, the royal physician, whose book *Idea medicinae philosophicae* (1571) was helping to legitimize Paracelsian medicine.[13] When Tycho came to Copenhagen, he visited shops of booksellers, printers and clockmakers, dined with university friends, stayed with another Paracelsian friend, Professor Johannes Pratensis, and visited Peter Oxe, Vedel and others at Copenhagen Castle.

He also spent time at Knutstorp, which had been rebuilt in 1551 as four brick buildings around a cobbled courtyard, surrounded by a lake and reached over a causeway and draw-bridge from an outer court on dry land.[14] Beate Bille resided there with Tycho's precocious youngest sister, Sophie Brahe.[15] One day, his mother told him that he had come into the world with a stillborn twin brother. Deeply moved, Tycho composed an Ovidian elegy in the voice of his twin 'on Olympus' and had it printed in Copenhagen in 1572 as his first publication.[16] Knutstorp's parish church was in Kågeröd. Pastor Jørgen Hansen had a son, Hans Jørgensen, who eventually succeeded him, and a daughter named Kirsten Jørgensdatter, of whom little is known except that Tycho was drawn to her.[17]

A morning's ride through oak and beech parkland brought Tycho to Herrevad Abbey, founded four hundred years earlier

by monks from Cîteaux. The austere abbey in the style of Fontenay had acquired a landed estate of some three hundred farms, half a dozen mills, iron forges, fishing rights and its own manorial court.[18] Since the Reformation, a married Lutheran lector had been teaching the monks to use a Lutheran breviary, and in 1565 the last abbot, Lauritz Severinsen, turned over the abbey keys to Tycho's uncle, Steen Bille of Wanås and Råbelev, who took charge as governor of the abbey and estate.[19] When Tycho came there, the last old monks still chanted the reformed office in Latin with Lutheran boys from the monastery school under Lector Canutus Joannis (Knud Jensen). The immense, three-storey Portal House, 30 metres (100 ft) long, was the residence of Steen Bille and his wife, Kirsten Lindenow of Sellerup.

Wandering the church aisles, Tycho would have seen the gravestone of his ancestor, Peter Brahe of Mickedala and

Rännesnäs, a fourteenth-century patron of the abbey.[20] From the south transept, a door led into a twelfth-century building with steps up to the monks' dormitory and infirmary above the chapter house and a library with a rich collection of manuscripts and printed books.[21] Somewhere, there was the monks' distilling house and apothecary. Schoolboys tumbled out of church wearing the white Cistercian habit, although their path led to service as noble courtiers and Lutheran pastors.[22] Tycho's youngest brother, Knud Brahe, spent his school days among them, for their father had relented and let his youngest son learn Latin.[23]

Tycho Brahe came frequently to Herrevad Abbey. He was fond of his learned uncles, Steen Bille and his brother Jens, who lived nearby at Billesholm. In their youth, Steen and Jens Bille had studied abroad for five years, and King Gustavus called their father, his cousin, a rank papist for sending them

14 Gerhard von Buhrmann, *Knutstorp Castle*, 1680, engraving published by Abraham Fischer, 1756.

first to Paris, not Wittenberg.[24] Both went on to serve the
Danish crown in peace and war.[25] During the late war, Swedish
raiders had pillaged and torched Steen's seat of Wanås Castle,
so he and Kirsten Lindenow resided at Herrevad for the rest
of their days.

This gentle knight was a very different role model from
the brusque and brilliant Peter Oxe, but Tycho looked to
both of them as he struggled to reconcile his high birth
with his love of natural philosophy. Steen Bille and Kirsten
Lindenow were court favourites and maintained a pious,
lively and learned household at Herrevad. Danish traditions
of balladry, vernacular poetry, music and dance must have
been part of their lives, for Jens and Steen Bille had written
and collected ballads as young courtiers in the days of King
Christian III, and Herrevad schoolboys like Knud Brahe
and Claus Lyschander, as well as Tycho, would carry these
traditions into the future.[26]

Steen Bille kept the Cistercian workshops in production
at mills along the Rönne River and at iron forges in the
forested uplands. Herrevad's workshops provided the crown
with a variety of products on demand, such as 60,000 bricks
in 1555, two hundred wheelbarrows in 1558, and eighteen
sets of wheels for naval gun carriages in 1563.[27] By 1576,
Steen had brought in a German papermaker named
Christopher Rotther to establish Denmark's first paper mill
in an abbey mill at Klippan.[28]

Eket Hammermill on the Herrevad estate was Denmark's
main source of domestic iron. Sparks flew as osmund iron
was pounded under a cam-driven trip hammer to transform
the glowing mass into wrought-iron bars, rods and plates for

15 Gravestone for Steen Bille and Kirsten Lindenow, *c.* 1586, St Maria
Church, Helsingborg.

the Copenhagen cannon factory and other royal workshops.[29] Farther up the horst ridge of Hallandsåsen, ore was extracted from bogs around Örkelljunga. Paracelsus had described how God created the element of water within the earth and placed within this 'matrix' the 'semina' of iron, where it gave birth to iron ore wherever the liquid tree of iron spread its branches, within the upland bogs of Skåne or the deep mines of Swiss mountains.[30] Tycho could watch the workers reduce this bog ore into osmund iron in charcoal-fired bloomeries at Östra Spång.[31] The blooms were cut up and sent to Eket Mill as 28-kilogram (60-lb) ingots of slag and iron, where they were forged into iron and steel.[32]

Tycho Brahe saw these marvels of divine chymistry and human industry on the Herrevad estate and grew eager to establish a chymical laboratory of his own. Steen Bille, Canutus Joannis or one of the old monks may have shared his interest, because his laboratory came to be at Herrevad and not at Knutstorp.[33] He had Pratensis send him laboratory equipment from Copenhagen.

Early in the year 1572, Steen Bille learned of a Venetian glass-maker at the Danish court.[34] German glass-makers made greenish bottle glass, but Venetian masters could spin out delicate goblets of pure cristallo flecked with gold and swirls of vibrant red, green, aquamarine, orange or yellow on fantastically shaped stems, and they could also make equipment for chymical laboratories. Steen Bille apparently persuaded King Frederick that Herrevad was the best place to locate a glassworks, because he issued an open letter on 10 April 1572 that allowed 'Master Anthonius de Castille Vinitziam' and his servants to establish Denmark's first Venetian glassworks at

Kvidinge near the abbey's Klippan mill.[35] Danish tongues soon reduced Maestro Antonio's florid name to 'Tønnis Vind' as he and his journeymen began to produce cucurbits, alembics, flasks, elegant glass bottles, bowls, drinking vessels and red window panes.

Tycho wrote for help in finding a laboratory assistant, and Pratensis recommended an odd fellow named Nicolaus Michaelis Wiburgensis, who was 'not unwilling' to consider the job. Pratensis' letter went on to refer playfully to Bacchus as the patron of Tycho's imbibing at Herrevad, Urania for his astronomy and Vulcan as the inspiration of his chymical forge, and he also mentioned Venus, perhaps thinking of Tycho and Kirsten from Kågeröd.[36]

Herrevad had gradually been transformed from a centre of monastic piety into an aristocratic Renaissance seat that promoted new forms of social interaction, literature, natural philosophy and technology. Its rather remote location – from everybody except the Skåne nobility – allowed Tycho to pursue his chymical studies undisturbed, supported by the glassworks, ironworks and other technical facilities. He enlisted the abbey's smiths, brass-founders and cabinet-makers to make a larger version of the sextant he had left with Paul Hainzel. Its arms of well-seasoned walnut were 155 centimetres (5 ft) long with brass tabs at the far ends and interchangeable 60° or 30° arcs attached to one arm.[37] With his eye close to the fulcrum, Tycho could measure angles between two celestial objects along the inner edges of the brass tabs and lock the movable arm in place with a thumb-screw. He soon realized, however, that the position of his eye was slightly behind the fulcrum, which produced an instrumental error of parallax that distorted the observed angle, and he constructed a table of corrections.[38]

Tycho's discovery of this principle of error grew out of his understanding of geometry and his habit of repeating observations. He soon learned that no two observations ever produced precisely the same results and came to realize that an observation was an approximation, not a determination, of an object's position. An observation was an experiment that needed to be verified. This insight, which now seems self-evident, had not been a regular part of astronomy, or of science, before Tycho Brahe.

During the summer in 1572, when few stars were visible in the endless Scandinavian light, Tycho spent his time in the

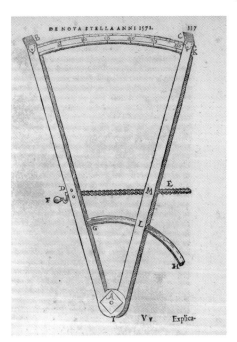
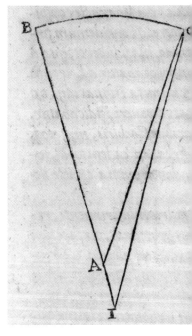

16, 17 Tycho's sextant with 30° arc and his diagram explaining its instrumental parallax.

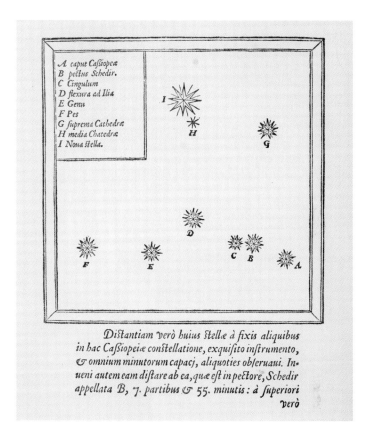

A caput Caßiopeæ
B pectus Schedir.
C Cingulum
D flexura ad Ilia
E Genu
F Pes
G suprema Cathedræ
H media Chatedræ
I Noua stella.

Distantiam verò huius stellæ à fixis aliquibus
in hac Caßiopeiæ constellatione, exquisito instrumento,
& omnium minutorum capacj, aliquoties obseruaui. In-
ueni autem eam distare ab ea, quæ est in pectore, Schedir
appellata B, 7. partibus & 55. minutis : à superiori
verò

spagyric laboratory between travels to court, Knutstorp and
Copenhagen. Gradually, the nights grew longer and darker.
By the autumn feast of Martinmas on 11 November, the sun
set at around four o'clock. The following evening, as skies
cleared, Tycho scanned the stars as he walked from his laboratory for the evening meal. Suddenly, he stopped. Directly
overhead, in the constellation Cassiopeia, was a brilliant new
star, shimmering with radiant light. Tycho could not believe
his eyes. He knew every star by name.

18 Tycho's map of Cassiopeia locating *Noua stella*, the New Star, *c.* 1573.

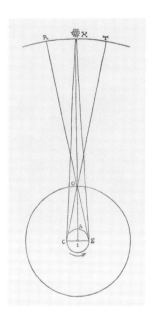

19 Diurnal Parallax. ACE is earth with the North Pole at the centre I. RXT is the sphere of the stars with the New Star labelled X. As earth rotated anticlockwise and Tycho's position moved from E to A to C every 12 hours, he would have seen an object at O appear to shift from R to X to T. This apparent shift is called diurnal (daily) parallax, but the new star had none, so it was as distant as the other stars.

20 Tycho's sextant mounted in an abbey window.

But when I pointed out the location and learned that others could also see it, I no longer doubted that a star actually appeared there. This was truly the greatest miracle in the whole of Nature since the beginning of the world . . . All philosophers agree, and reality itself declares unambiguously, that no alteration of generation or corruption occurs in the ethereal regions of the heavenly world, but that the heavens and the ethereal bodies therein neither increase nor decrease in number, magnitude, luminosity, nor in any other way, but are always the same and always will be the same, never worn down by the years, permanent.[39]

Tycho set aside his chymical experiments to study the new star. It was an exploding supernova, but nobody in the sixteenth century knew that, nor did they know what to make of it. Across Europe, some simply stared with gaping mouths; others used lengths of cord to line it up with other stars, or cross-staffs to measure distances between the bright new star and stars in the constellation Cassiopeia. Paul Hainzel used the great quadrant of Augsburg to measure its daily upper and lower culminations. Others used small hand-held astrolabes.

Tycho observed it with his sextant.[40] He kept observing the new star, day after day, month after month, verifying his results time and again. With his 30° arc, he measured angular distances between the new star and other stars and corrected the observed positions for instrumental parallax. He repeated these observations many times.[41] He was looking for diurnal parallax: if the new star appeared to shift among the stars in the course of the night, it was closer to the Earth than the other stars; if it shifted more than a planet, it could be in the sphere of fire below the Moon, where lightning, meteors, comets and other fiery phenomena flared up, and where followers of Aristotle believed that it would be.

It did not shift. It was a true star. But, stars in the high heavens did not come and go. So how could this be?

Tycho attached the 60° arc to his instrument and mounted it in a Romanesque window of the chapter house with the fixed arm horizontal, and then he carefully adjusted its alignment with a brass plumb line and shims. He mounted pinnules (brass tabs) at the upper and lower ends of the movable upper arm and observed the lower culmination of the star through aligned slits in these pinnules.[42] After each observation, he checked the plumb line for any deviation from the vertical. He observed the new star's distance from Polaris and other stars to plot its upper culmination. He kept observing on clear nights for as long as the star was visible. He used Regiomontanus' trigonometry to calculate its ecliptical latitude and longitude and noted that its nativity was in the House of Taurus.

Tycho's life was not all stargazing. Around February 1573, Kirsten Jørgensdatter became pregnant with his child. It was clear that their liaison could never lead to a wedding. No matter how well-bred, intelligent or charming this pastor's daughter might be, she had no noble quarterings nor any landed estate, and her children could hardly be nobles under Danish law. She was a commoner, and Tycho could not marry her. But like Orlando, who lost his wits for love of Angelica, he was unwilling to abandon his Kirsten.

As Kirsten waxed, the new star waned. Tycho kept observing the new star as it gradually faded away. He was confident that it actually was a star, but he struggled to explain it. He eventually rejected the Paracelsian view that it came from a seed planted at Creation and accepted Melanchthon's Lutheran version of Aristotelian physics, which emphasized that divine laws of nature rule the celestial regions and eternally reflect the wisdom of the Creator. This led him to conclude that the new star was a sign placed in the sky by God, contrary to the laws of physics, as a warning to humanity. It was a true star, unlike the Star of Bethlehem that guided the Magi.

Tycho wrote an essay on the star which he took to Copenhagen to discuss with Pratensis and others. Charles de Danzay, who was well versed in astronomy and whom Tycho liked because he was 'silent and true', invited all of them to dine.[43] During the meal, Tycho asked their opinions of the new star. None of them had heard about it, and Danzay thought he was joking, but Tycho simply smiled. Later that evening he took them outside, and upon seeing it they were astonished.[44] Pratensis was lecturing at that time on the *Natural History* of the Stoic philosopher Pliny the Elder and recalled that Pliny said Hipparchus had seen a new star. Tycho concluded that Hipparchus' star foretold the end of King David's dynasty and the rise of the Roman Empire, while this new star anticipated the seventh Maximum Conjunction, as Cyprianus Leovitius and others had foretold. Pratensis encouraged Tycho to publish his manuscript, but Tycho was aware that many frowned upon aristocrats writing books. Even the eminent Viceroy of Schleswig-Holstein, Heinrich Rantzau, a master of aristocratic self-promotion, used elaborate ruses and pen names to avoid the 'stigma of print'.[45] However, when a flood of books and manuscripts on the new star arrived from Germany and Tycho found most of them ill-informed, he agreed that something had to be done.[46]

As these events transpired, Otto Brahe's estate was finally settled. Knutstorp Castle and estate came into the joint possession of Tycho and Steen Brahe, although Beate Bille retained certain dower rights.[47] Steen Brahe returned from Saxony and quickly advanced at the court of Frederick II to the office of Cupbearer (*Hofskænk*) in charge of all royal breweries and wine cellars, table linens, silver, treasures and all court service of beverages.[48] In June 1573 he won the hand of Birgitte Ottesdatter Rosenkrantz, heiress of Næsbyholm and a great estate on Sjælland. The younger brothers, Axel, Jørgen and Knud Brahe, all served as knights in armour at foreign courts.

Peter Oxe urged Tycho to publish his manuscript and perhaps hide his name under an anagram, so Pratensis and Tycho went to Lorenz Benedicht in Copenhagen, who produced some of the most beautiful books ever printed in Denmark, and before long, Tycho's book was in print in an elegant format.[49] Latin poems by Vedel and Johannes Franciscus Ripensis ornamented the slender volume, which opened with a lively epistolary dialogue between Pratensis, who bubbled with Paracelsian imagery in trying to persuade Tycho to publish his work, and Tycho, who reluctantly agreed. The book went on to present evidence gathered by meticulous observation that 'this new star does not have its place in the elemental region below the moon, nor in the spheres of the seven wandering stars, but in the eighth sphere among the fixed stars.' It foretold great political and religious upheavals and would bring Jovial abundance and peace followed by Martial war and pestilence, and finally, Saturnalian sorrow and death. Tycho's astronomical and astrological reports were followed by a humanist oration in which he described the immense theatre of the universe as a dynamic, unified cosmos with Man placed at the centre to study the visible Creation and to learn to know the invisible, incorporeal majesty and wisdom of its Creator. Tycho announced his intention to remedy the short-comings of astrology as pointed out by Pico della Mirandola, and to achieve more precise observations and planetary tables in order to determine the order of the planets.[50] He went on to apply his new astrological methods to the forthcoming lunar eclipse of 8 December 1573 and commented on the uncertain state of meteorology.[51]

As part of his project of astrological reform, Tycho Brahe proposed a new system of coordinates that covered the entire celestial sphere surrounding Earth. His baseline was the vernal colure, the meridian running through the point of vernal equinox. Astrologers regarded this as the first point of Aries and the beginning of the zodiac, but Tycho saw it in astronomical terms as a great circle encircling the heavens through both hemispheres at right angles to the equinoctial. In time, these new equatorial coordinates were bound to weaken the connection between astronomy and astrology because they were not based on the zodiac, the foundation of astrology.

The final section of the book was an 'Elegy on Urania' composed by Tycho in the style of Ovid. In this long Latin poem, Tycho described himself wandering along the Rönne through a verdant countryside where the noble Steen Bille had put barbarism to flight and brought in pure crystalline glass like that of Venice, and also paper, never before produced there.[52] In this idyllic place, Urania suddenly appeared and summoned

Tycho to worship her instead of Vulcan. She granted that the Microcosm corresponded to the Macrocosm, that Earth also contains its stars and what is above is also below, and she asserted that the stars foretell but do not compel the rational mind. In her realm, however, 'high in the sky, above the clouds, I enjoy celestial ambrosia with Jupiter himself'. So then, why do you hesitate? *Ergo age, quid dubitas?* The phrase was echoed in Ripensis' opening poem. Tycho replied to this divine summons in the manner of Pico, as a Magus, a man made divine and able to participate in the intellect infused in nature: I am descended from Brahe and Bille, my mind is ardent for great and noble things. I strive to soar by the power of the mind to the peaks of thunder, see marvels created by God, and by the spirit gain power over the ethereal realm. Tycho's urge was for Hermetic *gnosis*: to soar through the spheres of heaven with the Creator, the omnipotent mathematical Lawgiver of Philippist Neoplatonism, and to gain control of the cosmos itself.[53]

Latin poetry, epistolary dialogue, astronomical *observatio*, astrological prophecy and humanist oration: all these genres of Renaissance rhetoric came together in Tycho's slender, elegantly printed volume. Embedded in a humanist package, however, was something quite unconventional, even unprecedented: a precise, verifiable study of a single star, based on methods of observation and data reduction of Tycho's own invention. Here was an empirical method with an eye cast backwards to antiquity but also, Janus-like, with great potential for the future. His Muse had summoned him to set his sights impossibly high. Tycho Brahe was determined to become a new Hipparchus. He would number the stars anew for posterity.

THREE

Finding a New Life, 1573–6

ITH HIS PATERNAL inheritance, Tycho Brahe was rich by 1573 and could afford better instruments than a wooden sextant shimmed up in a window-sill. He designed a quadrant with the elegance of Augsburg instruments, stable, precise and emblematic of the divine nature of astronomy-astrology. It was calibrated with a series of arcs in a new manner proposed by Petrus Nonius (Pedro Nunes): in the first scale 90°, then 89, 88, 87, down to 46, which meant that the *dioptre* (the rod carrying the instrument's sights, a Greek term that Tycho preferred to the Arabic *alidade*) would always fall on some calibrated point.

The quadrant was made of gilt brass by a Copenhagen master, probably the royal clockmaker, Stephen Brenner from Nuremberg. It was 39 centimetres (15 in.) in diameter, and Tycho designed new sights, which he named *pinnacidia* ('light-cutters'), to replace the traditional pinholes. The lower sight had two narrow slits collimated to the upper tab. This provided two parallel lines of sight. When the sights were precisely aligned, a celestial object looked the same through both slits. An emblem engraved on the arc bore a motto contrasting the fleeting pleasures of courtly life with knowledge of eternal celestial matters and another hidden motto contrasting the

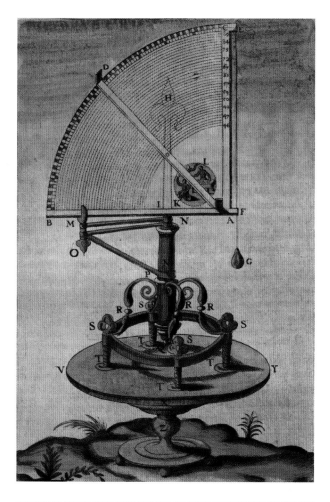

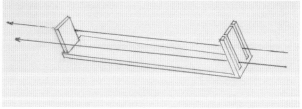

21 *Above:* Tycho's small quadrant of gilt brass, *c.* 1598, woodcut.
22 *Below:* Tycho's pinnacidia ('light-cutters') showing parallel lines of sight to a celestial object.

vanity of all human endeavours with the eternal merits of Christ.[1] This instrument rested on a sturdy base levelled with a brass plumb line and thumbscrews and was much more accurate than a hand-held quadrant of that size.

Tycho also commissioned Brenner to make a clockwork celestial globe of gilt brass to show phases of the Moon, diurnal solar movement, and times of sunrise, sunset and meridian transits.[2] Like the ancient planetarium of Archimedes, this instrument was a talisman to capture the divine order of the cosmos mechanically, 'not only to look at, but to ponder in the soul'.[3]

Tycho had much to ponder that autumn. Kirsten Jørgensdatter gave birth to a daughter, who was baptized Kirstine, on 12 October 1573. Two months later at Knutstorp he observed the lunar eclipse foretold in his book, using the new quadrant and assisted by his fourteen-year-old sister, Sophie Brahe, who was 'very fond of these matters by nature, took part eagerly, and helped where she could'.[4]

His first steel instrument was a sextant made the following spring of Eket steel.[5] A swivel-mounted rod on an adjustable base was attached to a 117-centimetre (4-ft) arm that carried a Nonian arc. The observer turned a long thumbscrew to adjust the angle between the arms as he sighted from the hinge, which was attached to a curved supporting rod. This instrument was stable, self-supporting, accurate and easier to use than the old wooden sextant, though a bit heavy.

Tycho's university friends wanted him to lecture on astronomy, but he refused, claiming it was beneath the dignity of a nobleman. However, when somebody persuaded a few noble students to petition him to lecture, and when King

Frederick approved and Ambassador de Danzay offered his Copenhagen mansion as the venue for the inaugural oration, Tycho finally agreed.[6]

The entire university community gathered in Danzay's great hall on Thursday, 23 September 1574. Noble students, some barely in their teens, swaggered in as professors in academic robes and commoner students filled the hall. Tycho held no academic degrees but stood forth as a nobleman to explain his natural philosophy and demonstrate that it conformed to the Philippist consensus of the Church of Denmark, whose most eminent theologian, Vice-Chancellor Niels Hemmingsen, rejected astrology and placed great emphasis on the doctrine of free will.[7]

Tycho's oration began with geometry and arithmetic, which Melanchthon, inspired by Plato, had called the 'wings of the mind'.[8] From geometry flowed plane and spherical trigonometry, optics, gnomics, geography, architecture and many mechanical arts. Tycho traced a genealogy of astronomical wisdom beginning with Seth, the son of Adam, and reserved special praise for Hipparchus, Ptolemy and Copernicus, who 'restored the science of celestial motion' but also advocated a Sun-centred system 'contrary to the principles of physics'.[9] He followed Melanchthon in emphasizing macrocosmic influences on the health of the human microcosm and extended these influences to the natural world in the manner of Paracelsus: 'There is no herb so insignificant, no mineral or metal so abject, no animalcule so vile that it is not endowed with some special and particular virtue.' Like Ficino, he distinguished between those humans who do not exercise their free will and have 'lowly, earthly minds, like those of cattle', and 'those in whom there is fiery vigour of heavenly origin', and who can use their rational free will to overrule the stars. Like Hemmingsen and Pico della Mirandola, he condemned black magic as inspired by the Devil but did not address the beneficent white magic practised by wise rural women and men, for which Hemmingsen expressed broad tolerance.[10] Tycho drew on the Paracelsian theory of *semina*, which Severinus had expounded at length, and asserted that fixed stars could influence the terrestrial world when 'aroused and impregnated by the seven wandering stars'. Tycho cautioned, however, that astrology was not an exact, mathematical science like astronomy, but that it drew its principles

> *a posteriori*, that is, from experience itself, and forms its conclusions from many particularly fallible observations, not unlike the way medicine works. Thus, for the same reason, astrology, no less than medicine, deserves to be counted among the physical sciences (*physicas artes*).[11]

In this way, Tycho drew a distinction between astronomical *observatio*, which provided exact mathematical descriptions of natural phenomena, and the *observatio* of astrology and medical case studies, which was expressed in the less precise medium of words.

Following the oration, Danzay invited Tycho and all the professors to a banquet prepared by his French chef. Good-natured banter enlivened the conversation. Danzay, 'with his suave and quick wit', remarked to Hemmingsen that Tycho raked all faculties over the coals, including the theologians, for scorning astrology. He added that John Calvin many years ago had persuaded him to give up horoscopes, and he now considered astrology to be harmful to Protestant religion.[12] Tycho smiled and replied that getting into politics could do much more damage than astrology. Hemmingsen listened and finally declared that he did not object to Tycho's views, insofar as Tycho did not restrict the ability of God to act freely and did not limit human freedom of choice by the influence of the stars. If these two points were granted, Tycho's views could be 'tolerated'.[13] Tycho had cited many authorities in the course of his oration but referred to the Bible more than any other source. He said that no astrologer, even in antiquity, ever denied that God acts freely. The human mind was not subject to the stars and could rise high above them, even rule

23 *Left*: Stephen Brenner's 1573 clockwork celestial globe, detail of illus. 52.
24 *Right*: Eberhard Baldewein's *c.* 1574 clockwork celestial globe.

over them, with the help of God. 'And with this,' said Tycho, 'we came to agreement'.[14]

Tycho Brahe's oration helped him stake out his place among the leading thinkers in Denmark. His view of natural philosophy, like theirs, was based on the eirenic Lutheran humanism of Melanchthon, which did not rule out Neo-platonic, Hermetic, Copernican, Paracelsian or Ramist ideas so long as they did not challenge the religious consensus

25 Tycho's portable steel sextant with Nonian arc, *c.* 1573. Illustration altered by the author.

demanded by King Frederick II, who sternly barred all
other forms of religion than Philippist Lutheranism from
his realms.

Following the success of his oration, Tycho lectured on
planetary theory to a small group of students during the
autumn and winter of 1574–5. He was the only nobleman of
his era who taught in the University of Copenhagen, but his
role as courtier-philosopher was modelled more on fellow
courtiers like Peter Oxe and Steen Bille than on his academic
friends. Other professors lectured on spherical astronomy, so
Tycho took up planetary theory. He used Erasmus Reinhold's
geocentric Copernican models and became one of the first in
any university to lecture on Copernican astronomy.[15] Tycho
owned a large house in the city and probably lived there with
Kirsten Jørgensdatter, who gave birth to a second daughter
named Magdalene in Copenhagen towards the end of 1574.[16]
A student named Peter Jacobsen Flemløse dedicated to Tycho
a witty pastoral dialogue in the style of Virgil's *Eclogues*, and
Tycho took him into his service.[17]

In the long run, however, the life of a university don was
not for Tycho Brahe. His tremendous innovative capacity
was not satisfied by explaining Copernicus to a handful of
students. He and his brothers, Steen and Axel, presented
themselves to King Frederick II on 20 December 1574 at Sorø
Abbey and took their leave of the court.[18] His brothers
planned to marry in 1575, and Tycho intended to abandon
the classroom to travel abroad.

King Frederick had begun to replace the old castle of
Krogen ('The Hook') in Elsinore (Helsingør) with a majestic
Renaissance fortress named Kronborg ('Crown Castle'). He

had recruited artists and artisans from the war-torn Low Countries and wanted Tycho to establish contacts with skilled artists, artisans and technicians in the lands he visited. That spring, Tycho set off with Flemløse while Kirsten Jørgensdatter and their two small daughters stayed home.[19] He had a private agenda, which he did not reveal to the king: he intended to search for a place to live as a natural philosopher among learned aristocrats and friends who would accept Kirsten Jørgensdatter as his equal.

Towards the end of March, he arrived at the court of William IV, Landgrave of Hesse-Kassel, a learned ruler who had decided as a young man, in the words of historian Karsten Gaulke, to pursue 'deep cognition of mathematics' as a political strategy.[20] The comet of 1558 had convinced the landgrave, as the conjunction of 1563 convinced Tycho, that celestial tables were hopelessly inaccurate. He brought Andreas Schöner from Nuremberg to design a high balcony observatory at Kassel Castle and Eberhard (Ebert) Baldewein from Marburg to build its instruments. By 1560 Landgrave William had compiled the first new star catalogue since antiquity and had commissioned an elaborate gilt brass clock with a rotating celestial globe on top to display the catalogue's 58 stars.[21] This great automaton eliminated the need for tedious calculation of celestial positions and made Landgrave William the leading authority among German princes on astronomy, astrology and clockwork devices.[22] In 1568 he commissioned two azimuth quadrants for simultaneous observation of a celestial object's altitude and azimuth.

Tycho Brahe arrived a few days before Easter, which in 1575 fell on 3 April. He and the landgrave observed, exchanged

26 Eberhard Baldewein's second planetary clock with a celestial globe on top, 1563–8, steel, brass (partially gold plated), silver (partially gold plated), enamel, copper, catgut.

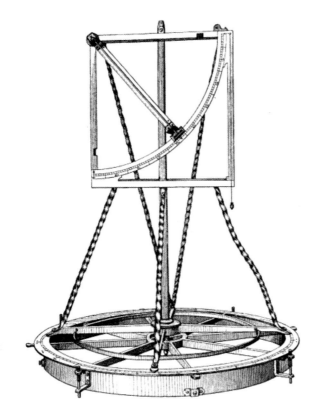

gifts and conversed for more than a week. Landgrave William gave Tycho a copy of his star catalogue, and Tycho gave him *De Nova stella*.[23] He admired the landgrave's azimuth quadrants, great celestial clock and Baldewein's small mechanical globe of 1574, the only such globe in Germany, which was strikingly similar to the one Stephen Brenner had made for Tycho in 1572.[24] He may also have seen George Labenwolf's fountain at the landgrave's pleasure house.[25]

Landgrave William's infant daughter, Sidonia, took ill on Maundy Thursday and died the day after Easter.[26] Tycho Brahe

27 Landgrave William's iron azimuth quadrant with brass arc.

offered his condolences and took his leave as the court went
into mourning. He travelled to Frankfurt am Main for the
semi-annual book fair, and on to Basel, where he stayed for
some time before crossing the Alps into northern Italy. Venice
was 'splendid and grand, the Emporium of all Europe' and
Tycho became acquainted with members of the 'very magnificent Senate and others of the nobility . . . I personally
heard a large number of men of the highest nobility discuss
elevated and philosophical topics with great shrewdness and
ingenuity,' he said.[27] These discussions may have taken place
in an exclusive 'academy' such as the Accademia Parutiana, or
perhaps in Palladio's Accademia Olimpica in Vicenza or the
Accademia dei Rinascenti in Padua, with its famous university
and gardens.[28] Tycho did not record the details, but aristocratic life in Venice and the Veneto made a strong impression
on him.

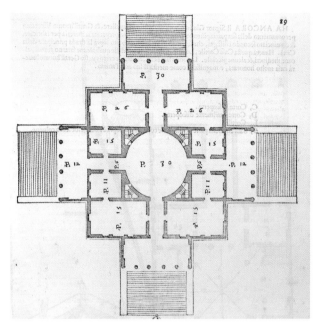

In late summer, Tycho and Flemløse travelled to Augsburg. The great quadrant had blown down in a storm in 1574, and Tycho was disappointed to find cracks in the wooden foundation of his large celestial globe, but he enjoyed spending time among friends and also met a portrait artist named Tobias Gemperle.[29] On 1 November 1575 Tycho attended the coronation in Regensburg of Archduke Rudolf of Habsburg as King of the Romans. Once again, he penetrated the innermost circles of power. He met the king's physician, Thaddeus Hagecius (Tadeáš Hájek z Hájku), who referred to Flemløse as his 'Achates'; and Jan Gregor van der Schardt, the court artist who staged the coronation.[30] Hagecius gave Tycho a treasured manuscript of the unpublished *Commentariolus* of Nicholas Copernicus.[31]

28, 29 Palladio's Villa La Rotonda, 1567–80, photographed in 2012, and its plan, 1570, engraving.

After the coronation they went to Nuremberg, where Tycho met Joachim Camerarius the Younger, visited the shop of the fountain-maker Georg Labenwolf, and must have seen the high balcony where Walther and Regiomontanus observed the stars on the house where Albrecht Dürer later lived. At Saalfeld in Thuringia, he visited Erasmus Reinhold the Younger, who showed Tycho his father's annotations in Copernicus' *De revolutionibus orbium coelestium* (On the Revolutions of the Heavenly Spheres).[32]

In Wittenberg, Tycho found the university community in chaos, every professor fired, new ones appointed, a former university rector dead after days of torture, and Melanchthon's son-in-law, Caspar Peucer, rotting in prison. Elector August had uncovered a 'plot' hatched – of all places – in Denmark, where Saxon theologians were accused of conspiring with Niels Hemmingsen to establish a Calvinist regime in the Electorate of Saxony after a bloodbath as brutal as St Bartholomew's.[33] The purged ones, Philippists to a man, were accused of 'Crypto-Calvinism'. Elector August had written in his own hand to inform King Frederick of the plot, using a Danish student named Jørgen Dybvad as his courier.[34]

By early November, news had spread across Europe that the Danish statesman Peter Oxe, formerly chamberlain to the Duke of Lorraine, had died on 24 October 1575. One of his last official acts, under strong Saxon pressure, had been to summon Hemmingsen and the entire faculty of the University of Copenhagen to answer the Elector's charges. Hemmingsen courageously refused to answer only to the King of Denmark, not to German theologians, to which Peter Oxe replied, 'I will convey your reply to my lord. No harm

shall come to you for my sake.'[35] Tycho heard more about
these events when he returned to Denmark towards the end
of the year, having secretly chosen Basel as the place to settle
for the rest of his life.

Tycho Brahe presented himself to King Frederick during the Yuletide festivities at Sorø Abbey and recommended
the painter Gemperle, the sculptor Schardt and the fountain
builder Labenwolf for the Kronborg project.[36] He reported
on courtly events in Regensburg, Kassel, Venice and perhaps
even Saxony. King Frederick was pleased and assumed that
Tycho would continue in the royal service. He offered a variety
of commands, but Tycho was non-committal. This puzzled
the king. Why would Tycho wait for a canonry in Roskilde
when he was offered much higher office?

To Pratensis, Tycho wrote, 'I did not want to take possession of any of the castles our benevolent king so graciously
offered me' and said he yearned for a tranquil 'Apollonian' life
among the Muses. 'You have often heard me complain that
I am dissatisfied with everything here, this way of life, these
customs, this daily chatter. When I am with people of my
own class, who congregate around my uncle at Herrevad or
visit me at Knutstorp . . . I waste a lot of time.'[37] Astronomy,
astrology and spagyric chymistry were his obsessions, and he
knew that the 'golden shackles' of courtly life left little time
for such endeavours.

Inspired by experiences abroad, he began to design new
instruments. First came a quadrant around 58 centimetres
(2 ft) in radius, which Victor Thoren called an innovative
'landmark'.[38] Constructed of heavy brass, it had a dioptre of
gilt steel and an azimuth circle like those in Kassel, but it was

calibrated with improved Nonian divisions and levelled with
thumbscrews and brass plumb lines.[39] The dioptre extended
beyond the fulcrum for ease of adjustment and was held in
position by a feather spring. It carried new pinnacidia with
parallel lines-of-sight through slits on all four edges, three
of which were now adjustable so the slits could be narrowed
for greater precision.

30 Andrea Alciati, *In Aulicos*, woodcut. *On Courtiers*: 'The courtly life you find
divine, and think that you are doing fine; you say that you can leave some day,
but golden fetters make you stay.'

31 Tycho's Nonian azimuth quadrant, c. 1576.

Then, it happened: the event that changed his life. Early on the morning of 11 February 1576, a royal page rode to Knutstorp Castle with a summons to court. Tycho left immediately and arrived that same afternoon at Ibstrup hunting lodge, where the chamberlain, Niels Parsberg – the brother of Tycho's duelling opponent in Rostock – showed him into the royal chamber. He and the king were alone. Stately and tall in his green hunting silks with gold buttons, King Frederick II was strong and athletic at 42 years old. Tycho Brahe, not yet thirty, barrel-chested and round-faced, with sweeping moustache, trimmed beard and terrible scars, bowed in homage. 'One of my courtiers reported that your uncle, Steen Bille, told him in secret that you are planning to return to Germany,' said the king. The truth was out. And it was out of the question.

King Frederick went on:

I was staying recently at the castle I am building in Elsinore, and when I looked out one of the windows, I saw the little island of Hven, lying in the Sound in the direction of Landskrona. No nobleman lives there. If I remember correctly, your uncle, Steen Bille, told me once – and this was before your last trip to Germany – that you liked its location. It occurred to me that it would be very well suited to your experiments in astronomy and distillation, because it is high and has an isolated location . . . if you want to live on the island, I would gladly grant it to you. There, you can live peacefully and carry out without disturbance the studies that interest you. And when I have built

Groseeck

the splendid castle that I have begun in Elsinore, I will
cross the sea to the island from time to time to see
your work in astronomy and distillation, and gladly
aid your efforts, not because I have any understanding
of astronomical matters or know what is involved in
it, but because *I am the King*, and you are in my kingdom and belong to a family I have always held dear,
and you are said to have considerable insight into such
matters. I see it as my duty to support and promote
things like this appropriately. What good would it do
for you to return to Germany and live as a stranger to
accomplish that which you can do just as easily in your
native land? We should assure instead that Germans
and people of other nations who want to know about
such things should come here to see and learn that
which they can hardly find elsewhere.[40]

32 Ibstrup Royal Hunting Lodge, detail of illus. 75.

Tycho was overwhelmed. The king seemed to read his mind and offer him exactly what his heart desired. How could he refuse? His grandfather had died fighting for the king's grandfather, his family had supported this king's ancestors in their times of trouble, his foster father had died from saving the life of this very king. Tycho knew that Landgrave William of Hesse-Kassel had urged King Frederick to support his research.[41] He knew that this Kingdom of Denmark was his home, and that his legacy was interwoven with its history.

He wrote to Pratensis and Danzay, who urged him to accept. 'Apollo wants it, Urania recommends it, Mercury commands it with his staff,' wrote Pratensis, 'Do you still doubt?'[42] He certainly also spoke with his mother and brother at Knutstorp, and with Steen Bille. One week later, on 18 February 1576, he rode to Frederiksborg Castle and accepted his sovereign's offer.

King Frederick immediately granted him a pension of 500 rixdollars a year, roughly equal to his income from Knutstorp.[43] On 23 May 1576 he received the island of Hven in lifetime fee, quit and free of any payments to the crown, with 400 rixdollars to construct a suitable residence.[44] His future would be as squire of this little island, not as a canon in Roskilde or a stranger in Basel.

One day earlier, on 22 May 1576, King Frederick had granted the fiery Manderup Parsberg command of another Danish island.[45] Manderup was sent to Hammershus Castle, bristling with 150 cannons, to rule the large Baltic island of Bornholm with its nineteen parishes. Hven had one parish. Tycho's grant was for life, however, and Manderup's was at

the royal pleasure. Bornholm was strategically located, far off
in the Baltic Sea. Tycho's island was within sight of Kronborg
Castle and intended to be its satellite, a new type of court
space. Tycho's charge was not to defend his little island but to
increase the *fama* and glory of the Danish realm by extraor-
dinary achievements in natural philosophy. He was eager
to begin.

FOUR

Treasures of the Sea King: Kronborg and Uraniborg, 1576–82

OUR DAYS AFTER accepting King Frederick's offer, Tycho Brahe climbed the coastal bluffs of Hven to survey a rolling winter landscape. A windmill rose above a village of thatched farmsteads amid fallow fields. On the western bluffs stood the thirteenth-century church of St Ibb's. The southern third of the island was uncultivated commons.

What could he make of such a place? Castles of his ancestors towered over Skåne, but Hven was no place for a castle. He would build a Renaissance villa as a satellite to the centre of power at Kronborg, where he could, as Palladio said, 'quietly apply himself to the study of books, or the contemplation of nature in imitation of those ancient Sages'.[1] Not a pinched and packed professorial household, but an aristocratic site of social luxury and philosophical activism like Herrevad or the villas of Augsburg and the Veneto, a magical home of Apollo and the Muses, drawing down cosmic energy to transform this island into a microcosm of the great universe.[2] He called it *domus Uraniae*, 'Urania's house', later *Uranienborg*, 'Urania's Castle', and, finally, *Uraniborg*, 'Celestial Castle'.[3]

Following Vitruvius, he took his architectural proportions from the human body and began with circles and squares.[4] On

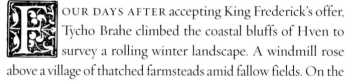

33 Leonardo da Vinci, *Vitruvian Man*, c. 1490, pen and ink over grey-washed paper.

a north–south axis, he laid out a circle, a square, and another circle, subdividing the square with a Greek cross of corridors meeting at a rotunda to create four rooms of the same diameter as the two circles.[5] The circles represented flanking towers serving Urania, not Mars. The building would be 5.5 square metres (60 sq. ft), the circular and square rooms 6.5 metres (22 ft) in diameter, with 1.5-square-metre (15-sq.-ft) entrance towers, centred on the eastern and western sides. Cellars under the towers swung out 9 metres (30 ft) from the central block. A square, walled garden would surround the site, 90 metres (300 ft) on each side, aligned to the cardinal points and divided into paths and beds composed of circles within squares. He was drawing the first unified house and garden plan north of the Alps, with harmonious ratios derived from *Musica theoretica*, the 'oldest of all quantitative physical laws', expressing the *virtus* of microcosmic man.[6] The plan was 'saturated with geometry', wrote two leading Danish authorities, 'but at the same time strikingly home-made in composition'.[7]

There were 46 households of tithe-paying peasants living in the village of Tuna on Hven.[8] Patriarchs met periodically at the village *Ting* (assembly) to decide communal matters, giving little thought to royal authority until Tycho Brahe personally brought *dominium regale* to the island. As patron of St Ibb's, he controlled glebe lands, the village mill and two-thirds of the tithes. The *Ting* became a manorial court under Tycho's bailiff instead of the village Oldermand, and Tycho demanded corvée labour under the law of lordship (*vorned-skab*). He ploughed up a large part of the commons for a grange farm and quickly constructed three buildings around

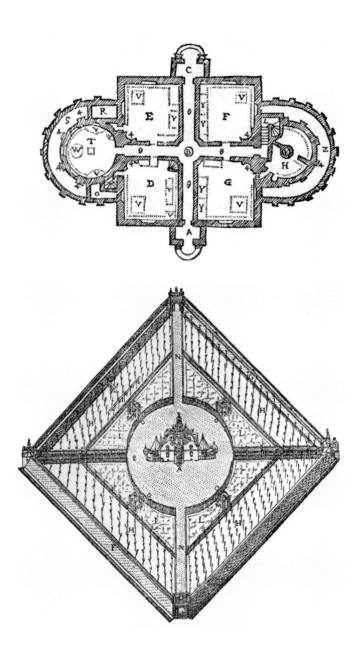

34, 35 Plan of Uraniborg, c. 1586.

a triangular courtyard. He and his household may have lived in the wing with the round tower at first.[9]

A skilled master mason, perhaps Hans Floris, could have built Uraniborg's vaulted cellars from Tycho's sketches.[10] By 8 August 1576, the cellars had risen to ground level, and Charles de Danzay came out to preside over a festive sunrise 'consecration' of Uraniborg's cornerstone as wine flowed freely.[11] Jan Gregor van der Schardt arrived in 1576, and George Labenwolf came to plan fountains for Kronborg's courtyard and Uraniborg's rotunda.

That summer, plague spread from Copenhagen to Helsingborg. It carried off Tycho's beloved, precocious daughter Kirstine, less than a month before her third birthday.[12] For safety's sake, Tycho took little Magdalene and Kirsten Jørgensdatter, who was pregnant again, out of Helsingborg and lodged them with a noble widow named Margrethe Gagge at Tågalycka (Taagelykke) manor.

36 Uraniborg grange, *c.* 1586, detail of illus. 67.

On 13 December 1576, the day before his thirtieth birth-day, Tycho observed the solar culmination on the winter solstice for the first time on Hven.[13] From this observation, he used Copernicus' obliquity of the ecliptic to calculate Uraniborg's latitude. He checked his solar result by observing Polaris and was troubled to discover a difference.[14] Which figure was right? It was essential to know, because the latitude of Uraniborg would be a factor in every observation he made.

The Nonian system of calibration was also a problem. It was awkward and unreliable in practice. Tycho found a better method in the dotted transversal lines on his old cross-staff. He proved mathematically that distortion on a curved arc

37 Jan Gregor van der Schardt, *Self portrait*, c. 1575, polychrome terracotta.

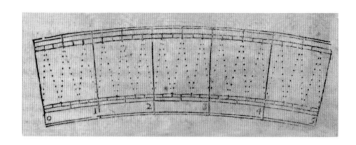

38, 39 Tycho's portable steel sextant. Transversal lines of dots (*above*) mark finer subdivisions of the calibrated arc.

would be negligible and applied this calibration to the azimuth quadrant and steel sextant.[15] Elimination of the Nonian arcs made the sextant much lighter and easier to use. In the spring of 1577, he also commissioned a clock inspired by those in Kassel, then three more by 1580, and began to test them for accuracy.[16]

Kirsten Jørgensdatter gave birth to a son on 2 January 1577 at Tågalycka manor, but the infant died after six days. Tycho never saw him, but composed a dolorous epitaph for his grave.[17] Queen Sophie gave birth to her first son on 12 April 1577, and Tycho spent the 'light nights' of Nordic spring and summer calculating Prince Christian's horoscope.[18]

That spring, the consistory of the University of Copenhagen elected a *Rector magnificus* to serve as its administrative and ceremonial head under the chancellor, as they did each year. In 1577, on Niels Hemmingsen's recommendation, the consistory broke precedent and elected Tycho Brahe, who held no academic degree and was not a professor. The Elector of Saxony was pressing King Frederick to purge Hemmingsen from the university, and Hemmingsen apparently hoped that a great court aristocrat like Tycho could protect him. But Tycho was focused on Hven and declined the honour.[19]

In August 1577 Tycho was granted the crown manor of Kullagården to provide lumber, charcoal and cordwood a short sail from Hven in return for maintaining Kullen lighthouse at the point of the wooded peninsula.[20] That summer, Uraniborg's red brick walls rose above the vaulted cellars to establish a sequence of interior spaces like a Palladian villa. Georg Labenwolf's son, Lienhart, came to lay out the villa's

hydraulics.[21] Schardt, Labenwolf and many artisans worked at Kronborg as well as Uraniborg.

Around sunset on 13 November 1577, Tycho was fishing when he noticed a bright star over the Sound.[22] As the sky darkened, long, ruddy rays gradually stretched away from the point of sunset, and he realized that it was a comet, the first he had ever seen.[23] He went for his cross-staff and later observed it with the steel sextant and azimuth quadrant.[24] He wrote to Petrus Severinus and begged not to be summoned to court while the comet was visible, because he needed to observe it carefully.[25] Three astronomer-astrologers were already at court: Severinus, Iver Bertelsen and Jørgen Dybvad, who rushed his prognostication into print after merely looking at the comet. This publication and Saxon pressures won Dybvad a mathematics professorship with the lucrative right to publish almanacs.[26]

Tycho observed the comet every clear night from 13 November 1577 to 26 January 1578, noting colour changes, measuring angular distances from prominent stars, and calculating the comet's changing latitude and longitude.[27] He applied Regiomontanus' methods to determine its parallax

40 Tycho's sketch of the comet on 13 November 1577.

and concluded, 'The comet was not in the region of the elements.'[28] When it faded from sight, Tycho wrote a secret report in German for King Frederick and Queen Sophie.[29] His starting point was Melanchthon's interpretation of Aristotelian natural philosophy in the light of Copernican and Paracelsian cosmology and his own observations. He asserted that his inductive method of 'assiduous observation and demonstration' (*durch vleißige obseruation vnnd demonstrattion*) was superior to the a priori method preferred by Aristotelians.[30] The Aristotelians had their

> knowledge and opinions, not from experience or any mathematical observation done with assiduous methods, but they have it from subtle arguments of reason alone, which . . . however embellished it might be with subtle arguments, is still only a good thought taken from human reason, which can be refuted by other arguments from human reason.[31]

Tycho based his own method on 'immediate observations through improved instruments' and trigonometrical analysis of the resulting data 'through the high science of triangles'.[32] The book of nature needed to be observed with methodical precision and written in the language of mathematics.

Tycho's method could produce irrefutable mathematical conclusions based on verifiable observations, but it had its limits: it could not claim to answer questions that went beyond empirical evidence, as the Aristotelians claimed to do. Sometimes, Tycho wrote, 'our limited and earthy understanding [provides] no real grounds and knowledge (*wissenschafft*)',

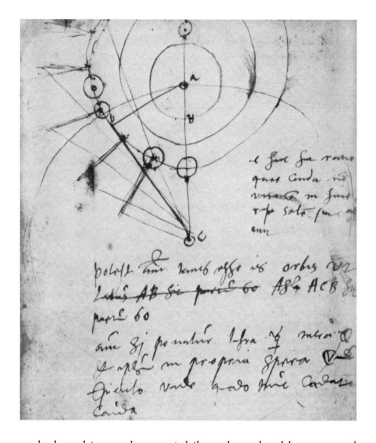

and when this was the case, 'philosophers should not quarrel uselessly about matters they cannot resolve but should all the more admit our *ignorantia modeste*'.[33] Tycho drew on Nicholas of Cusa's concept of 'learned ignorance' and used the German word *Wissenschaft*, the equivalent of the Latin *scientia*, to refer specifically to knowledge acquired by his method of 'assiduous observation and demonstration'. He placed his method in opposition to the Aristotelian view of astronomy as *scientia media*, intermediary between mathematics and physics.[34]

41 Tycho's 1578 sketch of the comet, Venus and Mercury orbiting the Sun.

Tycho's astronomy strove not simply to 'save the phenomena' with geometical models, but to explain the true nature of the physical universe, even as he granted that his method could not explain everything.

Tycho described the colour and movement of the comet and concluded that its tail was 'nothing but the rays of the sun, which have passed through the body of the comet'.[35] He placed it far beyond the Moon, closer to Venus than to the outer planets or fixed stars, and wondered whether it was in orbit around the Sun. Remembering that Martianus Capella in late antiquity had also put Mercury and Venus in orbit around the Sun, Tycho considered this alternative, but finally settled on a geocentric Copernican model like that of the *Prutenic Tables.*[36]

As for its astrology, Tycho said that the comet of 1577 'was so tremendously huge and had a malicious, saturnine appearance' that its effects would be immense, causing great human mortality and religious disruption.[37] These effects would last until the Great Conjunction of 1583, when the New Star of 1572 and the Maximum Conjunction of 1603 would begin their 'mighty operations',

> and then in the following years will take place great changes and Reformation, both in spiritual and worldly affairs, which perhaps will be more to the good than the worse for Christendom. But because this Maximum Conjunction is the seventh since the beginning of the world, which number belongs to the Sabbath according to the Hebrew Cabbala, it is expected that the eternal Sabbath of all creatures is at hand.[38]

King Frederick pondered the implications of Tycho's prognostication. He rejected Elector August's efforts to draw him into an ultra-orthodox Lutheran alliance and listened instead to Danzay, Landgrave William, and others who urged Protestant unity against growing Catholic aggression in preparation for the coming Apocalypse.[39] He rained favours upon Tycho, including augmentation of the Kullagården grant and the Norwegian benefice of Nordfjord with an income equal to Knutstorp's estate.[40] Honours flowed even more abundantly, however, to his brother, Steen, who soon became the youngest member of the sovereign Council of the Realm.[41]

Margrethe Gagge died on 7 October 1577, and Kirsten Jørgensdatter moved to Hven with little Magdalene.[42] Within a month, she was pregnant again. According to Danish law, when a man and woman lived together openly for three winters and she wore the keys to the household on her belt, they were legally married, even without a wedding.[43]

She wore the keys, but Danish law gave Tycho the same authority over his household that King Frederick exercised over the court. His learned students and assistants were part of his *família*, as he sometimes called his household. Tycho wielded his authority strictly, generously rewarding those like Flemløse who served him well.[44] He corresponded with friends across Europe to learn what astronomers like Michael Maestlin, Cornelius Gemma and Elisaeus Roeslin thought of the comet.[45] Moreover, he began to collaborate with other observers, especially Thaddeus Hagecius, by exchanging observations and ideas.[46] Meanwhile, he assigned Flemløse to triangulate angular distances between major fixed stars and establish their positions firmly. Flemløse sketched himself at

work in ancient Roman garb. By March 1578 he had established
a network of sixteen reference stars.[47]

On a visit to Kronborg, Tycho met a master mason named
Hans van Steenwinckel, who was experienced in architectural design and had a knack for drawing in perspective.[48]
Tycho invited him to Hven, began to teach him geometry
and astronomy, and introduced him to Vitruvian theories of
architecture.[49] He needed a man with Steenwinckel's practical
experience. Uraniborg's two round towers needed roofs that
could open to the skies. They flanked a cornice that swept up
to a central gable like the tripartite curved gables of Venice.
A light shaft ran up through the building from the rotunda to
an octagonal cupola still to be constructed. Roofs over eight

42 Peter Jacobsen Flemløse's self-portrait in Roman attire with the
improved steel quadrant.

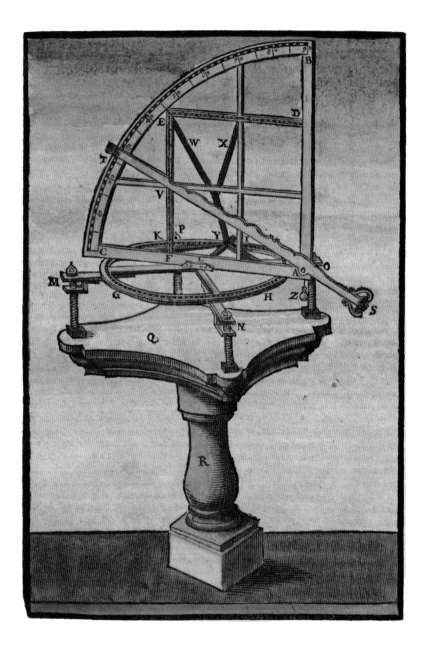

43 Tycho's azimuth quadrant enclosing Peurbach's gnomon square, *c.* 1578.

garret rooms would go out from the cupola to four gables. A rooftop gallery and balustrade would run around the cupola and out to four octagonal belvederes with mechanical statues of the four seasons. All of this needed to be built. Tycho had designed its symmetry and harmonious proportions. Was Steenwinckel the man who could make these complex structures a reality?

Tycho brought in five or six master artisans with various skills to build Uraniborg's instruments. His instrument factory came to have a horse-powered trip hammer, iron and steel smithy, brass foundry, engraving and gilding shop, cabinetmaker's shop and instrument-maker's shop.[50] One of the first new instruments was an improved azimuth quadrant with an open frame cast of solid brass. It was calibrated with transversal lines instead of Nonian arcs, and the square internal brace was calibrated like Peurbach's 'gnomon square' to show the value of the tangent to any angle measured on the arc.[51] After correcting a minor instrumental error, it was more stable and accurate than the old quadrant, although it was too small to measure fractions of a minute of arc, which remained Tycho's goal.[52]

He continued to find a disagreement of around $1\frac{1}{2}$ arcminutes between solar and stellar determinations of Uraniborg's latitude. The problem was how this would be resolved. The ancient Greeks never took what Frances Yates called 'the momentous step of experimental verification of its hypotheses', but this was precisely what Tycho was doing.[53] He recognized the potential for error in the very act of observation and set out to verify his observations by repeating them in order to see if the results could be replicated. This was an innovation of great significance for the future history of science. Some days, observations were 'not well seen'; other days, 'mediocre', 'not so great because of clouds', then 'good', 'better', and finally, 'precise' and 'exquisite'.[54]

Constant observation also made Tycho acutely aware that the Sun, Moon, planets and stars were physical objects that possessed volume and substance and moved through some kind of physical space. Any theory of astronomical movement would have to take these physical facts into consideration. In 1578 he began to explore the diameter and parallax of the immense Sun.[55]

On 8 August 1578 Kirsten Jørgensdatter gave birth to a daughter named Sophie. Tycho no longer referred to her as his 'natural' child, but considered her to be born in wedlock. At year's end, Queen Sophie gave birth to a son named Ulrik, and Tycho Brahe spent long hours calculating his nativity.[56] Around that time, one of Queen Sophie's noble maids of honour withdrew in disgrace, and Knud Brahe fled the court in dishonour with Tycho's covert assistance, not stopping until he had put the entire continent between himself and the wrath of King Frederick II. Seducing a royal maid of honour could be a capital offense, but once he was far away, Knud made light of it in the album of a friend by showing a huntsman pursuing more than a fox around the escutcheon of Brahe.[57]

Tycho finally received the canonry of the Chapel of the Magi in Roskilde in June 1579. Its endowment provided a substantial income and the patronage of several learned livings and scholarships. The interim grant of Nordfjord was withdrawn, but Tycho asked to retain it for a year and

also requested the next vacant canonry in Roskilde for his
assistant, Flemløse. Both requests were granted. When sailors
complained about the Kullen light, it was granted to another
lord, but Tycho protested and got it back. A year later, he lost
Kullagården and Nordfjord again, and Hven peasants complained of his lordship.[58] Presumably, they complained to
Christopher Valkendorf, the Master of Rents, but Tycho went
to the king, pled to retain Kullagården with the Kullen lighthouse and Nordfjord, and requested that royal commissioners
investigate the peasant complaints.

Kirsten Jørgensdatter gave birth to yet another daughter,
Elizabeth, in 1579, and Tycho's sister, Sophie, married Otto

44 Knud Brahe as a huntsman with the Brahe arms, 1580.

Thott, a prominent young courtier with two Skåne castles. That summer, the king and queen planned to bring Prince Christian home from Mecklenburg, where he had lived with his grandparents since his baptism. The Saxon Elector and Electress were still blustering over what they called the 'Crypto-Calvinism' of Niels Hemmingsen and the Danish church, and they would also be there. Shortly before departing, King Frederick exiled Hemmingsen from Copenhagen University to a canonry in Roskilde.[59] At Güstrow Castle, having silenced Saxon complaints about Hemmingsen, he faced down Saxon pressure to accept their militantly anti-Calvinist *Book of Concord* and displayed recent letters from Queen Elizabeth of England and King Henry of Navarre. Elector August was so offended that the entire Saxon court stormed off 'in a huff' the very next day.[60] In this way, King Frederick maintained the tolerant, eirenic Philippist humanism of the Danish church that allowed Tycho and others to explore the full range of Renaissance thought.

45 Tycho's emblems of *Astronomia* and *Chymia*.

That summer and the next, ramparts faced with stone were erected around the Uraniborg site with gatehouses in the east and west and outbuildings like smaller Uraniborgs in the north and south corners. Labenwolf's crew installed a fountain and running water in Uraniborg in late 1579. The cupola and roofs were erected, and a winged Pegasus on the highest spire was connected to an interior wind gauge. Obelisks, portals and other ornamental stonework were also installed. Above the east portal, flaming spheres and ecstatic putti gestured to a statue of *Astronomia* in repose, with a motto from the Emerald Table of Hermes Trismegistus – *Svspiciendo Despicio* ('By looking up I see down') – and at the west portal, *Chymia* and the motto *Despiciendo Svspicio* ('By looking down I see up').[61] These sculpted figures have been ascribed to Jan Gregor van der Schardt.[62]

Gradually, Uraniborg stood forth in red brick, sandstone and gleaming copper. The grounds inside the ramparts were articulated by fenced gravel paths, knots of herbal and ornamental gardens, and an orchard. Interior painting and panelling progressed, and Tycho hoped to move in before the end of 1580. If any building in northern Europe epitomized the late Renaissance, this was it.

Tycho observed a solar eclipse on 31 January 1580, but for the next ten months from February to November, only two brief observations were recorded beyond the usual solar culminations.[63] This was a festive year beyond all others at the Danish court, and Tycho was a courtier. That spring, Queen Sophie gave birth to her third daughter at Koldinghus Castle, but Tycho was not asked to prepare horoscopes for royal daughters. In May, however, he was very much involved in the pageantry of the formal election by the Council of the Realm of the three-year-old Prince Christian as successor to the throne, and the ceremonies were augmented by another in which the three Dukes of Schleswig-Holstein pledged homage to King Frederick. A feast in Odense Castle concluded these events on 3 May 1580, when King Frederick II established the Royal Order of the Elephant and bestowed a heavy golden chain and jewelled golden elephant on his brother, Duke Hans the Younger of Schleswig-Holstein; another was granted to Viceroy Heinrich Rantzau of Schleswig-Holstein, and others on six great lords, including Christopher Valkendorf, Jørgen Rosenkrantz, Steen Brahe – and Tycho Brahe.[64] This was the highest honour the Danish monarch could bestow.

A month later, King Frederick II addressed a moral issue that disturbed some of his theologians and advisors: he publicly chastised men who lived openly with women outside of marriage and banned them from religious sacraments until they mended their ways.[65] Tycho responded by refraining from Holy Eucharist. Eventually, he called the pastor of St Ibb's to live at Uraniborg as his chaplain and let out the glebe farm to a tenant.

That summer of 1580, a courier brought King Frederick a splendid copy of the *Book of Concord*, bound in velvet with gold ornamentation, as a gift from the Elector and Electress of Saxony. The king paged through it and found 'many new, puzzling, and unusual phrases and opinions, which could easily mislead and disturb the unity' of his church. In the middle of a sleepless night, King Frederick asked his groom of the chamber to make a fire: 'he had caught a Devil he wanted to burn. And when the fire was ablaze, he threw in the book and burned it up'.[66] He then banned the *Book of Concord* from all his realms under threat of death to violators.[67] This was a grave affront to Saxony, but it was high time for Denmark to seek a new alignment in the affairs of Europe.

A student of astronomy named Paul Wittich (1546–1586), 'very skilled in mathematics', arrived on Hven that July.[68] He owned a manuscript of Copernicus' *Commentariolus* in the author's own handwriting – a gift from his uncle, Balthasar Sartorius, who had studied under Copernicus' only disciple, George Joachim Rheticus.[69] Wittich also had four copies of Copernicus' *De revolutionibus orbium coelestium* (On the Revolutions of the Heavenly Spheres), each one full of marginal notes and numerous diagrams of world systems, 'residues of a once intense discussion' among astronomers.[70]

Wittich was not an observational astronomer, but he joined Tycho in freewheeling discussions of cosmology and planetary theory.[71] He showed Tycho all of his manuscripts, and Tycho displayed his own large library of annotated books and manuscripts. Tycho enlisted him as an assistant and 'revealed his whole enterprise'.[72] Wittich had considered a Capellan model in 1579, as Tycho had done in 1578, and Tycho argued that the new star of 1572 and comet of 1577 were both celestial phenomena, but Wittich placed them below the Moon.[73] On 10 October 1580 Flemløse spotted a small comet in the northern sky. Uraniborg sprang into action to plot its movements against reference stars and chart its altitude and azimuth with the quadrant.[74] Even Wittich had to help, to the amusement of Tycho's smiths, for he knew none of the constellations and 'argued that such knowledge

overleaf: 46 King Frederick ii receiving the homage of the dukes of Schleswig-Holstein in Odense in 1580, *c.* 1589, engraving.

Collatio rerum feudalium, qua Fridericus Daniæ rex feuda Duc
Ranzovio, vicario regio, nomine vero Ducis Johannis senioris Johanni de Wis
Odenschæ in

13

Confert ſuo quidē filiorumq̃ tanquam Holſatiæ Ducum nomine, Henrico
nedicto ab Aleſeldt Dñō. Haſeldorſij, Ducis Johannis junioris Johanni Blomen, facta
xx.

dilecta Deo rerum concordia nutr<x>.
Munera tu vitæ proſperioris habes.

was no more necessary for an astronomer than a knowledge of herbs was for a physician. Christopher Rothmann later noted that Wittich had poor eyes and should have stuck to geometry.'[75]

Tycho and his assistants observed the comet for as long as it was visible. Steenwinckel, 'my architect', joined them on 12 October.[76] Wittich's time to shine came when they began to reduce the observational data.[77] He knew how to transform complicated problems requiring multiplication and division into simple addition and subtraction by a formula called *prosthaphæresis*, first developed by Johannes Werner of Nuremberg, whose manuscript passed to Rheticus, who taught it to Sartorius, who taught it to Wittich, who brought it to Tycho and Flemløse.[78] Tycho immediately recognized its value and 'harnessed Wittich to the task of helping him compile a manual of trigonometry' for his assistants.[79]

They observed the comet until it vanished. Kirsten Jørgensdatter gave birth to yet another daughter, Cecilia, making four in all. In the midst of all this, they prepared to move into Uraniborg, while Wittich slaved away on the manual. One day, he came and said that his revered uncle Sartorius was ill, and that he needed to leave for Breslau (Wrocław). As a parting gift, Tycho gave him the most opulent book on astronomy ever published, Peter Apian's *Astronomicum Caesareum*, which had cost him the value of 70 grams of gold. In the protocol of exchange, such a valuable gift was a sign of high regard and implied reciprocal obligations.[80] Wittich accepted the gift but ignored the obligations. He had already brought *prosthaphæresis* to Uraniborg, and he carried Tycho's letter to Hagecius dated 4 November

1580, which said, 'God willing, we hope to move over to the new building next week.'[81] Back home in Breslau, Wittich 'exhibited a curious mixture of boastfulness and obsessive secrecy when questioned about his mathematical and astronomical work'.[82] His friend, Andreas Dudith, described him as muttering under his breath and claiming Tycho's theories and observations as his own, but Dudith added, 'you know what Wittich was like'.[83] And yet, Tycho valued him for the brilliant mathematician he was.

In November 1580, as they finally moved into Uraniborg, the benefice of Nordfjord was restored to Tycho Brahe. The Great Celestial Globe from Augsburg, covered with seamless brass plates and engraved with the equatorial and ecliptic, was placed in Uraniborg's 'Museum', along with Tycho's library, automata and painted portraits.[84] The panelled Winter Room was warmed by a tile stove and contained Tycho and Kirsten's four-poster bed and a massive oaken table with Tycho's high seat. Other ground-floor rooms were for guests, with running water in every room and privies off two rooms. A secret system of bells allowed Tycho to summon his servants as if by magic.

Uraniborg's first new instrument was an immense azimuth quadrant with a brass scale over 194 centimetres (6 ft) in radius, mounted within a steel frame, calibrated and subdivided with dotted transversal lines down to ten arcseconds. An enlarged version of Peurbach's 'gnomon square' on the steel framework showed the value of the tangent or cotangent of any observed angle from the horizon or zenith.[85] It was installed in the south tower and was larger than any instrument in Kassel.[86]

The problem was that it didn't work. On 10 December 1580, it got a trial run 'with the newly corrected calibration', but by 22 December, Tycho could see that something was wrong with the pinnacidia and that wintry blasts shook the instrument on its pillars, to say nothing of the fact that 'it could hardly be rotated without setting the whole instrument in motion'.[87] This grave disappointment led Tycho to reconsider his whole observational strategy. Bigger was not aways better.

Meanwhile, peasant complaints against Tycho were resolved by a royal ordinance of 8 January 1581 declaring Hven's islanders to be tenants of the crown, not freeholders, regulating corvée labour at around fifteen workers a day, and setting the *Ting* day as every other Wednesday.[88] This ordinance did not please the islanders. Three months later, Tycho

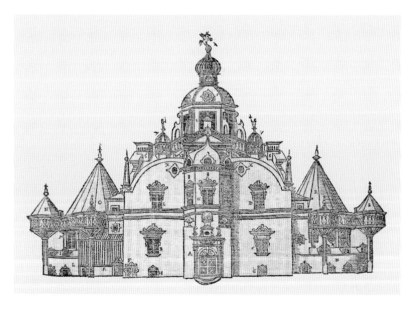

47 Uraniborg around 1580.

48 Tycho's Greatest Steel Quadrant, 1580–84.

was informed that his annual salary of 500 rixdollars would expire at the end of the year, but then, in June 1581, King Frederick II returned Kullagården to him and gave him a new bell for Uraniborg.[89] A tug of war between Valkendorf's goal of sound administration and the king's desire to reward a favourite must have lain behind this erratic granting and withdrawing of royal benefices.

Family events, obligations at court and other affairs kept drawing Tycho away from Hven. There was his brother Jørgen's marriage to Ingeborg Parsberg and the baptism of his sister Sophie's son, Tage Thott.[90] Anders Vedel retired from court and moved to Ribe, where Tycho attended his wedding in August 1581.[91] One week later, back on Hven, Kirsten Jørgensdatter gave birth to a son on 28 August 1581. He was named Tyge after Tycho's grandfather.

The disaster of the Greatest Steel Quadrant was followed in 1581 by a remarkably successful sextant that eliminated the problem of instrumental parallax and allowed precise sighting. Tycho reversed the instrument's orientation and brought the calibrated arc down to the observers, although this meant that there always had to be two observers. Two pinnacidia on dioptres moved along the arc and a circular post mounted at the fulcrum replaced a bronze tab as the upper sight. This allowed the observers to measure angles between two celestial objects over both sides of the collimated post. The Triangular Sextant had a radius of 155 centimetres (5 ft) and was comparatively light, due to Tycho's innovative use of laminated wood. Pieces of thoroughly dried walnut or hard spruce were glued together crosswise and covered with canvas, then painted with lead-based paint. The arc was graduated to single degrees and to fifteen arcminutes on transversal lines. The instrument rotated on a cylinder stabilized by internal springs, and it swung on its base to make observations quickly and accurately. Flemløse and assistants began testing it on 16 April 1581 against the steel sextant and cross-staff.[92] It soon became the instrument of choice for measuring angles between celestial objects and was improved by modifications over time. When Tycho realized that one observer could sight along the edge, he mounted pinnacidia at the zero end and removed the second dioptre. In January 1582, he mounted the sextant with one side horizontal and used it to measure altitudes.[93] In that year he replaced the cylinder mounting with a ball-and-socket held in position by eight spring-loaded pressure plates. Eventually, as we shall see, he adapted the Triangular Sextant to measure extremely small angles.

The Zodiacal Armillary was an ancient instrument used since Hipparchus and Ptolemy to measure celestial latitude and longitude. Tycho ordered one from Schreckenfuchs in 1575.[94] He clarified the design, reduced it to essentials, increased the size, and added pinnacidia and other innovations, always aiming for precision, stability and ease of operation. By 1577, he had simplified the usual five or six rings to four, ordered the rings in brass, and sent them to Herrevad to be mounted on an iron stand, but the smiths could not make sense of his instructions.[95] In 1581, he brought these graduated brass rings to Hven and built a zodiacal armillary with an angle of obliquity based on his own solar observations. When testing began on 2 November 1581, the instrument proved unsteady and unreliable, and this made

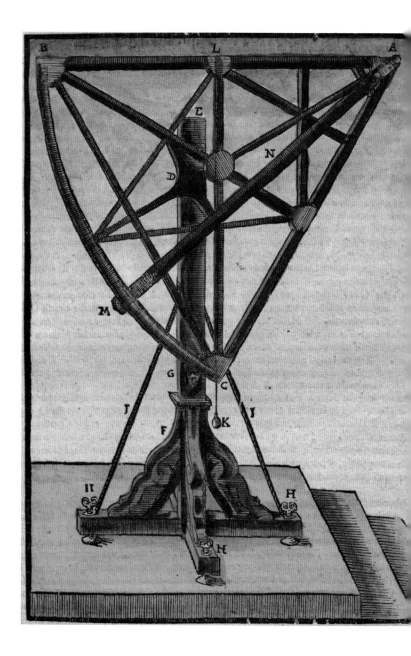

49 Tycho's Triangular Sextant mounted to observe meridian altitudes.

50 Tycho's Triangular Sextant mounted on a ball-and-socket.

him sceptical of observations by ancient astronomers who had used similar armillaries.[96]

Tycho's former tutor, Hans Aalborg, helped to observe between September 1581 and May 1582.[97] Anders Viborg, a prankster and wit, was assisting by December 1581, and Viborg's friend, Gellius Sascerides, soon after.[98] Johannes Stephanius, a learned and talented musician of peasant origins, arrived on 1 February 1582.[99] They and other assistants slept in the garret, dined at the long table in the Winter Room, learned Tycho's methods, worked and relaxed together. All of them cultivated Latin poetry and the fine arts. Flemløse took charge of observations when Tycho went off to court.[100]

A big, new clock was tested against observations of solar meridians and was 20 seconds fast after 24 hours on 30 December 1581.[101] On 5 March 1582, two crews observed the sun and recorded the time that elapsed until Venus passed the same longitude.[102] These observations and others soon to follow became Tycho's link between the day and night skies.[103] His crews observed the moon in all phases and observed planets all winter long with cross-staff, zodiacal armillary and triangular sextant, timing some observations with the clocks.[104] Tycho still needed to establish Uraniborg's true latitude and observed the upper and lower culminations of Polaris and other circumpolar stars simultaneously with several instruments without reaching a satisfactory result.[105]

By June 1582, Tycho's brass founders had cast an immense 90° arc with a radius of over 194 centimetres (6 ft), which was polished and graduated to ten arcseconds and by transversals to a single of arc.[106] Installed in the room across from the Winter Room, it faced due south. Removable pinnacidia,

Tycho's 'light-cutter' sighting devices, slid along the arc, and he used them to observe meridian transitions along collimated lines of sight over the upper and lower edges of a horizontal gilt brass cylinder in a small opening high on the wall.[107] Tycho was immensely proud of this instrument and called it 'Tichonicus', the Mural Quadrant. Rock solid, stable, protected from weather, quick and easy to use, it consistently surpassed his goal of accuracy within one minute of arc.[108] He kept testing it against simultaneous observations of solar culminations with three other quadrants from 10 June 1582 through the rest of the year.[109]

Knud Brahe remained in exile for three years, studying at universities in Italy and France and visiting many lands before he was restored to honour at the Danish court, where he soon rose to the high office of Cupbearer (*Hofskænk*), formerly held by his brother Steen. Tycho, Steen, Axel, Jørgen and Knud Brahe, and their brothers-in-law, Henrik Gyldenstierne, Councillor Christen Skeel and Otto Thott, were all active courtiers and royal administrators.

Then came a hard blow to Tycho. Marriage had always been a family affair, but King Frederik II and his clergy wanted to bring it under Church control. Part of the problem was that some people, nobles and commoners alike, entered into marriage without the ceremony of a church wedding. To deal with part of this problem, a royal ordinance of 19 June 1582 declared that children born to a noble father and commoner mother were not nobles, could not bear a noble coat of arms nor use a noble surname or inherit privileged noble land, but could only inherit their father's cash and personal property.[110] For the first time, Danish law clearly reserved noble rank to

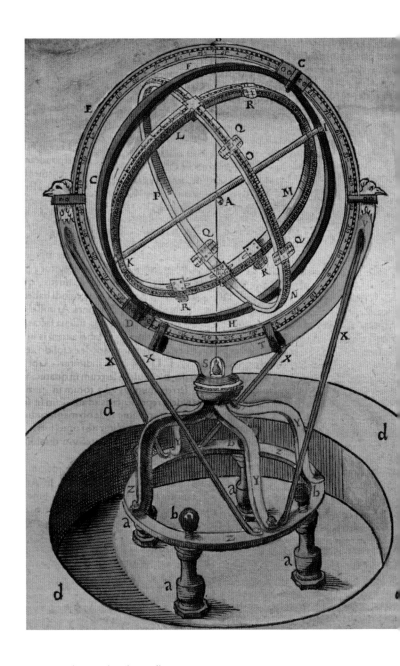

51 Tycho's Zodiacal Armillary.

52 'Tichonicus', the Mural Quadrant.

those of noble descent in all paternal and maternal lines.[111] Tycho's children were not Brahes and would never inherit Knutstorp Castle with its landed estate.

Three weeks after this stern ordinance, Tycho's 300 rix-dollars a year for the Kullen light was cut off because 'the king has discovered that it did not cost so much'.[112] The language reflected Christopher Valkendorf's principles of economy. King Frederick II did decide, however, to pay for repairs to the Chapel of the Magi instead of billing Tycho Brahe.[113]

By the summer of 1582 Tycho was well settled in Uraniborg, and Kronborg had become a heavily fortified castle of great splendour. On 22 July 1582, a large English delegation headed by Peregrine Bertie, Lord Willoughby de Eresby, arrived to invest King Frederick II with the Order of the Garter.[114] The investiture took place on 13 August in Kronborg's great hall, one of the most splendid in northern Europe, hung with tapestries of one hundred Danish kings designed by Hans Knieper.[115] The ceremony concluded with a deafening salvo from cannons atop Kronborg's great tower, and a gargantuan feast followed, 'seven or eight Hours together at one Meal', during which Lord Willoughby's Paracelsian physician, Dr Thomas Moffet, met and conversed with the renowned Petrus Severinus.[116]

Lord Willoughby, Moffet and many others sailed to Hven on 18 August, where Tycho Brahe escorted them up the bluffs and mastiffs barked as they passed through the gatehouse into the orchards and gardens. They saw the Great Celestial Globe and other treasures of the museum, went from the light-filled laboratory up to the observatories, and enjoyed rooftop views of the Sound with ships of many nations.

Uraniborg thus made its appearance on the international stage as a ceremonial space of the Danish court. From Kronborg Castle, distinguished visitors sailed the narrow waters to Hven in order to 'see and learn that which they can hardly find elsewhere' and returned more fully comprehending the splendour, wisdom and power of the Danish king, who ruled such far-flung realms and followed the divine footsteps of Nature.

53 Kronborg Castle, 2005.

FIVE

Star Castle: Going Down to See Up, 1582–8

N THE WINTER OF 1581–2, Tycho Brahe tried to force the warlike planet Mars to reveal whether Copernicus or Ptolemy was correct. In the Ptolemaic universe, Mars was farther away than the Sun as both revolved around Earth, but in the Copernican cosmos, Earth and Mars both revolved around the Sun, and when Mars was in opposition, it was closer than the Sun.[1] This meant that its parallax would be greater than the Sun's parallax. Astronomers generally used Ptolemy's figure of three arcminutes for solar parallax, and Tycho used this figure instead of determining it by his own observations.[2] If Mars revealed a parallax of more than three arcminutes, he would consider it closer than the Sun.

Tycho had just started to keep a journal of meteorological observations, and it shows how weather affected his ability to study the stars. Clear skies allowed him to observe Mars morning and evening on 26–27 December and again on 17 January 1583 to determine its diurnal parallax.[3] The results were inconclusive, because it was hard to measure such small angles. Tycho was determined to try again.[4]

A student named Elias Olsen Morsing arrived early in 1583 and learned to observe by assisting in the search for

Martian parallax.[5] Tycho had begun to test his assistants' skills and the accuracy of the instruments by using as many as five separate teams to observe solar culminations simultaneously with different instruments.[6] He brought an element of play into observation by encouraging the teams to compete and soon found that Morsing was one of the best.

Uraniborg's latitude was still unresolved. Using Copernicus' angle of obliquity and constant observation, Tycho reduced the difference between his solar and stellar determinations to around five arcminutes, but as Moesgaard pointed out, better observations 'were not a magic wand that moved astronomy forward on their own'.[7] Tycho was collecting more data than ever before in the history of science. The very volume of all his observations compelled him to keep on inventing new methods to process the data. As he worked through piles of solar data, Tycho gradually discovered a way to find what was later called the 'arithmetic mean'. He began to quantify the approximate accuracy of each instrument.[8]

At that time, his assistants were observing the constellation Cassiopeia, where the new star of 1572 had appeared, but its stars were so close together that two observers using the Triangular Sextant kept bumping heads. Tycho solved the problem by inventing the Bipartite Arc with two precisely equidistant brass cylinders and two graduated arcs at opposite ends of a 155-centimetre (5-ft) iron rod. It tested out to an accuracy of around 30 arcseconds. Then, Tycho had another idea. He installed a second brass cylinder on the Triangular Sextant so two observers with two movable pinnacidia could use it in the same way as the Bipartite Arc. He tested one instrument against the other, corrected a flaw in the sextant's new pinnacidia, and obtained splendid matches.[9] By early 1583 he had these two excellent instruments for observing very small angles.

Kirsten Jørgensdatter gave birth to a son, who was named Jørgen, that year, and Queen Sophie also bore a son. Tycho spent many hours preparing a horoscope for the infant Duke Hans.[10] If he also computed horoscopes for his own children, which seems likely, he would have devoted much time to nativities in 1583. Other events at court also took time. Georg Labenwolf's monumental Kronborg fountain arrived after eight years of delays and was installed that summer. On the day of dedication, Neptune Ruler of the Seas 'came alive' to festive choral and instrumental music and rotated atop a 6-metre (20-ft) column packed with spraying brass statues above an octagonal basin of black marble decorated with bronze bowmen and harquebusiers.[11]

The Great Conjunction approached that summer, and Tycho searched for Jupiter and Saturn in the bright summer skies, finding them $4°\ 11'$ apart on 11 June, but then the separation grew instead of shrinking. Had he missed the conjunction during earlier nights of overcast skies?[12] After extensive observation and calculation, he finally concluded that the conjunction took place in Pisces, bringing the eight-hundred-year cycle to an end, and that Jupiter was in opposition, brightest and closest to the Earth, at 12.50 a.m. on 5 September 1583.[13]

Late that year, his instrument factory turned out a huge version of the classical Greek *triquetrum* as another homage to his predecessors. As usual, Tycho redesigned the instrument and enlarged it for greater accuracy, but this time, he went

overboard. Ptolemy's slender hinged wooden rods were transformed into a monster that filled Uraniborg's north tower
with a rotating brass beam nearly 330 centimetres (11 ft) long
and an azimuth circle more than 466 centimetres (15 ft) in
diameter. Tycho tested it in December but was not able to
get satisfactory results.[14] The huge triquetrum was a costly
fiasco. Two great Uraniborg instruments, two failures. What
could he do now?

In November 1583, King Frederick gave Tycho a fully
rigged pilot's boat that allowed him to sail in any weather.
Foreign skippers were still complaining about the Kullen light
and other parts of the world's first system of lighthouses along
sea lanes, so King Frederick took steps to improve the entire
system.[15] Changes came to Queen Sophie's court in 1584,
when Inger Oxe retired as Stewardess and Tycho's mother,
Beate Bille, succeeded her.[16] That summer, young Prince
Christian was hailed as the future king in each province of
Denmark. Tycho Brahe swore his solemn oath of loyalty at
Lund on 20 July with the entire Skåne nobility, followed by
representatives of the clergy, burghers and peasants. The long
ceremony concluded with a festive banquet for all.[17]

Tycho wanted to set up a printing office at Uraniborg.
There were many good reasons for this, including the need for
close oversight to protect his intellectual property, assure the
accuracy of highly technical texts and woodcut illustrations,
and guarantee that the books had an elegant humanist format. As historian Sachiko Kusukawa points out, 'it was very
rare for an author to be in full control of the production of
both images and text', but Tycho had the will and the means
to achieve such control.[18] Tobias Gemperle was skilled at

54 Tycho's Bipartite Arc.

cutting woodblock illustrations. Tycho hired a printer named
Joachim, obtained type fonts at the Frankfurt Book Fair, and
sent Joachim to Wittenberg that summer to buy a press and
additional equipment.[19] In the autumn, the printing office
was set up in the 'little Uraniborg' at the southern corner of
the ramparts.

After observing at the summer solstice of 1583, Tycho
finally realized that the difference between his polar and solar
determinations of latitude had to be due to refraction. He
became the first astronomer to take refraction into consideration and was finally able to establish Uraniborg's latitude as
$55° 54' 15''$.[20] Now, he could begin to build his model of solar
motion. He no longer aimed to choose between Copernicus

55 Tycho's Large Triquetrum.

56 Georg Labenwolf's Kronborg Fountain, 1730.

or Ptolemy but set out to create a geometrical theory of his own, using combinations of circles and epicycles familiar to Renaissance astronomers but based entirely on his own observations.[21] He took the approach of Copernicus, who had calculated his solar theory on the basis of the time it took the Sun to pass through a selected segment of its orbit, but Tycho wanted to minimize the effect of refraction, so he chose two segments near the summer solstice instead of Copernicus' winter segment.[22] By early 1584 he had worked out an entirely new solar theory and calculated ephemerides to test its predictive ability.

He now suspected that Copernicus and others had set the obliquity of the ecliptic too low by ignoring refraction, and he decided to launch a scientific expedition to discover whether this was true. He sent Morsing to Frauenburg (Frombork) with a Triangular Sextant and the meteorological notebook. Morsing arrived on 13 May 1584 and lodged near the cathedral's West Tower, where Copernicus had observed.[23] When overcast skies cleared on 17 May, he mounted the Triangular Sextant to observe the solar meridian culmination; by 5 June, he had recorded eleven solar culminations.[24] On 25 May, an astronomer named Matthias Menius arrived and invited Morsing to visit Königsberg (Kaliningrad), which he did, establishing the latitude of the Prussian capital in a manner that corrected the *Prutenic Tables* by 26 arcminutes.[25] Back in Frauenburg, he observed four more solar culminations. Canon Johann Hannow presented him with a wooden triquetrum made by Copernicus, 2.5 metres (8 ft) long and calibrated in ink with a quill pen, and he apparently also acquired a portrait of Copernicus, possibly a self-portrait.

Morsing was back on Hven by 23 July. Tycho was so excited to have Copernicus' triquetrum that he composed a Latin poem in its honour and displayed it by his own immense triquetrum.[26] Morsing's observations showed that Copernicus' calculations had to be adjusted for an error of around two and a half minutes of arc for the latitude of Frauenburg, and his obliquity of the ecliptic had to be raised. Tycho also needed to revise his own solar theory to take these new figures into consideration.

He was disappointed to discover that the great Copernicus lacked a strong commitment to observation.[27] Tycho began to realize the significance of his own work when he saw that he was superior to Copernicus as an observational astronomer. He designed a 1.5-metre (5-ft) brass version of Copernicus' simple instrument and equipped it with pinnacidia and a

57 Frauenburg (Frombork) Cathedral. Copernicus' tower was beyond the row of buildings to the left of the church.

brass cylinder instead of peephole sights, installed a spring to hold the rulers in position and a levelling plumb line protected from wind inside a tube, and mounted the instrument on a sturdy, adjustable base. It was displayed next to Copernicus' triquetrum to demonstrate Tycho's innovations in instrument design.[28]

Tycho now realized that Uraniborg's high, windy site made observation difficult. Moreover, the failure of the triquetrum and Great Steel Quadrant taught him that instruments could not be enlarged without taking ease of use and the strength and weight of materials into consideration. He needed a new observatory and a new instrument-maker. Hans van Steenwinckel sketched a plan for the observatory, and Tycho recruited a Westphalian instrument-maker named Hans Croll, who had exceptional imagination, technical skills

58 Tycho's improved Triquetrum.

and very sharp eyesight.[29] That busy summer of 1584, on an open site seventy paces from the southern gatehouse of Uraniborg, corvée labourers dug a deep pit and masons began to build an underground observatory protected from Hven's winds. Tycho named it *Stjerneborg* (Star Castle).

Anders Sørensen Vedel came to visit, and they discussed plans for the future. On 1 July 1584 Tycho dictated as Vedel wrote down a proposal for a royal grant of the island of Hven to Tycho Brahe and his posterity as a permanent centre for the study of mathematics.[30] Tycho's sons were still toddlers, but he intended to raise them as mathematicians, experimenters and natural philosophers. His daughters could marry men with similar interests. They could run Uraniborg as a private research institution and carry on their father's investigations into nature. This plan would provide a future for his children as commoners. At some appropriate point, Tycho

59 Site of Stjerneborg's Great Steel Quadrant, 1962 photograph.

discussed it with King Frederick, who approved but did not implement it immediately. They may have anticipated objections from the University of Copenhagen, the Council of the Realm or the Master of Rents.

Tycho's proposal was unprecedented and strikingly innovative. Much of his genius was expressed in his ability to organize and lead teams of technicians and researchers in investigations of the natural world.[31] Uraniborg later came to be seen a model for seventeenth-century research institutes. In some ways, it resembled contemporary 'academies' like the Pléiade at the court of France, Giambattista della Porta's scientific Academia Secretorum Naturae in Naples, or the learned households of Ulisse Aldrovandi in Bologna, John

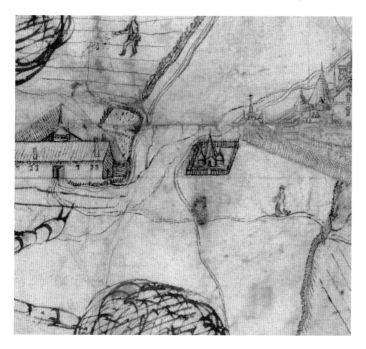

60 Stjerneborg, *c.* 1586, detail of illus. 67.

Dee at Mortlake, and the 'Wizard Earl' of Northumberland in England. Uraniborg went far beyond any of these others, however, in its organized pursuit of innovative natural philosophy. The academy in Naples encouraged members to report on individual experiments but pursued no organized programme of research. Uraniborg, on the other hand, was organized and centrally directed for teamwork towards clearly articulated goals. Tycho worked with and led a large staff of highly trained professional technicians and university-educated mathematicians, astronomers and chymists, all of whom participated in advanced education at Uraniborg.

Daily life at Uraniborg centred on Tycho's family and the *família* of all those young mathematicians, artists and artisans, who also served as his secretaries and tutored his children. Top university students signed on for three or four years, while others came for shorter stays. Tycho met daily with his students and assistants over a leisurely supper, shoulder to shoulder on benches in the Winter Room, passing the beaker, discussing work, planning their next activities, and joking with Jeppe the dwarf jester. Privacy was largely unknown in that era, manners were frank, quick-witted and courtly, and there was plenty of close physical contact.[32] Some evenings they composed poetry, played lutes and recorders or the positive organ, sang Danish ballads, German lieder, polyphonic Italian madrigals, French chansons or Latin motets from Johannes Stephanius' collections and other song books, or they pushed aside the furniture for vigorous Renaissance dancing.[33] Some nights after supper, visitors and residents alike shivered in the observatories or sweated in the laboratory. Many days, mathematicians reduced observational data by *prosthaphæresis* while others laboured in the printing office or instrument factory. In summer, they occasionally dined in Uranborg's garden pavilions or bowled and played games in the open air among pleasant aromas.

This was far different from university studies. European universities did not have observatories or research laboratories, and universities north of the Alps did not have aviaries or museums, although a few had begun to lay out botanical gardens.[34] Uraniborg had all of these facilities, plus an unprecedented array of astronomical instruments. In Tycho's learned spaces, hands-on techniques and problem-solving took precedence over theoretical, academic learning. Students worked with Tycho and collaborative experimenters and technicians like Flemløse, Morsing, Croll and Steenwinckel and learned how to produce and verify new knowledge.[35] This lively, innovative household laid down models for the rest of their lives and became the prototype of future scientific academies real or imagined.

In the summer of 1584, Tycho took the radical step of breaking the link between observational astronomy and astrology by designing an instrument to measure coordinates that did not follow the zodiac. This was the Equatorial Armillary. It took Earth, the domain and dwelling place of Man, as its starting point and used coordinates of declination, measured north or south of the equator, and right ascension, measured eastwards around the equator from the point of the vernal equinox. These equatorial coordinates grew out of the system Tycho had first proposed in 1573.[36] The instrument's steel outer ring, over 155 centimetres (5 ft) in diameter, was mounted on Renaissance cabinetry of laminated hardwood

61, 62 Tycho's first and second Equatorial Armillaries.

painted with portraits of Ptolemy, Albategnius (Al-Battānī) and Copernicus, and Tycho now included himself to express his new confidence in his own achievements. The inner rings were made of laminated, brass-covered wood, fixed at right angles and turning on an axis aligned like the Earth's axis to the celestial north and south poles. Tycho tested the instrument on 20 August 1584 and sent it back for adjustments while he went off to Jutland to celebrate his brother's wedding.[37]

Knud Brahe and Margaret Lange were married at Bygholm Castle on 23 August 1584. The host was Margaret's brother, Erik Lange of Bygholm, who was obsessed with goldmaking by alchemical transmutation. With his close friend, Falk Gøye, also an alchemist, Erik had survived the horrors of the St Bartholomew's Day Massacre in Paris. Falk's sister was married to Tycho's brother, Axel Brahe.[38]

A month after the wedding, Erik Lange visited Uraniborg with other 'barons and noblemen' including an Austrian astrologer and alchemist, Baron Siegfried von Rindscheid of Friedberg, and probably also Falk Gøye. Lange brought along his secretary, Michael Walter, and his mathematician, Nicolaus Reymers, Heinrich Rantzau's former surveyor, who now wanted to study astronomy.[39]

Tycho entertained them in robust Renaissance style. Eventually, 'Erik grew tired of Bacchus's drops and wanted to spend some time with my Urania'. The others left, and talk turned to cosmology. Lange asked Tycho to explain various theories of the planetary system. 'Erik's boy', Reymers, stood there among the servants, but Tycho was suspicious of him, so Lange sent him away. Tycho 'grabbed a piece of chalk', drew and criticized the systems of Ptolemy and Copernicus, and then,

> I sketched and explained in broad lines the one I had
> worked out myself for this purpose. Afterwards, I wiped
> it out again – as well as I could, for I had sketched it
> on the green cloth that covered the table. But this nosy
> busybody [Reymers] got a whiff of what we had hidden
> from him . . . he sniffed around and gained informa-
> tion about many other things of mine.[40]

One day, at lunch, Tycho noted that Reymers was behaving oddly and said, 'Those German fellows are all half-cracked.' Years later, Reymers still chaffed under the insult.[41] Finally, Tycho asked Anders Viborg to see whether Reymers was snitching information, and Michael Walter later reported that Anders

> spent the night in [Reymers's] room [and] found four
> whole handfuls of tracings and writings . . . When
> [Reymers] woke up in the morning . . . Like a rav-
> ing maniac, he ran around shrieking, weeping, and
> screaming so that he could hardly be calmed down.[42]

Tycho assured him that anything belonging to him would be returned. After two weeks, Erik Lange and his servants left, and he soon dismissed the troublesome Reymers.

Tycho was dismayed by Erik Lange's futile pursuit of gold-making. After they left, he composed an Ovidian epistolary elegy intended to be a *remedia amori*, a remedy for misplaced love. The poem urged Lange to abandon his carnal alchemical love of gold and turn instead to the healing, spiritual chymistry of Paracelsus. Come back to Uraniborg, where this true love will seize you and we can cultivate astronomy, chymistry and poetry together.[43] Tycho also composed an epistolary elegy to Falk Gøye and dashed off a third to a nobleman named Jacob Ulfeldt who happened to visit.[44]

The printing office was ready to go.[45] Tycho gave the elegies to Joachim, who set them in type and locked up the frames so Tycho himself could print the first publication of the Uraniborg press under auspicious skies at 10.45 a.m. on 27 November 1584. The epistolary elegy to Erik Lange was first, but of the three elegies, only the printed one to Ulfeldt survives.[46]

Tycho went on to promote his own self-image in poetry by placing himself within a circle of eminent friends in a series of epistolary Latin elegies to patrons of high rank (Kaas, Rantzau, Danzay), academic scholars in mathematics, chymistry and medicine (Pratensis, Ripensis, Claus Scavenius), and the three learned aristocrats (Lange, Ulfeldt, Gøye).[47] He also printed woodcuts, probably by Gemperle, of Uraniborg, two instruments, and his *imprese* of *Astronomia* and *Chymia*. Hans Aalborg distributed all of these broadsides at the Frankfurt Book Fair in 1585. Tycho acquired additional type fonts in 1585 and offered to print books for Rantzau and Hagecius but had to renege for lack of paper when Hagecius sent him a manuscript.[48] The shortage of paper became a chronic problem.

The Equatorial Armillary was installed in Uraniborg's South Observatory in October 1584. Tycho soon made a new version out of Herrevad steel for the North Observatory, covering the rings with brass plates and projecting the pinnacidia on both sides of the arc to provide each observer with four parallel lines of sight. In January 1585 Tycho used these two equatorial armillaries and the Triangular Sextant to observe Mars in opposition. The observations were better than earlier ones, but something was still wrong with the data. He decided he needed to examine refraction more thoroughly.[49]

During that winter of 1584–5, he revised his solar theory. By this time, his observational methods, in Moesgaard's words, 'created a new standard for objective precision, not only for modern astronomy but for all later exact science'.[50] Tycho worked out history's first table of refraction, extending from the horizon up to 20°, above which he assumed that refraction was negligible. He continued, however, to use Ptolemy's exaggerated figure of three arcminutes for solar parallax, which compromised the accuracy of his table.

On 11 December 1584, King Frederick inquired about a compass he had sent back for repairs, which he needed to use in his vast hunting reserves. He wanted Tycho to make two more just like it.[51] He also wanted a handbook on weather forecasting from signs of nature, which Tycho assigned to Flemløse to compile.[52] Every year, Tycho prepared an astrological calendar for King Frederick and Queen Sophie. In 1585, since his press was up and running, he decided to print the calendar and assigned Morsing to work on it, then asked Heinrich Rantzau for enough paper to print 2,000 copies.[53] The calendar was in press when Morsing spotted a small, fuzzy comet low on the horizon on 18 October 1585, which they

observed diligently. Tycho decided to add a discussion of the comet to the calendar.[54] Victor Thoren noted that the accuracy of these cometary observations finally exceeded Tycho's goal of ± 1 arcminute.[55]

The calendar was calculated in accordance with Tycho's solar theory and dedicated to the nine-year-old Duke Christian.[56] It placed the comet in the *aether* of the high heavens and described astrological effects foretelling the 'Mystical

63 King Frederick II's silver sundial and compass, 1573.

Sabbath' to come. This first book from the Uraniborg press was distributed far and wide. Acute readers quickly realized that Tycho had written much of it himself, and some wondered why he bothered to print something so full of astrology, even under the name of another person.[57]

In the summer of 1585, Stjerneborg was nearly complete. An Ionic portal of black porphyry led down to a domed warming room and three round crypts.[58] The Greatest Equatorial Armillary, one of the finest instruments Tycho ever designed, was installed in the large crypt. Its semicircle of brass-covered steel was nearly 350 centimetres (12 ft) in diameter and could be adjusted precisely to the plane of the celestial equator. Within this semicircle was a 272-centimetre (9-ft) circular armilla on a steel axis resting on a sculpted Atlas and celestial globe, parallel to the axis of the Earth and held on top by an iron wishbone. This instrument became an immense icon of the universe, capturing the coordinates of the heavens in observations and simultaneously giving physical shape to the divine geometry of the cosmos in steel, brass and carved Gotland marble.

The stability, accuracy and ease of use of this instrument testified to the collaborative skills of Tycho and Croll. When the dome swung open, an observer could sight from the armilla to measure declination along collimated lines of sight over a central brass cylinder, then flip over the whole armilla and observe from pinnacidia on the other side to verify the observation. The observer could sight from pinnacidia on the graduated semicircle over the edges of the axis to measure equatorial distances east or west of the meridian of Uraniborg, and two observers with two pinnacidia could determine right

ascension from an object of known right ascension.[59] Tycho
began testing it on 9 June. In July, he began to distrust the
pinnacidia and tested them time and again on the armillary and Tichonicus. These 'light-cutters' were apparently
an improved design of spring-loaded pinnacidia that could
narrow the sighting slits on all sides with the turn of a single

64 Hans Knieper, King Christian IV at age seven, 1585.

65 Tycho's Greatest Equatorial Armillary.

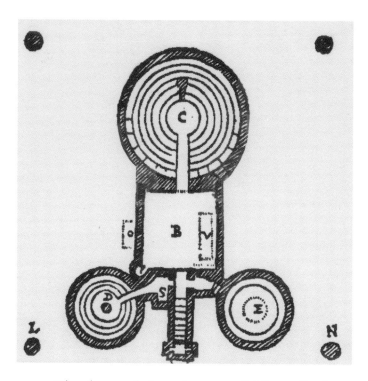

screw. The observer balanced two parallel lines of sight an inch apart and carefully narrowed the slits, sometimes until they were narrower than the pupil of the eye, which allowed him to surpass the normal limits of naked-eye observation. By autumn, these new pinnacidia worked to precision.[60] Tycho's large Zodiacal Armillary was placed in the other small crypt but seldom used, although Croll made it 'strong and stiff' to hold an observed position.[61] Above ground, Stjerneborg was enclosed by a square picket fence.

Landgrave William IV had not heard from Tycho for a decade. He wrote to Rantzau to ask after Tycho, and to say that his astronomer, Christopher Rothmann, had observed

66 Plan of Stjerneborg in 1585.

the comet of 1585; he also mentioned that Paul Wittich had recently visited Kassel, where he helped to make the instruments much more accurate.[62]

Where had Wittich learned to improve instruments? He was no observational astronomer. Had intellectual property been stolen from Uraniborg? Tycho was an advocate of open collaboration among astronomers, but respect for intellectual property rights was a corollary of collaboration. Tycho and others claimed a right to profit from intellectual property within an economy of courtly exchange that measured profit in *fama*, not royalties. He decided to send Flemløse to investigate and gave him a letter to the Landgrave dated 1 March 1586, along with his observations of the comet, new solar ephemerides and the woodcuts of Uraniborg, the Triangular Sextant and second Equatorial Armillary.[63]

Astrology was never far from politics for court astronomers like Tycho.[64] Catholic military aggression, foretold by the stars, was leading King Frederick to display 'an unprecedented degree of militancy' in opposition. He organized a conference of German Protestant rulers to meet with the envoy of King Henry of Navarre, who was fighting for his life in the War of the Three Henrys.[65] While the king was away, Queen Sophie visited Uraniborg on 27 June 1586 with her court, headed by Tycho's mother.[66] The young queen shared her father's interests in astronomy, astrology, chymistry, scientific instruments and cartography, and she had studied Tycho's horoscopes, annual almanacs and secret papers on celestial phenomena.[67]

Tycho escorted her into Stjerneborg through the portal of black porphyry and down the stairs to see those immense instruments. They strolled through Uraniborg's knot gardens as the animated rooftop statues sprayed and Pegasus turned high above. Tycho led her into the villa and down a corridor decorated with epigrams to the sunlit atrium with the Aquarius fountain that represented the spring of Hippocrene and source of wisdom. In the Museum, she saw his mechanical marvels, the Great Celestial Globe, and portraits of Italian Renaissance philosophers, as well as of King Frederick and herself. Queen Sophie saw the chymical laboratory with its sixteen furnaces of grey Norwegian steatite piled with vials and cucurbits of Herrevad glass, and she was escorted up the grand staircase to the circular observatories flanking the bright Summer Room with its floral decoration. They entered the octagonal Yellow Chamber of Uraniborg's royal apartment, the Queen's Blue Chamber, and the King's Red Chamber. From the cupola and rooftop galleries high above, they surveyed five Danish cities and billowing sails of countless ships from many lands plying the Sound. Tycho Brahe, courtier and servant of King Frederick II, had built this magical satellite of Kronborg Castle as a royal microcosm, where all the world could 'see and learn that which they could hardly find elsewhere'. Queen Sophie and her court experienced all its marvels.

That evening, in the Summer Room, Tycho's musicians and servants entertained the queen and her court at a grand feast. A storm broke and continued the next day with thunder, lightning and high seas. They passed the time with 'all kinds of wise talk and conversation over the table'.[68] Anders Vedel was present, and Tycho mentioned that he had brought 'many old Danish Ballads, to which Your Grace remarked to have a special pleasure and joy to read'.[69] Among courtly

ballads of Danish chivalry were three Nordic tales of the evil
Queen Grimhild, which Vedel had transposed to the island
of Hven, adding a dimension of *Nibelungenlied* legends to the
mythos of Uraniborg.[70] The ballads delighted the queen, who
wanted Vedel to send all of them to her, and he later published one hundred ballads dedicated to Queen Sophie. As
the storm raged, talk must also have turned to astronomy,
astrology, chymistry, the Comet of 1585 and even the Great
Sabbath of All Creation.[71] In the end, the queen and her court
stayed another night and departed on 29 June, after the storm
had passed.[72] King Frederick soon returned from Lüneburg,
where he had met with a formidable power bloc of Protestant
princes from 16 to 22 July but was left frustrated when the
conference ended without resolution.[73]

Many distinguished visitors came to Tycho's island that
summer. In August, Queen Sophie returned with her parents,
Duke Ulrich of Mecklenburg, Duchess Elizabeth, and their
nephew and heir, Duke Sigismund August.[74] That day could
hardly have passed without discussion of chymistry, conjunctions and coming threats. In September, flashes of *chasmata*,
aurora borealis, which Aristotle described as blood-red cracks
in the sky, appeared over Denmark. King Frederick was ill,
and weeks of adverse winds delayed the Mecklenburg court's
departure until Duchess Elizabeth also took ill and died on
15 October.[75] During the period of mourning and impending
danger, King Frederick secretly donated an immense sum of
money to support the Protestant cause in France.[76]

Flemløse returned in October 1586 with letters from
Kassel and a supply of paper from Frankfurt, perhaps also
bringing a new printer, Christopher Weida. Finally, Tycho

could begin to print his manuscript on the Comet of 1577.[77] The Kassel astronomer-astrologers were eager to collaborate, and Flemløse brought part of Rothmann's recent manuscript on the Comet of 1585, the Landgrave's observations of the New Star of 1572 and his star catalogue of 1562.[78] Tycho learned that Nicolaus Reymers had been in Kassel, calling himself Ursus.[79] Was it he or Wittich who brought Uraniborg's form of *prosthaphæresis* to Kassel?[80]

 Correspondence between Kassel and Uraniborg began to flow as regularly as postal couriers and courtly obligations allowed.[81] Adam Mosley remarked, 'these men anticipated a real benefit from the exchange of data obtained at their different locations.'[82] They wrote with astonishing openness and a collaborative willingness to share.[83] Their common aim was the advancement of astronomy and cosmology.[84] Observational techniques were matchless at both Hven and Kassel, but Tycho had a more complete research institute that included a printing press. Landgrave William displayed his star catalogue by engraving it on an automaton globe, but Tycho was the one who published it, and he also printed the Landgrave's letters and those of Christopher Rothmann, besides publishing his own works.

Rothmann was a generation younger than Tycho and had been educated to make different assumptions about the starry heavens. He had matriculated in Wittenberg at a time when the Aristotelian worldview was collapsing and Tycho was proving that celestial change occurred beyond the Moon. Rothmann went on to learn his observational astronomy at Kassel.[85] His correspondence was peppered with stimulating ideas, which Tycho relished as fully as his daily discussions with assistants and visitors.[86] Rothmann brought in new strains of Stoic thought, while Tycho drew on the chymical cosmology of Paracelsus.[87] Both rejected celestial spheres and wondered whether celestial space was simply air, as Rothmann thought, or the celestial element *aether*, as Tycho believed. Both were Lutheran Philippists, but Rothmann argued that the Bible was written for ordinary readers and did not speak with authority on natural philosophy, while Tycho continued to interpret the Bible literally. Rothmann defended Copernicus' heliocentric cosmology, while Tycho, seeing the universe in physical terms, was staggered beyond belief by the immensity of space demanded by a heliocentric universe.[88] When Tycho realized in the course of their correspondence that planetary orbits were simply paths through open space, unbounded by spheres, he saw that there was no reason why one orbit could not pass through another.

> And if magnetite and iron, terrestrial and lifeless as they are, may naturally and without violence attract each other, even through an interposed body, why should such things not be likely to happen in the heavenly bodies which by the Platonists and the more judicious philosophers were believed to be animate?[89]

This opened the way to his final version of the Tychonic System. Meanwhile, Tycho's correspondence with the Kassel astronomers circulated, and Rantzau thought their letters ought to be published.

Tycho's income continued to fluctuate. He lost Nordfjord in 1586 but received compensation of 300 rixdollars per

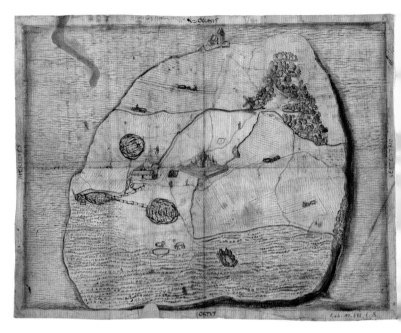

annum. When he protested that Nordfjord gave 500 rixdollars, the king ordered Valkendorf to raise the compensation
to 400 rixdollars. Valkendorf apparently objected, so the king
shifted the payment to the Tollhouse of Elsinore, which
Valkendorf did not administer.[90]

As his fortieth birthday approached, Tycho summoned
three of Denmark's finest artists to paint a collaborative work
of art on the wall above Tichonicus. Hans van Steenwinckel
contributed perspective views into all levels of Uraniborg's
activities, Tobias Gemperle painted a portrait of Tycho at
work, and Hans Knieper added a landscape across the top.
Tycho was immensely pleased with this painting, now known
only through a later engraving (see illus. 52).[91] Tycho commissioned Steenwinckel to soar in the imagination and capture

67 The Island of Hven, c. 1586.

a magical bird's-eye view of Hven: this became the first estate map in Scandinavian history, and Tycho's friend and patron Heinrich Rantzau sent a copy to the publisher George Braunius in Cologne.

Tycho also posed for a woodcut portrait in a high-collared cape, lace ruff, golden chains and Order of the Elephant, holding a glove like a Roman *mappa*. The portrait radiated a commanding aura of *sprezzatura* (Tobias Gemperle was probably the artist but died of the plague soon after it was completed). Steenwinckel may have drawn the Roman arch bearing Tycho's sixteen quarterings.[92] Tycho commissioned Hendrick Goltzius in Haarlem to make an engraving from this woodcut.

On his fortieth birthday, 14 December 1586, Tycho began to install the Revolving Azimuth Quadrant in Stjerneborg's stepped eastern tower. It was tested with old and new 'light-cutters', adjusted by Croll, and came through with flying colours by March 1587. Constructed of laminated hardwood reinforced with steel and brass, it turned on an adjustable steel base, had a radius of 155 centimetres (5 ft) and an azimuth circle 233 centimetres (7.5 ft) in diameter, and rigorous testing found it accurate to within around fifteen arcseconds.[93]

In February 1587, at a remote hunting castle in Jutland, King Frederick II secretly received two Austrian barons and a third person who turned out to be Archduke Matthias, the emperor's brother.[94] The Archduke may have had his eye on the vacant Polish throne, and all three visitors were known to favour toleration of Protestants in Habsburg lands. The king wrote in his journal that Archduke Matthias sought the hand of his eldest daughter, Princess Elizabeth of Denmark.[95] In

68 Tobias Gemperle (ascribed), *Tycho Brahe*, 1586, woodcut.

August, the Poles elected a Swedish prince, Sigismund Vasa, whose mother was the descendant of Polish kings.[96] The two barons, Herberstein and Liechtenstein, visited Uraniborg and apparently told Tycho that Paul Wittich had died. Tycho asked them to see if they could purchase his manuscripts and library for Uraniborg, and they tried without success.[97]

Scottish diplomats came frequently to the Danish court. Denmark had revived fifteenth-century claims to the Orkneys, and King James VI was seeking a match with a Danish princess. Ambassador Peter Young of Seaton visited Uraniborg in 1586 and 1587, gave Tycho a portrait of the Scottish humanist George Buchanan, and they became friends.[98]

Mature Danish, Norwegian and Icelandic students from the University of Copenhagen continued to enter Tycho's service. Jacob Mikkelsen Lemvig signed a three-year contract to serve as chaplain and assistant, but Tycho generously released him early to take a better call, and the talented Christian Hansen Riber took his place. Hans Buck was killed in a student brawl in Copenhagen after leaving Uraniborg. Tycho brokered a coveted Regius Stipend for Gellius Sascerides, to be used for study abroad when he finished his studies on Hven.[99] Others came and left without leaving a mark.[100]

Some students came from abroad. 'Joannes Hamon Dekent' (Dr John Hammond), a mercurial and musical young Englishman, served Tycho for three months in 1587, and Radulphus Meherentius (Raoul Méhérent) from Sées in Normandy served him for six months in 1588, then both went on to stay with Dr John Dee at Třeboň Castle (Wittingau) in Bohemia.[101] Duncan Liddel stayed for a week in 1587 and witnessed a spectacular show of observational precision by five of Tycho's teams on 29 June.[102] He went to Rostock and became the first in Germany to teach the Tychonic planetary system, then visited Uraniborg again the following summer.[103]

Meherentius reported that Tycho's book on the Comet of 1577, *De mvndi aetherei recentioribvs phaenomenis, Liber secvndvs* (On the Most Recent Phenomena of the Aetherial World, Book Two), was off the press and ready for the bindery before the end of 1587.[104] Most of the manuscript had been written around 1578–80. Tycho's long critical reviews of other works on the comet were added later, and Tycho decided in 1587 to add a description of his Tychonic System and his instruments and methods. The book was labelled 'book two' because Tycho planned a 'first' volume to deal with the New Star of 1572 and a third to treat comets after 1577. A total of 1,500 copies were printed.

This book presented astronomy and cosmology with the astrology left out, as Copernicus had done, and it presented much that was new. Tycho's innovative use of equatorial co-ordinates; his precise locations of reference stars; his cosmos of planets soaring through open space in a revolutionary plan-etary system with the Sun and the Moon orbiting the Earth, planets orbiting the Sun, Mars cutting through the Sun's path, and comets sweeping through on egg-shaped heliocentric orbits; as well as Tycho's emphasis on the immensity of the physical universe and his new methods to assure that astron-omy was based on verifiable empirical data, as he demanded that it had to be, all opened the way to revolutionary new vistas in astronomy.

By 1588 Stjerneborg had been rebuilt extensively with two new crypts and new roof designs. The deep eastern crypt

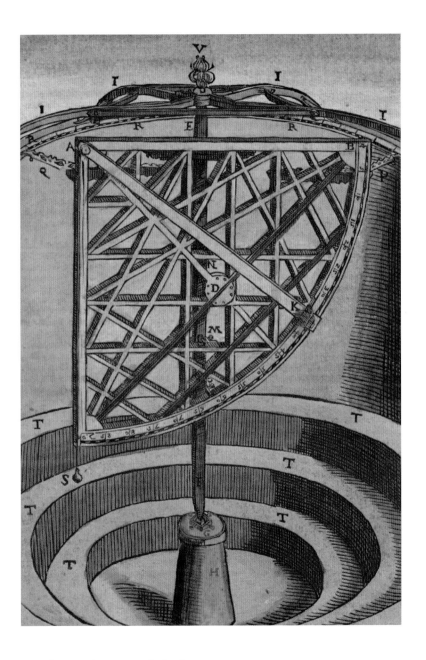

69 Tycho's Revolving Azimuth Quadrant.

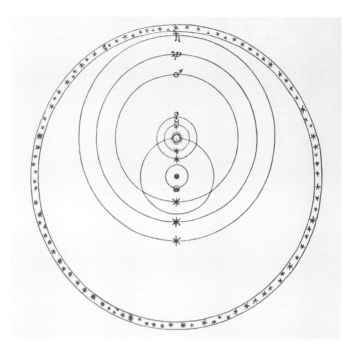

held a ball-mounted Triangular Sextant, the stepped western crypt a redesigned Great Steel Quadrant. Tycho had instructed Croll to take down the flawed Uraniborg quadrant, reinforce and flip its frame to bring the arc to the observer's side, and install a new dioptre with improved pinnacidia.[105] A 350-centimetre (11.5-ft) azimuth circle encircled the crypt, and the instrument tested out to an accuracy of ± 10 arcseconds.[106]

Stjerneborg's central warming room had a stove, long table, clocks and alcove bed surrounded by portraits of eight great astronomers, past, present and future, including Tycho pointing to the Tychonic System on the domed ceiling and asking, *Quid si sic?* (How about this?) All crypt roofs swung open to the skies. A barbed quatrefoil palisade around the site

70 The Tychonic System.

contained open-air stations for instruments.[107] The warming room's roof was a grassy 'Parnassus' with an automaton statue of Hermes Trismegistus as Mercury, probably by Jan Gregor van der Schardt.

In the autumn of 1587, Tycho submitted an expanded astrological calendar for 1588 to King Frederick II.[108] Duke Ulrich of Mecklenburg also wanted to know his prognostication for that fateful year.[109] Tycho replied to the duke's noble messenger with disarming frankness: 'I cannot as a friend hide from you my view that I do not like to get involved in *Astrological* matters', adding that he preferred to be involved only with *Astronomy*:

> These *Astrological* predictions are like a *cothurnus* [the high-heeled boots worn by tragic actors in ancient Greece] that fit any foot, large or small, as you like. Therefore, I have never thought much of them. But each year I humbly and obediently deliver such an *Astrological Prognostication* to His Royal Majesty my Gracious Lord, because I must obey His Majesty's wish and command, even though I do not care much for it myself and would prefer not to be associated with such doubtful predictions, the actual truth of which cannot be investigated thoroughly, as *Astronomy* can be built with *Geometry* and *Arithmetic* with the help of careful *observation* of the course of the Heavens.[110]

Tycho Brahe still pursued his own arcane astrology of conjunctions but seemed quite sceptical of horoscopes and almanacs.[111] He recognized that *observatio* in astrology (and

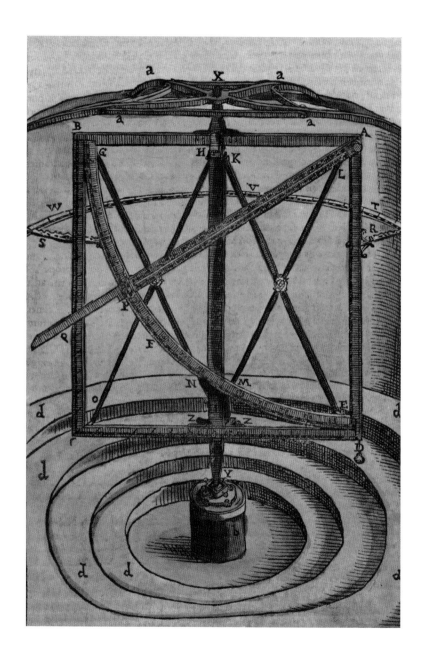

71 Tycho's Great Steel Azimuth Quadrant.

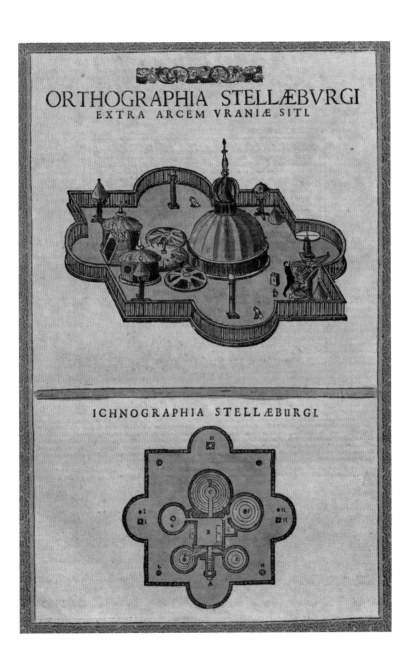

72 Plan of Stjerneborg in 1588.

medicine) could lead to case studies and even syndromes generalized in words, but astronomy was a more exact *scientia* because it could reduce the phenomena of nature to mathematical precision.

King Frederick was growing old, weakened by catarrh and a constant cough, depressed by the recent deaths of

73 Melchior Lorck, *King Frederick II*, 1582, engraving.

eight family members, haunted by victories of the 'Roman Antichrist' in France, the Netherlands and the Rhineland, and threatened by the invincible Armada poised to strike the English Channel and perhaps advance towards the Sound. In February 1588 at Sønderborg Castle, he was so exhausted at the wedding of his brother, Duke Hans, that he retired to his rooms instead of attending the celebration. A week later at Haderslevhus, he hosted the wedding of the bride's brother, Prince John George of Anhalt-Dessau, but was too weak to attend the wedding feast. The court set out for Frederiksborg and Kronborg, but at Antvorskov Castle, the king took to his bed. For a month, he lay there, drifting in and out of fever. On Maundy Thursday, 4 April 1588, around 4.30 in the afternoon, King Frederick II rose up in bed and then fell back and was dead.[112] Tycho Brahe's regal, open-handed patron was no more.

The news sent a chill over the island of Hven.

SIX

On the Move, 1588–99

When King Frederick II died, the Council of the Realm quickly put the fleet on alert and formed a four-man Regency that excluded Queen Sophie, tilting the Danish dyarchy back towards aristocratic oligarchy.[1] King Christian IV, the eleven-year-old successor, remained at his studies. Once the Spanish Armada was destroyed, the Regents withdrew from foreign affairs and left Queen Sophie to negotiate prestigious matches for her daughters.

Tycho acted quickly to reap benefits from his friends and kinsmen in power. He persuaded the Regents, Council of the Realm and Dowager Queen Sophie to support the permanent endowment of Uraniborg under a member of Tycho's family.[2] Meanwhile, his book on the Comet of 1577 was eliciting bewildered replies that led to increased correspondence.[3] Georg Rollenhagen of Magdeburg worried that Mars and the Sun might collide in Tycho's system, and so did Hagecius.[4] Gellius Sascerides delivered a copy to Kassel and was astonished to see a mechanical model very like Tycho's system, which Joost Bürgi, the landgrave's clockmaker, had made after Ursus described 'his own' system. When Gellius came face to face with Ursus in Strasbourg, he accused him of plagiarism.[5]

That summer, Flemløse left Uraniborg to become physician to Tycho's kinsman Axel Gyldenstierne, who became Viceroy of Norway. Two able Copenhagen students, Christian Sørensen Longomontanus and Cort Aslakssøn, came to study at Uraniborg, and Tycho promised to recommend Cort for a Regius Stipend.[6] Dutch map-makers, the brothers Arnold and Hendrik Floris van Langren and Willem Jansz. Blaeu, came to study because they wanted to commercialize astronomical knowledge, and Tycho eventually gave them information they could put on their globes and maps.[7] These and other students benefited from their Uraniborg experiences, and many of them later enjoyed Tycho's patronage. Few would have agreed with Georg Ludwig Frobenius, who visited in 1591 and found Tycho to be distant, frightening and tyrannical.[8]

Tycho was ready to begin printing *Astronomiæ instavratæ progymnasmata* (Introduction to the Instauration of Astronomy), his major work on the New Star of 1572. The word *instauratio* had implications far beyond astronomy, conjuring universal reform and a millennial revival of learning that included rebuilding Solomon's Temple and the Second Coming of Christ.[9] Tycho acquired a second printing press and began looking for a new master printer. His plans for a 'Theatre of Astronomy' now included the three original books and seven more describing Hven's instruments and mathematics, catalogues of stars, the Sun and Moon based exclusively on Hven observations, Tycho's new theories of the Sun, Moon and planets, and a final volume on the ecliptic latitudes of each planet.[10]

Late in 1588 he was pleased to receive an engraved map of Hven and bird's-eye view of the 'Hellespont of the North' published by Braunius and Hogenberg in Cologne from

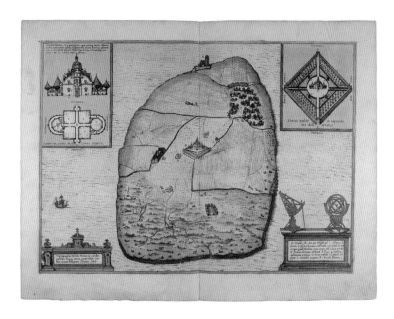

material submitted through Rantzau.[11] Such maps were
'instruments of power' confirming boundaries and possessions, proclaiming the wealth of regions, and guiding travellers
on land and sea.[12] Tycho had carried out a triangular geodetic
survey of the Øresund region and made an astonishingly
accurate map of Hven. Anders Vedel wanted him to map all
of Denmark and borrowed Morsing to begin surveying in
1589.[13] When Tycho mentioned this to King Frederick II,
the king sent Copenhagen Castle's entire map collection to
Uraniborg.[14] Flemløse was measuring latitudes of places in
Norway and visited Bishop Anders Foss of Bergen, who
mapped his entire diocese including Nordfjord.[15] Tycho's portable azimuth quadrant was a good surveying instrument, and
he later commissioned Peter Jachenow to make an odometer
for measuring distances.[16]

74 The Island of Hven, 1588.

In 1589 he brought out a Kronborg contractor, Valentine Spangenberg, to excavate a series of ponds, dams and sluices in geometrical shapes to provide waterpower for a paper mill on Hven. Hans van Steenwinckel designed the mill house and a high-pressure jet to turn an 8-metre (26-ft) overshot water-wheel, but this large project took several years to complete.[17]

By 1590 Erik Lange had piled up immense debts in his search for alchemical gold. He barely eluded debtors' prison by selling his share of Engelsholm to his sister Margaret and Knud Brahe. Morsing was gravely ill at the time and expired in the arms of Longomontanus on 11 March, just as Sophie Brahe, a widow not yet thirty years old and hopelessly in love, betrothed herself to Erik Lange.[18] They were constantly at Uraniborg and were present when King James VI of Scotland,

75 The Sound with Kronborg Castle and Elsinore, Hven, Kullen Lighthouse, and the Danish cities of Helsingborg, Landskrona, Malmö and part of Copenhagen (Frans Hogenberg, 1588).

recently married to Princess Anna of Denmark, visited Hven
with his court on 20 March 1590.

King James and Tycho chatted away in Latin and the
Scottish court trailed along to see the marvels of Uraniborg
and Stjerneborg followed by a boisterous feast.[19] Brimming
beakers of wine went from hand to hand in the Danish fash-
ion, and each recipient proposed a toast, sang or improvised
an epigram before swigging. Chancellor Maitland's witty Latin

76 Peter Jachenow, odometer.

epigrams delighted Tycho.[20] Great smorgasbords of rich food ranging from venison and salmon in rich sauces to spices, fruit and sugar cakes were laid before them, and guests chose whatever they liked from each array.[21] The visit was a great success, and King James later granted Tycho a Scottish copyright for his publications.[22]

Such visits of royalty and high officials enhanced the *fama* of Tycho Brahe and linked Uraniborg to courtly and learned networks that spanned the continent. Tycho's correspondence grew by leaps and bounds. He knew, however, that princes were mercurial and courts dangerous. Duke Henry Julius of Brunswick-Lüneberg-Wolfenbüttel, recently married to Princess Elizabeth of Denmark, arrived in May and was so taken with Stjerneborg's automated statue of Mercury-Hermes that he demanded to have it. Tycho reluctantly gave it up when the duke promised to replace it with a copy, which he never did.[23] Later that day, the haughty, thin-skinned duke stormed off without a farewell.[24]

Professor Niels Krag visited that summer and took Tycho's eldest son to enrol at Sorø Abbey, now an elite academy for thirty noble and thirty commoner students. Three years later, Tycho's younger son would join him among the commoners.[25] Christopher Rothmann also visited for the month of August 1590.[26] His conversations with Tycho left no record and were interrupted when other visitors arrived, including the powerful Scot George Keith, 5th Earl Marischal, and Hieronymus Megiser, the envoy of Archduke Charles II of Austria.[27] Tycho later claimed that Rothmann eventually accepted the Tychonic system. On a visit to Skåne with Tycho and the aristocratic botanist Lauge Urne, Rothmann admired

Sophie Brahe's garden at Eriksholm Castle – it surrounded a
'distilling house' where she prepared Paracelsian elixirs, per-
fumes, cosmetics and 'hermetically' sealed jars of preserved
fruit.[28] Back on Hven, Rothmann and Tycho teamed up to
observe with a Triangular Sextant and the Greatest Equatorial
Armillary.[29] When Rothmann left, he went to his birthplace
of Bernburg in Anhalt instead of Kassel, which surprised
both Tycho and the landgrave.

77 Gheyn's 1590 portrait of Tycho with too many golden chains.

L. S.

Towards the end of 1590, Tycho received the engraved portrait by Jacques de Gheyn II from the Goltzius workshop but thought there were too many golden chains and wanted it redone. He sent off another portrait sketch and included instructions for correcting the heraldry to include the royal arms of his Vasa ('Stormvase') ancestors in the proper place.[30]

Uraniborg had been whitewashed and domes erected above the entrance portals in 1589, and now, Tycho redesigned

78 Sketch of Tycho Brahe, *c.* 1586 (ascribed to Tobias Gemperle).

the ramparts in the shape of a barbed quatrefoil and enlisted
Sophie Brahe and her gardener, 'Giorg. F', to help him transform his knot gardens into boxwood parterres. The first
cuttings were put out in March 1591.[31] By summer, raked paths
led to a circle around Uraniborg from the four cardinal points,
aviaries filled the air with birdsong, an orchard of three hundred fruit and nut trees encircled the site, and pavilions
beckoned from the rampart semicircles. The new parterres
of medicinal, herbal and floral plants reflected the four

79 Uraniborg whitewashed.

corners of the world and demonstrated mastery over nature.
The garden's source of flowing water was the Aquarius fountain in Uraniborg, and garden statuary was massed in the
flaming spheres, putti, obelisks and statues adorning the villa.
Uraniborg seemed an island of peace and wisdom churning
with learned activity.

In one corner of the garden was the printing office and
a printer, Hans Gaschitz, with nothing to do. About half of
Astronomiae instavratæ progymnasmata was printed, but crucial parts
were still not written, so Tycho took out Flemløse's manuscript on weather forecasting and dictated an introduction as
Longomontanus wrote it down. He described an immense but

80 The Gardens of Uraniborg by 1591.

not infinite universe, the splendid, visible Creation of God, surrounding a small Elemental sphere of earth, water and air, which received celestial influences that affected plants, animals and creatures of the sea, but which humans could resist by means of reason. He spoke of celestial *aether* but did not mention fire as the fourth terrestrial element.[32] The book appeared in Danish and German versions in 1591.

Tycho could not hold the worries of the world in abeyance. He had to dismiss his stern Dutch bailiff in Nordfjord and turn out the tenant of Gundsøgaard manor near Roskilde and later imprisoned both of them without writ or warrant, for which the Regents chastised him.[33] They also ordered him to repair the tottering vaults of his Chapel of the Magi in Roskilde Cathedral, which he neglected to do.[34] In late 1591 Inger Oxe died and left a fortune of 90,000 rixdollars, but how much came to Tycho is unknown.[35] That summer, Knud Brahe and Margaret Lange tore down Engelsholm and built a new manor on a centralized plan that reflected Knud's wide experience of Renaissance life in Italy and France.[36]

Tycho's catalogue of stars was taking shape. He and Flemløse had established an astonishingly accurate 'skeleton' of reference stars as early as 1589, and Tycho had then put Longomontanus in charge of observing the entire sky with Stjerneborg's instruments. By 1592 the catalogue contained 777 stars at four levels of magnitude.[37]

Young King Christian IV had long been eager to visit Uraniborg. He finally arrived on Monday 3 July 1592, fifteen years of age, to enter Stjerneborg and see instruments so enormous he could step into them, then marvel as Uraniborg's towers swung open to reveal other huge instruments on

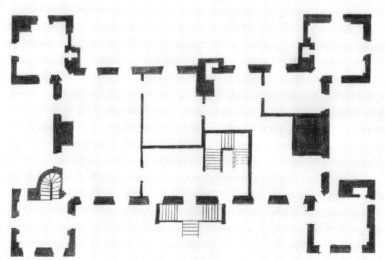

81 *Above*: Engelsholm, 2002, photograph.
82 *Below*: Engelsholm ground floor plan, 2018, drawing.

elevated platforms. Tycho led him from wonder to wonder. In the museum, he saw portraits of his parents, and Tycho raised the cover to reveal his gigantic, gleaming Celestial Globe. Tycho took down the precious silver-gilt globe, wound it up to show the phases of the Moon and daily movements of the Sun, and impulsively handed it to the king as a gift.[38] With the same spontaneity, King Christian took off a heavy golden chain with his own royal portrait and hung it around the neck of his worthy courtier.[39]

A year later, the young king came to Roskilde, expecting to see the resplendent alabaster and marble tomb of his grandfather in the Chapel of the Magi and the place where a similar tomb would soon be erected over his father.[40] Instead, he stepped into a nightmare of rotten timbers, collapsing vaults and a leaking roof. Angrily, he sent a courier galloping towards Hven to demand to know immediately when and how Tycho Brahe would make repairs.[41] Reprimand followed reprimand, but nothing was done.[42]

Sometime in these busy years between 1588 and 1594, Tycho tried to set up a wardship for his children but failed.[43] Some of his noble relatives may have refused to sign on because they thought it would weaken their future claims to his landed wealth. His bitter response was to sell his rights in Knutstorp to Steen Brahe, retaining only the style 'of Knutstorp'. Steen had two castles, three manors and hundreds of farms by then, on his way to acquiring eight manors and castles in all. Tycho had no landed property but now possessed considerable wealth in treasured movables and money market investments, which his children had every right to inherit.[44]

His sister Sophie was at her wit's end. After borrowing everything she could give him, Erik Lange had absconded from all his debts and skipped off to foreign parts in search of gold. How could she persuade him to return? Tycho knew that Latin poetry was the hallmark of a classically educated man like Erik. In 1594 he took time out to write a long chymical and astrological poem in Ovid's classical genre of *heroïdes* (letters from mythological heroines in hopeless love). In the economy of courtly exchange, a poem was a gift that required repayment, and this poem spoke with the voice of Urania (Sophie), demanding the return of Titan (Erik).[45] Peter Zeeberg unlocked its brilliant layers of erudition and wit, which another scholar called 'unequalled in sixteenth

83 The Chapel of the Magi as King Christian IV hoped to see it, with King Christian III's tomb (*left*) and the later tomb of King Frederick II (*right*).

century Danish Latin literature'.[46] The verses described how
Titan's 'Stygian' potions breathed smoke and exploded, kill-
ing his companion, but Erik crossed the Alps to seek greedy
golden lumps in Venice and wasted fortunes, all the while
ignoring the Golden Fleece of healing chymistry awaiting
him in Urania's garden. At one point, Urania brashly reinter-
preted the pristine wisdom of the Emerald Table of Hermes
Trismegistus as a bawdy chymical allegory of separation and
reunion, her earthly stability interacting with his mercurial
energy to produce not a dormant clump of gold, but a living
child in the athanor of her womb. Soaring into the higher
realms of astrology, the poem explained that Titan's horoscope revealed him as mercurial, charming, unstable, too close
to Venus, his honeyed eloquence masking bitter gall, while
Urania drew solace from Pallas Athena's gift of the love of
arts and sciences, like Penelope and her loom. Urania's pillar
of support was Apollo (Tycho), born under placid Aquarius,
loyal, humane, endowed with jovial discretion and quick, alert
Solar energy, which gave him the strength of Hercules. Tycho
the poet may have drawn upon his sister's horoscopes to write
the poem, but none of its poetic charm and erudition sufficed
to bring Erik back to Denmark.

Landgrave William IV was eager to compare Tycho's star
catalogue with his own, but nowadays he wrote more often
about his menagerie of wild animals and pulled Tycho into that
expensive, time-consuming aspect of courtly gift exchange.
Tycho said that he would gladly send a young elk (*alias* moose)
to Kassel, and the landgrave offered a Hessian horse in exchange, but when Tycho brought his pet elk from Knutstorp
to Landskrona Castle, it wandered about, entered the great

hall during a feast, and drank so much strong beer that it fell down the stairs, broke its leg and died. The landgrave's last letter, a month before he expired, was another request for a breeding pair of elk.[47]

Tycho was working on his lunar theory. Since 1590 he had become the first astronomer to observe the Moon systematically outside of syzygy (alignment with the Sun and Earth) and quadrature (45° from syzygy), and this led to his discovery of a predictable pattern of acceleration and deceleration, which he called the 'variation'. This was the first discovery of a new celestial motion by any astronomer since the ancient Greeks.[48] He went on to discover that the axis of the Moon's orbit wobbled, causing the lunar latitude to vary, and this 'nutation' also had to become a part of his lunar theory.[49] Finally, he deduced a 'nodal oscillation' of the line from the axis to the ecliptic and had to account for that in the theory.[50] These three discoveries, one of them a 'completely unprecedented' discovery by deduction, revealed the profound theoretical potential of Tycho's methods, but they also complicated his lunar theory to the point of bewilderment.[51]

New students arrived, including the Dutch trio of Johannes Pontanus, Adriaan Metius and Frans Gansneb genaamd Tengnagel van de Camp, who had studied together in Franeker and Leiden, and Elizabeth Paulsdatter of Elsinore, a chemist like Sophie Brahe and her own aunt, 'Doctoress' Barbara Thiisen.[52] Tycho's students chatted and disputed daily over the supper table. Disputation was a normal part of academic life, not only as table talk and formal academic debate, but in correspondence and print. Tycho's cordial disputes with Rothmann were beneficial to both parties. John Craig became his true-blue Aristotelian, whom Tycho cast as the 'Simplicius' of a real-life dialogue concerning two world systems, which he hoped to publish.[53] His disputes with Ursus were bitter and unpleasant, and Tycho preferred to pass them off to his assistants.[54] Religion provided grounds for many sixteenth-century disputes, but not for Tycho Brahe, who continued to practice the eirenic tolerance taught by Melanchthon and Niels Hemmingsen.

His dispute with Gellius Sascerides, however, turned bitter and sparked tension between Uraniborg and the University of Copenhagen. Gellius was the son of a university professor. He returned to Denmark in the spring of 1593 with a Basel doctor of medicine degree after five years in Padua and Basel and often came to Uraniborg. Gellius and Tycho's eldest daughter, Magdalene, soon became friends. She was twenty and he was 32 when they became betrothed in 1594. Gellius seemed just the man to take over Uraniborg until Tycho's sons came of age, but he soon got cold feet. Over the next two years, the match fell apart in acrimony that stained Tycho's honour.[55] The university was losing many fine students to Uraniborg, and the university mathematicians, as well as theologians who disapproved of Tycho's common-law marriage, lined up behind Gellius, while the faculty's physicians and the historian and diplomat Niels Krag stood with Tycho.[56] Long hearings before the university consistory compounded ill will and wore down Tycho's health.[57] His last stalwart patrons, Chancellor Niels Kaas and Regent Jørgen Rosenkrantz, died in these years, and a new regime came to power.

The coronation of King Christian IV took place on 29 August 1596, followed by days of festivity. Two of Tycho's brothers, Steen and Axel, now sat on the Council of the Realm, and all four brothers played their parts in the coronation and competed in festive jousts while Tycho networked with guests that included the Hohenzollern court astronomer-astrologer Johannes Müller.[58]

King Christian IV was nineteen years of age. After winning piles of honours in the coronation tilts, he was eager to do battle in the political arena. Christopher Valkendorf had been squeezed off the Regency, but King Christian brought him back in the high office of Steward of the Realm, while Christian Friis of Borreby became Chancellor. The king and his men began to develop grand plans for the Royal Navy and the capital city of Copenhagen.[59]

First of all, however, the young monarch wanted to demonstrate his power over the aristocracy by striking down entrenched abusers of office. One greedy leviathan was Ludvig Munk, the brother of Valkendorf's enemy, Admiral Peter Munk. Ludvig Munk had draped himself in ermine when he had been Viceroy of Norway, but King Christian sacked him from all offices and stripped away his wealth with immense fines. Next, Erik Lange was deprived *in absentia* of Bygholm Castle and charged with grave crimes. Tycho Brahe was confident that this would not happen to him. Any day now, he expected the king to endow Uraniborg as a permanent research centre. Less than a month after the coronation, however, his largest benefice, Nordfjord, was transferred to the Governor of Bergen.[60] For the first time in his life, Tycho seemed paralysed by the loss. Months rolled by, and he did not act.

Meanwhile, the Uraniborg presses stamped away, printing his correspondence with Kassel as a dialogue of changing ideas that showed the hard path to seeking truth about the stars.[61] These were not short, witty Ciceronian epistles but long, technical letters, sometimes in German, usually in Latin, rambling from subject to subject like conversations between friends and often accompanied by manuscripts or

84 Jacques de Gheyn II's corrected engraving of Tycho Brahe.

thick packets of observations.[62] The correspondence had been in press since 1590, but Tycho kept adding new letters as they arrived. By the end of 1596, the book was finished as *Epistolarvm astronomicarvm libri quorum primvs* (Astronomical Letters, Book One). Gheyn's new engraving had arrived, and Tycho pasted it on the back side of the title page in many copies. He made plans to print two more volumes of correspondence.[63]

On the very last day of 1596, Tycho finally pulled himself together and wrote a long letter in Latin, not to the young king but to Chancellor Christian Friis of Borreby, who had visited Uraniborg and was interested in astronomy. He enclosed a copy of *Epistolarvm astronomicarvm,* requested to keep Nordfjord, and asked that Uraniborg be permanently endowed as the late King Frederick had wished.[64] Three weeks later came a curt reply: King Christian IV could not pay for preservation of astronomical instruments, and the Governor of Bergen needed the income from Nordfjord.[65] All Tycho's hopes and dreams were crushed in an instant. What could he do now?

In February and March 1597, Tycho decided to move into his mansion in Copenhagen, a substantial Renaissance structure with a bay window and clock tower above the portal and outbuildings around a rear courtyard.[66] An adjacent ruined tower on the town wall served as his observatory and had rooms for his assistants.[67] He told Vedel he intended to finish the remaining tasks of a lifetime as a private citizen in the tranquillity of his own house.[68]

In Copenhagen, however, Valkendorf and Friis knew that Tycho would still attract the best students and that this would

weaken the university at the very time when they were planning to strengthen it.[69] Valkendorf sent the chief constable to
tell Tycho that he could no longer use the tower as an observatory, and he was forbidden to use his chymical laboratory.[70]
To Tycho, who was out of touch with the new administration,
this seemed 'Machiavellian'. His only contact at court was
Jørgen Rosenkrantz's young son, Holger, who could tell him
nothing.

On Tuesday 15 March 1597, Tycho made his last observations on Hven.[71] Three days later, his annual pension was
terminated.[72] On 9–10 April, Chancellor Friis came to investigate peasant complaints over religious practices and other
matters.[73] The next day, Tycho Brahe and his entire household
sailed away, leaving his bailiff, David Pedersen, in charge.[74]
But the Muses found no peace in Copenhagen. Tycho had
offended many people, and city gossip had stained his honour.
He summoned his sons, Tycho and Jørgen, from Sorø Academy.

On 14 April 1597 came yet another blow. Friis' visit to
Hven led to charges that Tycho's chaplain, Pastor Jens Jensen
Wensøsil of St Ibb's, had violated the Church Ordinance and
failed to reprimand Tycho Brahe for living with a 'concubine'

85 *Left to right:* Copenhagen's southeastern bastion, the ruined tower, and the
courtyard buildings with Tycho's towering mansion beyond them. Detail of
Jan van Wijk, *Prospect of Copenhagen*, 1611.

and abstaining from Holy Communion for eighteen years. Wensøsil was found guilty and would have been beheaded if Tycho's influential friends had not intervened.[75] To a high churchman like Chancellor Friis, Kirsten Jørgensdatter, the love of Tycho's life, was nothing but a whore, and his children were bastards without rights.

After a great deal of careful preliminary planning but without informing the king, Tycho Brahe departed from Copenhagen on 2 June 1597 with a household of twenty and all his portable possessions: astronomical instruments, chymical equipment, printing presses, books, papers and more.[76] Their destination was Rostock, where he still had many friends. The day they left, the professors Thomas Fincke and Iver Stub were sent to Hven to investigate reports that peasants had damaged the Stjerneborg instruments.[77] They were overwhelmed by the splendour of the remaining Stjerneborg instruments but did not consider them of any value to the university.[78]

Tycho had barely arrived in Rostock when he learned that the canonry of the Chapel of the Magi had been awarded to Chancellor Friis.[79] Convinced that Valkendorf and Friis wished him harm, he decided to write directly to King Christian IV, the only person in Denmark who could restore his honour. His letter explained that he had been drawn to the reform of astronomy in his youth, and that King Frederick II urged him to pursue this goal on Hven and promised to perpetuate his enterprise. He hoped that King Christian would fulfil that promise and consent to be his 'gracious Lord and King' so he would not have to seek a patron abroad. The letter went off around 10 July 1597. First Secretary Sivert Grubbe normally opened all incoming correspondence, but Tycho's letter lay undelivered for three months.[80]

In late July, Tycho spoke with Duke Ulrich of Mecklenburg, who wrote and urged his grandson to allow Tycho Brahe to work in a way that would shower honour upon Denmark.[81] Duke Ulrich also borrowed a princely sum from Tycho in return for a secure mortgage on the entire province of Doberan Amt.[82] Tycho had not left Denmark impoverished.

When the plague hit Rostock, Tycho accepted Heinrich Rantzau's offer of temporary asylum. He and his entourage left Rostock on 8 September and within the month had moved into Rantzau's Wandsburg Castle on the outskirts of Hamburg, where Tycho lived in grand style and travelled about in a coach drawn by six horses.[83]

His letter to King Christian IV was finally delivered in early October 1597. The king's reply was relentlessly harsh in reciting a long list of Tycho's administrative abuses, religious violations and transgressions of the law. Far from leaving Denmark for lack of money, the king had heard that he was able to loan thousands of rixdollars to lords and princes and advised him that if he wanted to 'serve as a Mathematicus, to offer your services humbly . . . and not lay out your views with such wilful words'.[84]

Tycho sank into a mood of dark despair. At long last, he began to write and found solace in composing an elegy in the style of Ovid. Its first word was the name of his beloved homeland: *Dania.* 'Denmark, what was my offense? How did I hurt you, my native land? . . . Was it wrong to spread your fame abroad?' The elegy began as a bitter jeremiad deploring Danish ingratitude for what he described as his herculean

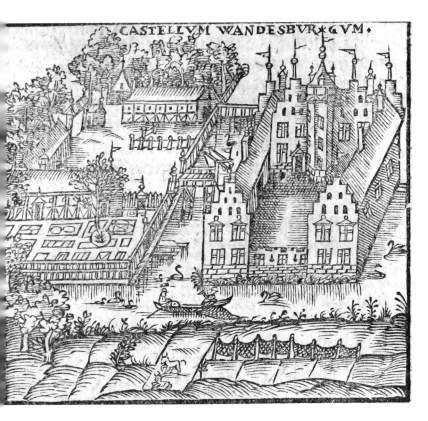

achievements, but the words gradually became therapeutic, leading him out of the dark wood of despair into the light of a reversal of values that brought hope and liberation. At last, he exclaimed: 'Sum tamen haud exul, Libertas obtigit ampla:/ Exilium in Patria verius ante tuli': 'I am no exile but win a greater freedom: my exile was when I lived in my native land.'[85]

He finished the elegy on 20 October 1597, sent copies to Rantzau and a few others, and then with a simple cross-staff resumed the observations he had abandoned at Uraniborg

86 Wandsburg Castle, 1591.

'against my will' around the time of the vernal equinox.[86] He found a portrait artist and commissioned several copies of an oil portrait with the legend, 'Tycho Brahe at the age of fifty, when after a long period of exile in his native land through divine providence he regained the liberty he had sought.'[87] He used these portraits as gifts to friends and potential patrons.

87 Tycho Brahe at the age of fifty, 1596, oil on canvas.

Tycho was ready to move on. He decided to publish a description of his instruments and facilities on Hven with an autobiography and an agenda for future achievements under a great monarch, perhaps an emperor, willing to support such unprecedented marvels. He set up his printing press at Wandsburg and brought in a Hamburg printer named Philip von Ohr, together with copperplate engravers, calligraphers, manuscript illuminators, bookbinders and others to produce fine books and manuscripts.[88] The book was entitled *Astronomiae instauratae mechanica* (Instruments for the Instauration of Astronomy).

Around the time it went to press, King Christian IV arrived in the Duchy of Schleswig. An outbreak of plague had moved his wedding to Princess Anna Catherine of Brandenburg to Haderslevhus Castle, where it took place in November.[89] After the wedding, Rantzau arranged for Tycho to meet the bride's parents.[90] Elector Joachim Frederick and Electress Catherine shared his interests in astrology and Paracelsian chemistry.[91] They received him warmly, agreed to write to Queen Anna Catherine and King Christian IV on his behalf, and sent Johannes Müller to study with him until the summer of 1598, but their letters to King Christian had no effect.[92]

Tycho was in frequent contact with other astronomers. One day, a courier arrived with a new book by the Imperial Mathematician in Prague, none other than Nicolaus Reymers Ursus. It contained vicious attacks on Tycho and Rothmann and a laudatory letter from somebody named Johannes Kepler. The same courier brought a letter from Kepler.[93] Ursus's foul attacks angered Tycho, but he praised Kepler's ingenious use of Platonic solids to establish intervals between planets. Another talented astronomer, David Fabricius, visited Wandsburg that summer and later corresponded with Tycho from his observatory in Esens. Christian Hansen Riber visited and became Tycho's courier for gifts to Joseph Scaliger in Leiden. Longomontanus returned after inquiring about Wittich's library on Tycho's behalf, Frans Tengnagel came back from a visit to the Netherlands, and a Danish student named Claus Mule joined the *família*.[94] Tengnagel and Mule were noblemen and became Tycho's couriers to princely courts. Holger Rosenkrantz, torn by religious anxiety, came to seek counsel with Tycho. After returning to Denmark, he announced his betrothal to Sophie Axelsdatter Brahe. Drawing on his personal experience, Tycho replied that the chains of matrimony were much more pleasant and less ungrateful than those of the court.[95]

He wanted Holger to deliver his new book and star catalogue to King Christian IV, but this was prevented by conditions at court.[96] Tycho complained of the 'Machiavelianism, injury, hatred, envy, malice, slander, disparagement, and contempt'.[97] He said that the 'two chancellors', Christian Friis and Chancellor of the Realm Arild Huitfeldt, colluded with each other, 'for one raven will not pluck out the eyes of the other'.[98] One was a 'neophyte of Niccolò Machiavelli' but was learning daily from the master Machiavellian at his side.[99]

By August 1598, however, he 'no longer cared'. Having failed to penetrate the shield of enemies around King Christian IV, he turned to other courts and especially to that of Holy Roman Emperor Rudolf II in Prague.[100] He corresponded with Hagecius and other brokers of imperial patronage as his

calligraphers lettered sumptuous manuscript copies of the
star catalogue, now expanded to 1,000 stars, with the finest
copy on vellum for Emperor Rudolf.[101]

Heinrich Rantzau advised him to get in touch with Duke
Ernest of Bavaria, Archbishop-Elector of Cologne, a man of
arcane interests and the emperor's cousin.[102] In June 1598
Tycho sent Tengnagel to present Prince Maurice of Orange
and Elector Ernest with sumptuously illuminated and autographed copies of his latest works. The Elector was astonished
to learn that Tycho had left Denmark. Tycho was renewing
astronomy for the first time in more than a thousand years.
How could King Christian IV allow this to happen? He asked
how much Tycho Brahe cost the Danish crown. Tengnagel
had lived in Tycho's household for three years. He estimated
that Tycho went through around 4,000 rixdollars a year.

'What?' erupted the Elector. 'Should such a man leave the
country for so little money? What a disgrace! A lord gambles
away more in an evening. Gold one can always get, but not
always such people.' He said he would commend Tycho Brahe
to Emperor Rudolf II and wanted to meet him personally.
'Tell that good, honourable man I wish him everything good,'
he said, 'and I will treat him hereafter as if he were my own
dear brother.' He heaped costly gifts on Tengnagel and immediately wrote to urge Rudolf II to take Tycho Brahe into his
service, which the emperor was eager to do.[103]

Astronomiae instauratae mechanica was dedicated to Emperor
Rudolf II.[104] It contained 22 woodcuts and engravings of
Tycho's instruments, a new engraving of Uraniborg, and
woodcuts of Hven, Stjerneborg and Tycho's *imprese*. Tycho's
innovative methods for collecting and verifying observational

data were laid out in detailed descriptions of instruments. He pasted the new engraved portrait in some copies, while others contained watercolour portraits showing a haggard, weary and bald old man with a cataract in one eye. When this book was finished, Tycho had Ohr print the manuscript of his lunar theory as another chapter in *Astronomiae instauratae progymnasmata*.

Around Michaelmas of 1598, Tycho and his *família* departed Wandsburg Castle in a caravan of at least four coaches surrounded by retainers.[105] At Harburg Castle, he autographed a copy of the instrument book for Duke Otto II of Brunswick-Harburg, who added his commendation of Tycho to those from Elector Ernest and Duke Ulrich.[106] The caravan moved up the Elbe and stayed a week in Magdeburg, where Tycho conversed with George Rollenhagen. Erik Lange turned up, but Tycho refused to allow him to accompany them and tempt the emperor with his latest futile gold-making scheme.[107]

The season was growing late. Tycho stored his heavy baggage in Magdeburg, had Longomontanus take his wife and daughters back to Wandsburg, and sped on with his sons and Tengnagel to Dresden. After a month in the Electoral Saxon residence city, he was warned of plague in Bohemia and advised not to proceed to Prague. He and his sons went back to Wittenberg, and he sent Tengnagel off to Italy with gifts for the rulers of Venice and other Italian states. Early in 1599, he summoned the rest of the family to Wittenberg, where they lived in the house of Philip Melanchthon, now the home of Professor Johannes Jessenius (Ján Jesenský) with his wife, Maria, and her brother, Daniel Fels.[108] Tycho was received as a celebrity, handed out his publications, set up a laboratory

88 Tycho Brahe, c. 1599.

and rushed to complete the remaining parts of *Astronomiae instavratae progymnasmata*.

Celestial globes using Tycho's stellar positions were start-ing to appear from the shops of Willem Jansz. Blaeu, the Langrens and Jodocus Hondius, setting a new standard for celestial cartography.[109] Ohr's press run of the lunar theory, however, was full of errors and had to be discarded. Tycho worked with Professor Melchior Jöstelius, who found a bril-liant way to improve *prosthaphaeresis* and published a pamphlet using Tycho's lunar theory to predict circumstances of a lunar eclipse on 31 January 1599.[110] The prediction was off by half an hour, which meant that Tycho had to repair his lunar theory.[111] Tycho had never formally matriculated in Wittenberg, but he and his sons did so on 1 February, together with an assistant, Johannes Eriksen. He presented a new *album amicorum* to his son, Tycho, who began filling it with signatures and arms of noble students in Wittenberg.[112]

Tycho continued to correspond with many power brokers at the imperial court, including Hagecius, Rudolf Coradutz, Wolfgang Rumpf zum Wullroß and the emperor's most trusted confidant, Johannes Barvitius. His summons to Prague arrived in a letter from Coradutz dated 27 January 1599, but Magdalene was seriously ill, and by the time she recovered, spring thaws and rain rendered roads impassable.

Emperor Rudolf grew extremely impatient. When would Tycho Brahe arrive?

SEVEN

The Emperor's Astrologer and his Legacy, 1599–1687

ycho Brahe and his household left Wittenberg on 14 June 1599 and moved up the Elbe in the direction of Prague. They spent the first evening at Castle Pretzsch as guests of the Saxon hereditary marshal, Hans Löser, and arrived the following day in Dresden. Kirsten and the daughters stayed there with Johann Tauchmann, a Saxon court official, while Tycho crossed the Ore Mountains with his sons and Claus Mule and rode into the 'golden city' of Prague.[1] As they arrived, Ursus fled the city.

More than 1,000 courtiers wandered the sprawling complex of Prague Castle on the heights above the city, but the reclusive Emperor Rudolf II was nowhere to be seen.[2] Raised in the austerity of the Spanish court, he had been Holy Roman Emperor since the age of 24. A good horseman, in his youth he liked to hunt stags and joust in armour and cultivated the fine arts and occult wisdom with a brilliance that attracted artists, philosophers, aristocrats and beautiful women. In his late twenties, however, something snapped. He began to fly into violent rages and then sink into deep depression, and he no longer met with any of the imperial bodies except the Privy Council (*Der Geheime Rat*).[3] This small group included his Steward (*Obersthofmeister*) Wolfgang

Rumpf, Court Marshal (*Obersthofmarschall*) Paul Sixt Trautson, and his closest advisor, Secretary Johannes Barvitius, as well as Rudolf Coraduz (Corraduc, Corraducius) and a few others. The emperor generally spent his days in seclusion with artists like Giuseppe Arcimboldo, physicians like Thaddeus Hagecius, and his clever valets, alchemists and wizards, many of them corrupt, of whom his first valet, Hans Popp, was the 'apple of

89 Hans von Aachen, *Emperor Rudolf II*, 1590s, oil on canvas.

his eye'. In his apartment and *Kunstkammer* and the attached private garden, library, workshops, stables and laboratory, Emperor Rudolf II laboured to distil the secrets of governing, *arcana imperii,* from the *arcana naturae*, in order to control the turbulent world by mere manipulation of microcosmic forces.[4] Tycho Brahe would surely help him unlock arcane secrets that others had failed to master.

Barvitius met Tycho in the gardens of Belvedere palace and bade him a hearty welcome on behalf of the emperor and Privy Council. A few days later, he was received in Prague Castle by Rumpf, who expressed astonishment that the Danish king had let such a man depart, to which Tycho replied that divine providence may have played a role. Barvitius took him to the Renaissance palace and gardens of the late Vice-Chancellor Jakob Kurz von Senftenau (Curtius) and said that Tycho could have this place as his residence unless he preferred a rural abode. Tycho replied that he had formerly lived on a peaceful island.[5]

On the day of his imperial audience, his carriage rolled into Prague Castle as Emperor Rudolf peered down from a high window. Barvitius and Tycho the Younger waited in the imperial antechamber: 'I went in to the emperor alone and saw him sitting in the room on a bench with his back against a table, completely alone in the whole room, without even an attending page.'[6] Tycho was arthritic, hard of hearing, his eyes watery and nose distorted, but his golden chains and manners revealed the polished courtier.[7] Emperor Rudolf was a little man, quick and athletic, dressed in the black silks of the Spanish court. His face radiated dignity and pleasure as he motioned for Tycho to approach and graciously shook his hand.[8] In a short Latin speech, Tycho requested his favour and presented his recommendations, which the emperor opened, laid aside, and said how agreeable Tycho's arrival was to him,

> and he promised to support me and my research, all the while smiling in a most kindly way, so that his whole face beamed with benevolence. I could not take in everything he said because he naturally speaks very softly.

Tycho requested to withdraw to the antechamber for his book and manuscripts, which he then presented. Barvitius later reported that the emperor studied them far into the night. As he left the audience, Barvitius mentioned that his odometer interested the emperor, and Tycho turned it over as his first gift of an instrument.[9] His other gifts were the manuscript star catalogue and ephemerides of the Sun and Moon prepared in Wittenberg, and the elegantly bound and illuminated copy of *Astronomiae instauratae mechanica*.[10] This book's dedication reviewed the long history of astronomy since the time of Adam, which aimed to capture the 'mysteries of the celestial theatre' with 'instruments that are not liable to error' and use geometry to arrange these observations into 'continuous quantities and a motion that is both circular and uniform'.[11] Tycho explained that he had designed instruments of unprecedented accuracy to collect and verify observations taken directly from nature. He had transformed the observation of nature into a collective activity by widespread correspondents and had organized teams of assistants working in pleasant, diligent competition.[12] He mentioned his unprecedented contributions to celestial refraction, solar

theory and lunar theory but did not mention establishing new
celestial coordinates to a patron who was an avid astrologer.
The book described each of his instruments in turn, its size
and material, advantages, shortcomings and verified standard of deviation, concluding with the Great Celestial Globe
that displayed precise positions of 1,000 stars. He described
Hven, Uraniborg and Stjerneborg. All in all, this book illustrated how Tycho Brahe had transformed astronomy from
an academic exercise into a courtly public endeavour, and he
added that he also knew secrets of spagyric chymistry too
powerful to put on paper.

During late July and early August 1599, Tycho unpacked
a brass azimuth quadrant and brass sextant to observe solar
meridian altitudes and culminations of Polaris. On 22 July,
he sent Johannes Eriksen up the tower of Charles University
to observe an eclipse.[13] These displays attracted attention,
and Tycho began to consort with great aristocrats at court.

The Privy Council was stunned when the emperor proposed that Tycho receive an annual salary of 3,000 florins in
hard currency with a down payment of 2,000 florins.[14] The
florin was originally a gold coin, but Emperor Rudolf meant
the silver 'Carolus gulden' equal to an imperial rixdollar
(*Reichsthaler*) of 25.984 grams silver-weight (also roughly equal
to a Danish *rigsdaler*).[15] Where was this money to come from?
Imperial finances were chaotic and corrupt, and salaries were
often in arrears, as Tycho's soon would be.[16]

The emperor also promised to grant Tycho a hereditary
estate, perhaps even make him a baron, and said he would
nominate his entire family for enrolment in the Bohemian
nobility. That last part was a dream come true to Tycho. In

the meantime, as a temporary residence, Emperor Rudolf offered Tycho his choice of large hunting castles at Brandeis and Lysá nad Labem or a smaller château at Benátky nad Jizerou ('Venice on the Iser'). Tycho chose Benátky and was escorted there in late August.[17] He summoned his family from Dresden and sent Tycho the Younger and Claus Mule to deliver a thick packet of letters to Denmark and return with Stjerneborg's huge instruments. He also planned to retrieve the instruments, library and other baggage stored in Magdeburg.

In August, Emperor Rudolf was compelled to leave plague-ridden Prague for Pilsen, and Tycho sent him the formula for his Paracelsian plague medicament.[18] Tycho stayed in Benátky and drew up plans for an observatory and chymical laboratory connected to the château, but the conscientious captain of Brandeis and Benátky, Caspar von Mühlstein, had scant means to fund such projects, so construction dragged.[19] In September, Tycho began to determine Benátky's latitude.[20] He was short of assistants but had enlisted the young Silesian nobleman Daniel Fels, whom he had gotten to know in Wittenberg, as his agent at court.[21] Tycho's cousin, Claus Steensen Bille from Herrevad, came to visit with a travelling companion who took ill and died soon after they arrived. The plague had reached Benátky. Tycho and his *família* took refuge for seven weeks during November and December 1599 in the fortress of Jiřice (Girsitz) near Kostelec but were back at Benátky when Tengnagel returned from his travels.[22]

Emperor Rudolf hated being away from his quarters and collections in Prague Castle. His violent rages returned, he made erratic decisions, dismissed many high officials,

and even replaced Hans Popp with a new first valet, Jerome Makovský. In December, Daniel Fels wrote from Pilsen that Barvitius wanted something to occupy the emperor's troubled mind, and Tycho sent the printed parts of *Astronomiae instauratae progymnasmata*, which calmed him for a fortnight.[23]

Around that same time, Tycho the Younger returned from Denmark with Christian Longomontanus, who was drawn back by Tycho's promise of an appointment as imperial mathematician. Tycho learned that Johannes Kepler was in Prague and summoned him to Benátky on 4 February 1600.[24] Tycho had many irons in the fire. Calculators were working on some of his projects in Wittenberg, and Matthias Seiffert had come to assist at Benátky.[25] His younger son, Jørgen Brahe – called George or Jiři in Bohemia – probably helped to set up the chymical library. Johannes Müller arrived with his wife in March 1600, expecting an imperial salary, but when that failed to come through and there was no room for a separate

90 Benátky nad Jizerou château.

household at Benátky, Tycho put them up in Prague and had Müller work on refuting some of Ursus' views.[26] The learned Rabbi David ben Solomon Gans came from Prague three times and stayed five days each time to discuss cosmology and philosophy. He later described Tycho's observatory as a long gallery with a dozen instruments, each in its own room, possibly with roofs that swung open like those of Stjerneborg.[27] Tycho and his assistants began to observe with an equatorial armillary, a couple of sextants and two azimuth quadrants, including Stjerneborg's Revolving Azimuth Quadrant.[28]

Eriksen, Tengnagel, Seiffert and Longomontanus knew what to do, but Kepler, like Wittich in his day, had little interest in observation and even harboured predatory desires. 'This is what I think of Tycho,' he had written earlier to Maestlin, 'he is very rich, but he does not make proper use of his riches, like most rich people. Therefore, we must wrest his riches from him' – adding, as if on second thought, 'and beg him to publish his observations, all of them'.[29] Tycho had welcomed Kepler in a 'gracious and most friendly' manner but expected him to join the team. Kepler's intention was not to help Tycho but to use him – and his observations. He was a loner by nature and felt extremely uncomfortable in the sociable, collaborative atmosphere of Tycho's unfamiliar *família*.[30] Tycho asked Longomontanus to help the new man fit in, and he set Kepler to calculating the orbit of Mars in reference to the true sun. Kepler made a hopeless mess of it in two long, complicated attempts, and then, as James R. Voelkel explained, Longomontanus pointed him to Dogma IV in the Uraniborg manual of trigonometry, and it was done in a snap.[31]

Kepler worked on Mars while Longomontanus worked on Tycho's lunar theory and had problems modelling the extremely complicated path of a Moon that wobbled through open space at changing speeds due to variation, nutation and nodal oscillation. Tycho's final version used five circles, two of them rotating around rotating centres and two turning on centres attached as 'epicycles' to other rotating circles. Kepler said that Tycho's theory was 'rendered unintelligible' by this complicated arrangement of circles and epicycles and urged him to try his new version of Ptolemy's equant, which considered a celestial body's motion to be uniform, not with respect to its own centre but from another, imaginary point.[32] Tycho saw the advantages of Kepler's approach but said he was too old to start over again. His solar theory was already in print. He needed to finish the lunar theory and move on, not go back. He was feeling his age.

Kepler kept pestering him for a formal contract. He wanted to be exempted from observational activities, live in Prague, receive a salary from the emperor, and have unrestricted use of Tycho's observations with the freedom to work at his own pace in his own way, which meant assuming Copernican rather than Tychonic cosmology and using equants instead of epicycles.[33] Kepler wanted Tycho to arrange all of this for him. Longomontanus told him he was asking too much.

When Kepler said he had written a critique of Ursus for the Bavarian chancellor, Tengnagel asked him what he had written.[34] He responded with a brief essay that dealt primarily with planetary models and avoided observational astronomy, although he did imply at one point that Tycho's understanding

of celestial space went beyond Copernicus, who thought that celestial orbs actually existed.[35]

Tycho wrote to Kepler's patron, Baron Hans Frederick Hoffmann of Grünbühel and Strechau, and suggested that the three of them meet to discuss the matter of Kepler's contract. Before that happened, Johannes Jessenius showed up, and Tycho enlisted him to mediate an agreement with Kepler. Jessenius did so on 5 April 1600, but Kepler was not

91 Unknown artist, *Johannes Kepler*, 1610, oil on wood.

pleased with the terms. That evening, Kepler got roaring drunk and began to rant 'like a mad dog' in the presence of the *família* and guests until Tycho finally responded in anger. Kepler's rude behaviour offended everybody, even the amiable Longomontanus.

The next day, Kepler flared up again, apologized, and then left Benátky and rode to Prague with Jessenius. From the city, he sent yet another vitriolic letter to Tycho. What was wrong with him? The courtly Tycho was appalled by Kepler's rude behaviour and wanted nothing more to do with him. A few days later, however, Kepler wrote a servile apology brimming with pious phrases. Tycho read it, mulled it over, and after three weeks, took him back.[36]

Tycho was unrelentingly generous in dealing with Kepler. He agreed to negotiate with Privy Councillor Coradutz to assure that Kepler continue to receive his Styrian salary while working for Tycho and living in Prague. When Kepler needed a ride home to Graz, Tycho arranged for him to travel with his cousin, Frederick Rosenkrantz, who had spent the spring at Benátky.[37]

At the beginning of May 1600, Tycho attended Caspar von Mühlstein's wedding in Prague. He became well acquainted with several Protestant aristocrats, including Baron Ehrenfried von Minckwitz, who visited Benátky, and Baron Siegfried von Rindscheid, the alchemist who had visited Uraniborg with Erik Lange.[38] Minckwitz blazoned the same arms as Tycho's Ulfstand grandmother, and they came to regard themselves as kinsmen.[39] Jessenius created a sensation that summer by dissecting a corpse before an audience of 1,000 in the courtyard of Reček College. This was the first dissection ever conducted at the University of Prague, and it paved the way for his move to Prague from Wittenberg.[40]

On 10 June 1600, Emperor Rudolf returned to Prague.[41] Barvitius advised Tycho to move there as well with his entire household.[42] They left Benátky and were hastily lodged in a noisy, crowded hostel named the Golden Griffin, five minutes from the castle. Johannes Müller and his wife had returned to Berlin with Tycho's parting gift of 200 florins.[43] Soon after Tycho arrived in Prague, the emperor summoned him to a long private audience and called him back for yet another audience the same day. Emperor Rudolf soon found a better residence for Tycho's household near the Hoffmann mansion, but even that location provided no room for observations.[44]

Christian Longomontanus, fast approaching forty years old, gave up on an imperial appointment and took his leave of Tycho and the *família* on 4 August 1600, handing over to Johannes Eriksen his manuscript of Copernicus' *Commentariolus*. By September, the Stjerneborg and Magdeburg instruments had arrived in Litoměřice (Leitmeritz), the head of navigation on the Elbe, and were sent overland from there. When the instruments and Tycho's library finally arrived in Prague, they were installed at Belvedere Palace near the castle, where the emperor could contemplate them at his leisure. The hazy, unclear air over the city, however, meant that Tycho was unable to observe for five months of 1600.[45] He set up his press and began to print the remaining parts of *Astronomiae instauratæ progymnasmata*. In addition to discussing the New Star in detail, the book now contained his star catalogue and solar and lunar theories.

Courtly affairs took much time, but Tycho, Tengnagel, Fels and Eriksen also worked on astronomy with Seiffert, Ambrosius Rhodius and peripatetic students including Willebrord Snell from Leiden.[46] Tycho's aged friend, Thaddeus Hagecius, died 1 September 1600. In October, the troubled emperor fired the faithful Rumpf and Trautson and ordered them to depart within two days, which they did. Access to the emperor was largely controlled now by Jerome Makovský, soon elevated to Baron Makovský of Makové.[47] That autumn, an embassy from Shah 'Abbas of Persia, which included the English adventurer, Sir Anthony Shirley, arrived and was received by the emperor. They stayed in Prague for three months and became acquainted with Tycho and his family.

Emperor Rudolf II purchased the Curtius mansion and began refurbishing it to serve as Tycho's residence. The only known image of the mansion is from a later time and shows it in ruins with several outbuildings around a garden enclosed by a high wall and entered through a Renaissance portal. Probably in the courtyard garden, Tycho erected a large pedestal for instruments with images that celebrated princely patrons of astronomy: King Alfonso the Wise of Castile above Ptolemy and Al-Battani, Emperor Charles V above Copernicus and Peter Apian, Emperor Rudolf II above Tycho alone, and King Frederick II of Denmark over an image of Uraniborg.[48]

That autumn, the emperor's militant cousin, Archduke Ferdinand II, expelled all Lutherans from Styria on short notice. A feverish and extremely distraught Johannes Kepler stumbled into Prague with his family in October, and they were put up in the Hoffmann mansion. Tycho offered him

employment discrediting Ursus' astronomy, as Müller had
done in part.[49] This was to support a legal case against Ursus,
and it became Kepler's task for the winter and the spring of
1601.[50] Forced against his will to become a team player and
perform a task assigned to him by the team leader, Kepler
gradually learned to understand the advantages of teamwork. He may even have become more courteous, although
he still liked to ridicule people behind their backs. Kepler and
Tycho had similar world views as Philippist Lutheran astronomers immersed in Platonic and Hermetic philosophy. Kepler
gradually began to understand that Tycho Brahe was the one
who had elevated astronomy from an elementary academic
subject into a prestigious focus of courtly natural philosophy, and that Tycho's leadership and generous willingness

92 Belvedere Palace, Prague.

to collaborate had transformed astronomy into a collective endeavour linking courts and philosophers across Europe.

A year earlier at Benátky, Kepler still thought in the academic terms he had learned from Michael Maestlin when he wrote his essay for Tengnagel. Now, in Prague, his 'Apology for Tycho against Ursus' showed what he had learned from the experience of working on Tycho's team and dining at Tycho's table. Instead of comparing abstract geometrical models, he dealt with the broader question of how astronomers work in community, using Tycho's dynamic, collaborative household and its web of connections as his model. Kepler now began, as Tycho began, with observation. Although still

93 The Kurz (Curtius) mansion in ruins in 1672.

not an observational astronomer himself, he had come to realize that his theoretical work was dependent upon the accomplishments of observational astronomers. 'The fact is,' he wrote, 'that observation of the celestial motions guides astronomers to the formation of hypotheses in the right way, and not the other way around.' Kepler described a three-step process in which

> the record of [celestial] motions is . . . the practical and mechanical part of astronomy; to discover their true and genuine paths is . . . the task of contemplative astronomy; while to say by what circles and lines correct images of those true motions may be depicted on paper is the concern of the inferior tribunal of geometers.[51]

This was a concise description of Tycho's approach: first, carry out precise, verifiable observations; second, move from observation to natural philosophy in order to interpret observational data in the context of physical celestial space; and third, establish mathematical hypotheses that combine positional astronomy with celestial physics. Kepler said that the astronomer 'ought not to be excluded from the community of philosophers who inquire into the nature of things'.[52] At one point, he even speculated about a celestial force akin to magnetism, as Tycho had done in 1587.[53] He argued that 'Tycho has provided us with a more perfect astronomy than [the ancients] left behind'. Kepler revealed a clear understanding of how Tycho had arrived at a system that dissipated 'those clouds of solid orbs' and linked planetary orbits to the Sun within a dynamic, physical celestial space through which comets occasionally came sweeping, declaring that

> in the Tychonic [hypotheses] there is not only a mutation and transposition of the Copernican [hypotheses]; they contain many new things peculiar to them derived from the appearances themselves. And if Copernicus wanted to incorporate these things he would have to correct and amend his own hypothesis, something which I, indeed, who follow Copernicus on the main points, think should be done.[54]

Kepler's manuscript 'Apology' became part of an ongoing dialogue within Tycho's *familia* on how to study the world of nature. They worked, disputed and celebrated together. During the fourteen days of Christmas 1600, they celebrated the betrothal of Frans Tengnagel and Elizabeth Brahe, and the betrothed couple then shared a bed.[55] Early in the new year, Emperor Rudolf II formally submitted a request to the Bohemian Diet that Tycho Brahe and his sons be accepted as noble citizens of the Kingdom of Bohemia.[56] When Shirley and the Persian embassy departed for Italy, Tycho arranged for Tycho the Younger to travel in their entourage, carrying gifts and an introduction to Grand Duke Ferdinando de' Medici of Tuscany, whose consort, Christina of Lorraine, was the great-granddaughter of King Christian II. Tycho wanted his son to stay in Siena, learn Italian, and then lead an expedition to Egypt to determine the precise latitude and longitude of Alexandria.[57]

On 25 February 1601, Tycho and his *família* finally moved into the Curtius mansion, where separate quarters were found for the Kepler family. Seven teams simultaneously observed the meridian culmination of the Sun on 28 February 1601 with the mural quadrant, two Stjerneborg quadrants, three sextants and an improved 'Ptolemaic' cross-staff. Kepler departed for Graz in May 1601 to deal with pressing financial matters, leaving his quarrelsome wife and family in Prague, but the *família* now included Seiffart, Rhodius, a Danish student named Paul Jensen Kolding, and two skilled observers, Simon Marius, who arrived in May, and David Fabricius, who came for three weeks in June.[58] Tycho's son, George, ran the laboratory. This large staff observed the planets throughout the summer months.[59] The Muse, Urania, had found a new home on the Hradčany heights in Golden Prague.

Tycho proudly sent out invitations to the June wedding of 'the Honourable and Wellborn Elizabeth Brahe' and the nobleman and imperial courtier Frans Tengnagel of Camp.[60] He called in his loan of 10,000 rixdollars from the dukes of Mecklenburg and planned to buy a château and landed estate in Bohemia.[61] His daughter's wedding was attended by court aristocrats, and the newlyweds departed with Johannes Eriksen to spend a year with the Tengnagel family in the Netherlands. The three noble families of Brahe, Fels and Jessenius gathered in 1601 to celebrate the betrothal of Tycho's daughter, Sophie, to Daniel Fels.

That summer, Elector Ernest of Cologne and others who preferred Archduke Albert as Emperor Rudolf's successor tried to persuade Tycho to cast a horoscope to present to the emperor showing that the heavens also preferred Albert.[62]

From April to July, this plot took up Tycho's time, but whether he ever actually presented the horoscope is unknown.

Meanwhile, Kepler sent another rude letter of complaint from Graz, which Eriksen answered with striking authority on Tycho's behalf. Tycho remained level-headed and generous in his support of Kepler through all these undeserved outbursts.[63] For his part, during much of his spare time in Graz, Kepler worked on a problem in optics suggested by Tycho's studies of refraction.[64] Nicolaus Reymers Ursus had died, but Tycho still pursued his case against him, and in the end, the archbishop of Prague confiscated and burned all copies of Ursus' *De astronomicis hypothesibus*.[65]

By then, Kepler had returned to Prague in good health and eagerly accepted Tycho's invitation to collaborate in compiling new tables of the planets, the Sun and the Moon. Tycho brought Kepler to court and presented him to Emperor Rudolf, proposing that he be appointed the next imperial mathematician. Tycho added that he planned to prepare planetary tables based on his own observations and wanted permission to name them the *Rudolphine Tables* in honour of the emperor, just as the *Alphonsine Tables* had been named for Emperor Rudolf's ancestor, King Alfonso X of Castile and Leon. Emperor Rudolf was pleased to grant his gracious permission.[66]

Soon after, on 13 October 1601, Tycho and Baron Ehrenfried von Minckwitz went together to a feast at the palace of Bohemia's greatest nobleman, Peter Vok von Rosenberg (Petr Vok z Rožmberka). The custom was to dine at six, beginning with soup, perhaps a wine soup, almond soup, pike soup or one of many other varieties. Then came a course of boiled beef, veal, mutton or lamb, followed by a course of prepared meats, then a course of roast meats, and then an abundance of game served with vegetables. Each course was accompanied by salads, sauces and visual displays and was consumed with immense quantities and varieties of alcoholic beverages. The meal concluded with sweets and fruit. Such feasts were why great Bohemian nobles suffered 'all kinds of vascular, digestive and urological difficulties' and had to seek the waters of spas.[67]

On that evening, Tycho Brahe ate, drank and conversed with gusto. In the course of the evening, he had difficulty holding his water, but etiquette did not permit leaving the table. When he returned home in pain, he could not pass water, and his agony was intense. The agony increased through a sleepless night, then a whole day, another sleepless night, and yet another – five days and nights of agony without sleeping. The agony turned to fever and delirium. Lady Christina Brahe, as Kirsten Jørgensdatter was now called, was at his bedside with Magdalene, Sophie with Daniel Fels, Cecilia and George. Kepler, Colding and all the other servants and assistants were there, but Tycho the Younger was in Dresden on his way home from Italy, and Tengnagel and Eriksen were in Deventer with Elizabeth, who had just given birth to Tycho's first grandchild, Ida Catherina Gansneb genaamd Tengnagel van de Camp, baptized on 28 September 1601.

Even in his pain, Tycho could not be deterred from eating. On the seventh day, 20 October, Count Erik Brahe of Visingborg, a distant Swedish relative through both Brahe and Vasa lines, visited and ate with him. The count called four days later to learn that Tycho had been delirious all night long, softly repeating the phrase, *Ne frustra vixisse videar* (Let my life not be in vain). By morning, Tycho was exhausted but no longer delirious. He sat up, took his leave of Christina and his daughters, encouraged his son and assistants to carry on their studies, and urged Kepler to finish the *Rudolphine Tables* according to the Tychonic and not the Copernican system. Around nine that evening, 24 October 1601, Count Erik Brahe held him in his arms, and Johannes Kepler later said, 'I saw the greatest of men expire.'[68] Kepler composed a moving account of Tycho's agony and peaceful death as the last entry in the observational journal.[69]

Two days after his death, Barvitius came to inform Kepler that Tycho's instruments and papers, including the observational journals, were to be placed in his care and that he would be the new imperial mathematician with an annual salary of 500 gulden.[70] Kepler had no idea what to do with all those instruments, but he was eager to seize the ten volumes of observational journals and 24 volumes of fair copies of observations arranged by year and celestial object.[71]

Erik Brahe stayed for three days, and then, 'I left the Lady Brahe.' On 4 November 1601, mourners proceeded from the Curtius mansion in solemn procession behind a man bearing a black damask banner that displayed Tycho's titles and coat of arms in gold, followed by Tycho's horse draped in black, another black banner and another fine horse in black. A procession of men in black followed at a solemn pace with Tycho's gilt sword and dagger, black helmet with the Brahe crest, gilt spurs on a pillow of black silk taffeta, and an escutcheon with Tycho's quarterings. Next came bearers of immense candles with armorial shields of Tycho's quarterings ahead of the

coffin, which was borne by twelve imperial guards. George
Brahe walked behind it, escorted by Count Erik Brahe and
Imperial Councillor Baron Ehrenfried von Minckwitz, all in
long black robes, followed in turn by privy councillors and
other nobles, Tycho's students and servants – Kepler and
the others – in long black robes, and finally, Lady Christina
Brahe, escorted by two fine old royal councillors, followed by
Magdalene, Sophie and Cecilia Brahe in turn, each escorted
by two distinguished gentlemen and followed by many noble
women and maidens and other leading women of the city.
Throngs of onlookers watched the solemn procession move
through Malá Strana along the river, across Charles Bridge to
Týn Church of the Utraquist Hussites, the greatest church in
Prague, which was packed with counts, countesses, noble maidens and many others, both nobles and commoners. Johannes
Jessenius preached a funeral sermon that reviewed Tycho's
distinguished birth, life and achievements and described his
death in a manner that pointed to uraemia, a diagnosis with
which modern experts agree.[72] Tycho's descendants eventually
erected a splendid grave monument in the church. Colding
and Kepler commemorated their master in Latin elegies.[73]

Tycho Brahe's privileged birth and upbringing made him
self-confident, demanding and competitive, with a strong
feeling of entitlement, but he was never your typical rich and
privileged noble.[74] He came from an extremely talented family and was far more intelligent than most people of any social
class. Full of ideas and open to the ideas of others, he was an
innovator and an activist who was willing to go his own way
and took pride in being self-taught. His marriage for love
was evidence of an independent mind, loyalty and willingness

to defy social conventions. It caused him endless social, religious and legal trouble, but Kirsten Jørgensdatter, now Lady Christina Brahe, this able pastor's daughter of whom we know so little, was the anchor and refuge of his life, she and their children. Tycho Brahe was a born leader, a gracious courtier, an extremely innovative organizer, and a demanding but kind and loyal master who did much to make teamwork enjoyable and promote the careers of his former assistants.

Tycho took hard blows in his lifetime, from the cuts of Manderup Parsberg's sword to the ridicule of Gellius Sascerides and others and what he perceived as the Machiavellian rejection of King Christian IV's servants. The comfort of friends and admirers in Germany and Bohemia, the stimulation of brilliant new assistants, and his family's acceptance as nobles in Bohemia helped him weather the crisis of old age, which often came early in the Renaissance.

His eirenic Lutheran faith made him open to all, and his hierarchical Platonic and Hermetic world view led him to see every individual as a microcosm of the universe, capable of finding a place within it. By force of a complex, powerful personality and brilliant intellect, Tycho Brahe did truly soar above his fellow creatures here on earth, and his legacy has endured.

A few months after his death, his daughter, Sophie, lost her betrothed when Daniel Fels died of Hungarian fever on 4 February 1602.[75] She and Magdalene would never marry. The following month, Tycho's sister, Sophie, dressed in tatters with holes in her stockings, having drained her great wealth for her wayward beloved, met Erik Lange in the Baltic port of Eckernförde. They were married and spent a dozen years dodging creditors until his death, when her son, Tage Thott, still immensely rich, brought Sophie home to dignified retirement in Elsinore with a housekeeper who had served at Uraniborg.[76]

Tycho's heirs sold the printed sheets of *Epistolarum astronomicarum* to Levinus Hulsius, a Nuremberg publisher and instrument-maker, who reissued the book with a new title page in 1601. Hulsius also bought Tycho's woodcuts and engravings of instruments for a reset 1602 edition of *Astronomiae instauratae mechanica*.[77]

The Tengnagels and Eriksen returned to Prague with little Ida Catherina in 1602. When Tengnagel learned that Kepler had Tycho's valuable observational manuscripts, he demanded their return and told Emperor Rudolf that he could complete the *Rudolphine Tables* in four years. As a result, he was named director of the project and the manuscripts were returned to him, except that Kepler purloined the Mars observations.[78]

Astronomiae instavratae progymnasmata on the New Star of 1572 was finally published by Tengnagel with Kepler's assistance in 1602. It was intended to be astronomy without astrology like *De mvndi aetherei recentioribvs phaenomenis*, Tycho's book on the Comet of 1577, but Kepler stumbled across an old manuscript, written in 1592 and locked away in a separate place, which foretold in detail the astrological effects of the New Star. Without obtaining anybody's permission, Kepler stuck it into the book. At the very end, he added in sincere homage, 'Certainly, if that star did nothing else, it announced and gave rise to a great astronomer.'[79]

In 1603 Tengnagel reissued *De mvndi aetherei recentioribvs phaenomenis* with a new dedication to Barvitius. After the death of Levinus Hulsius, Gottfried Tampach of Frankfurt am Main acquired the remaining printed sheets of this work, *Astronomiae instavratae progymnasmata*, and *Epistolarum astronomicarum*, and reissued all three volumes in 1610. The demand for Tycho's writings remained strong.

Various rulers wanted to buy Tycho's instruments, but Emperor Rudolf would not allow them to leave Prague. Tycho's widow and children moved to the Old Town and brought the instruments there for safekeeping, and then they negotiated to sell them to the emperor on the condition that the Privy Council guarantee payment. These negotiations eventually settled on 20,000 rixdollars for the instruments and observational manuscripts and 6 per cent interest on any unpaid remainder. Emperor Rudolf commended Tycho's sons to the Bohemian Diet for enrolment in the Bohemian nobility and promised a down payment of 8,000 rixdollars, but actually paid only 4,000 in 1603.[80] In 1604 Archduke Matthias persuaded Emperor Rudolf to have Kepler escort Tycho's instruments to the University of Vienna, where they passed into the hands of the university superintendent, Dr Matthias Pühelmayr, and the university's competent Jesuit astronomers.[81]

Tycho's heirs settled into their new status as noble Bohemian gentry. Christina Brahe purchased a dower estate near Schladnig (České Zlatníky) in the German-speaking Biela (Bílina) valley near the Saxon border, and her children became acquainted with the local Lutheran gentry. In March 1604 Tycho the Younger married Margaret Vitzthum von Eckstädt, a noble widow on the neighbouring estate of Patokryje (Pattogre), and they apparently took over his mother's estate when she died that same year.[82] The Tengnagels and Tycho's daughter, Sophie, converted to Roman Catholicism that year.

When Tengnagel began to work on the *Rudolphine Tables*, he discovered that Kepler had stolen the Mars observations and demanded their return. The emperor's confessor, Johannes Pistorius, stepped in to mediate an agreement of 8 July 1604 that let Kepler use Tycho's observations in return for promising to obtain approval from the heirs for every publication based on them and to complete the *Rudolphine Tables* first of all.[83] Because of this agreement, Kepler cast his next book on optical theory and his 1609 study of Mars, which contained his first and second laws of planetary motion, as preliminary steps to the *Rudolphine Tables*.[84]

Bohemia was under the shadow of civil war and foreign incursions for more than a generation from 1609 until 1648. Tengnagel survived until his death in 1622 as a Habsburg councillor and Kepler remained the imperial mathematician through thick and thin, but the entire kingdom of Bohemia was forcefully converted to Roman Catholicism after the Battle of White Mountain in 1620, and Johannes Jessenius was publicly beheaded in Prague's Old Town square in 1621.[85] Among the occupying imperial troops in Prague after White Mountain was a young soldier named René Descartes, who sought out sites associated with Tycho Brahe, spoke with people who had known him and searched in vain for his instruments.[86]

Tycho's instruments seemed to vanish in the chaos of those harrowing decades. One Triangular Sextant may have gone to the University of Ingolstadt, where it appeared in a portrait of a Jesuit astronomer named Cysat. Another Jesuit astronomer, Christopher Scheiner, hauled the Great Celestial Globe to Freiburg im Breisgau, where he built a small observatory on the university roof and tried to acquire Tycho's observational manuscripts.[87] Tengnagel would have handed them over, but the brothers Brahe refused, arguing that Kepler needed them to complete the *Rudolphine Tables*.[88] Scheiner moved in 1623 to Neisse (Nysa) in Silesia to establish a Jesuit college and brought along the Great Celestial Globe, then left it there when he went on a mission to Rome.[89]

It seemed almost miraculous that Tycho's family and manuscripts survived those violent decades when most of his instruments disappeared and only one Protestant member of the Brahe family was permitted to remain in Bohemia.[90] The emperor still owed the heirs 15,000 rixdollars at a rate of interest reduced to 5 per cent, but payments of the interest finally began to trickle in when Tycho the Younger was authorized to collect dues (*Kammerzinsen*) from four cities near his seat in the Biela valley.[91] His son, Otto Tycho Brahe, later wrote a status report on the family:

> Anno Domini 1627 the 2nd September, Lord Tycho Brahe's eldest son, Lord Tycho Brahe the Younger, gently departed this world in a worthy Christian manner, may God Almighty grant him and all true Christian believers a joyous resurrection. [He] was married in the year 1604 to the honourable, noble and virtuous Lady Margaretha Rasitzky of Pattogre, widow, born Vitzthum von Eckstedt, and [they] were blessed with 5 children together, of whom 4 are alive, and the eldest daughter

in 1628 was married to Lord Heinrich Abraham von
Salhausen, but the other three are still unmarried.
The aforesaid Lord Tycho Brahe the Younger's sister,
Elizabeth Brahe, was married to the noble and stern
knight, Lord Franz Gansneb genannt Tengnagel zum
Camp, Appeal Court Justice (*Appelations Rat*) to Roman
Imperial Majesty Rudolf of most commendable mem-
ory, likewise Aulic Councillor (*Reichshofrat*) to Emperor
Ferdinand II, and Archduke Leopold of Austria's
Privy Councillor, and they had 5 children, of whom
three are alive, and the eldest sister is married to a
Polish noble officer named Sigmund Wybrandsky, and
the aforenamed Franz Gansneb genannt Tengnagel's
first wife Anno 1613 was carried off by death in
Regensburg during the Imperial Diet . . . The aforenamed Lord Franz Gansneb genannt Tengnagel's
wife's sister, named Cecilia Brahe, was married to the
Wellborn Lord, Lord Gustav Sparre, Baron of Sundby,
His Royal Majesty of Poland and Sweden's Colonel
over a regiment of infantry, and the highly respected
princely highness Archduke Leopold of Austria's
Chamberlain and [they] have had several children,
departed to God . . .⁹²

George Brahe, who never married, took over as the family's contact with Kepler after the death of his brother, and
they had a good relationship. He eventually turned over all of
Tycho's observations to Kepler, who published the *Rudolphine
Tables* in 1627 and died in 1630, entrusting Tycho's manuscripts
to his son, Ludwig Kepler, and daughter, Susanna Bartsch.

After the great Protestant victory at Breitenfeld in 1631, Tycho's prophecy on the New Star of 1572, which Kepler had inserted into *Astronomiae instavratae progymnasmata*, was seen as a prophecy of this triumphant 'Lion of the North', King Gustavus Adolphus.[93] The following year, Saxon allies of the Swedish king swept into Bohemian Silesia with Duke Ulrik of Denmark, 21 years of age, serving as a colonel in command of a regiment of horse that was garrisoned in Neisse. In the abandoned Jesuit college, Duke Ulrik found the Great Celestial Globe, seized it as booty and sent it to his father, King Christian IV, explaining that its 'Author was the renowned Mathematicus Tycho Brahe, and presumably no equal to this Work of Art can be found in Europe or in any other part of the World'.[94]

George Brahe continued to ride the rounds of the four Bohemian cities twice a year to collect the interest payments. In 1638 he ran into an enemy patrol near Rakonitz and galloped hell-bent for life towards Pürglitz Castle (Křivoklát) with the patrol in hot pursuit. The next morning, his friend, Wenceslas von Elsnitz, the forester of Pürglitz, found his broken body outside the castle gate and the emperor's bond for 15,000 rixdollars lying on the ground.[95]

From then on, Tycho the Younger's son, Otto Tycho Brahe, a non-commissioned officer (*Wachtmeister*) in the imperial dragoons, took over the collections until his death without issue in 1662 on his estate at Těchlovice near Hradec Králové (Königgrätz). His sister, Christine Barbara von Sahlhausen née Brahe, died among other exiled Sahlhausens in Zittau on 7 January 1657, but whether she left issue is unknown.[96]

The last family member to collect interest payments from the four Bohemian cities was Rudolf Tycho Gansneb genannt Tengnagel von Camp, who inherited his grandfather Tycho Brahe's stocky build and reddish blonde hair and was accepted into the Bohemia nobility in 1622 despite his lack of eight quarterings. He rose to become Commandant of Prague Castle and Malá strana (Lesser Town) from 1650 until his death on 25 March 1672, leaving two daughters with his wife, Baroness Elisabeth Franziska Berzkowsky von Ssebirzow (Beřkovský von Šebířova). His youngest daughter, Elizabeth Ludmilla (Alžběta Lidmila), married Baron Adam Rudolf von Lissau, wrote a family memoir, and gave birth to fourteen children at Stránov Castle.[97]

Kepler's son and daughter lugged Tycho Brahe's observational journals from place to place amidst these years of warfare, tenaciously protecting them and resisting the pressures, threats and attempted thievery of Jesuits and imperial agents. In desperate poverty as a widow, Susanna Bartsch was forced in Dresden to pawn Tycho's 24 volumes of transcribed observations, where the emperor's chancellor tracked them down and brought them to Vienna.[98] They repose in the Austrian National Library to this day. Ludwig Kepler brought the ten volumes of Tycho's original observational journals to Königsberg in a trunk and sold them in 1662 to King Frederick III of Denmark, the grandson of Tycho's patron, for 500 rixdollars.[99] They are now in the Royal Library in Copenhagen.

After leaving Prague, Christian Longomontanus returned to Denmark and taught for forty years at the University of Copenhagen. Chancellor Christian Friis was so eager to recruit

him that he initially paid his salary out of his own pocket.[100] Many seventeenth-century universities remained pedantic bastions of theology, but Friis and Christopher Valkendorf were determined to invigorate the University of Copenhagen by building research facilities and recruiting Tycho's former assistants. Tycho had mistaken this desire, accompanied as it was by Friis' drive to force him to conform to ecclesiastical discipline, for a 'Machiavellian' plan to destroy Uraniborg, while their aim was actually to save its legacy by transplanting its staff and empirical methods to the university.

  By the time Longomontanus joined the faculty in 1605, a majority of the endowed Copenhagen professors were friends and former assistants of Tycho Brahe. One of them, Cort Aslakssøn, remained Longomontanus' colleague until his

94 Stránov Castle, Czechia.

death in 1624, earnestly striving to reconcile biblical theology
with Tychonic astronomy.[101] Longomontanus, in his four decades on the faculty, saw colleagues establish a botanical garden,
a museum of natural history and an anatomical theatre, while
making important empirical discoveries in human anatomy
and refraction and training scientists like Nicolas Steno, the

95 Willem Jansz. Blaeu's 1615 quadrant for Willebrord Snell.

founder of geological stratigraphy and crystallography, and the astronomer Olaus Roemer.[102]

Willem Jansz. Blaeu had made a large quadrant in 1615, modelled on Stjerneborg's Revolving Azimuth Quadrant, and Willebrord Snell had used it when he set out to measure a degree of latitude. It reposed in Leiden when Christian Longomontanus laid out the requirements and programme for the first planned university observatory in the world in 1639.[103] King Christian IV had wanted to give a church to the University of Copenhagen, but the professors said they needed a new library and an observatory, so the king summoned his architect, Hans van Steenwinckel the Younger, and they sat down to design a structure with all three functions.[104] King Christian thought of it as a new Temple of Solomon designed by a wise and pious ruler. The church would be the 'Temple of Faith'; above the sanctuary would be the 'Temple of Wisdom', a spacious hall containing the university library, with Tycho Brahe's Great Celestial Globe standing by the entrance; and the massive brick tower would be the 'Temple of Science', with the observatory perched on top and named *Stellaeburgi regii hauniensis*, the 'Royal Stjerneborg of Copenhagen', in homage to Tycho Brahe.[105] In 1642 Christian Longomontanus became this observatory's first director at the age of eighty. Other observatories were laid out like Uraniborg with great quadrants on their meridians at Paris in 1671 and Greenwich in 1676. In Beijing in 1673, Jesuit astronomers built another reproduction of Stjerneborg on the walls of the imperial city.

Uraniborg was also emulated in scientific academies across Europe. When the French Académie Royale des Sciences sent out its first scientific expedition in 1671, its destination was

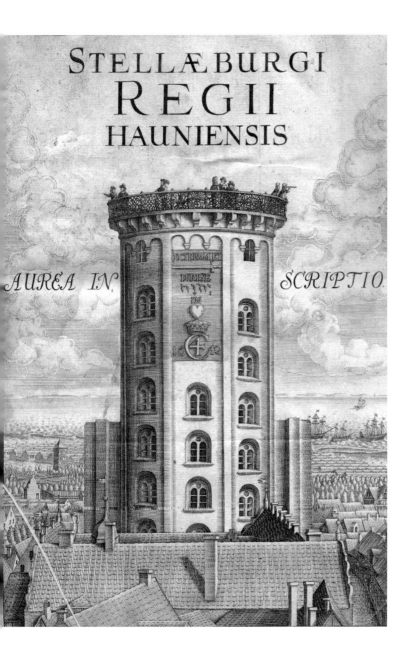

STELLÆBURGI
REGII
HAUNIENSIS

AUREA IN, SCRIPTIO

96 *Left*: Tycho's Great Brass Celestial Globe, 1598, engraving.
97 *Right*: H. A. Greyss, The Round Tower Observatory, 1646, engraving.

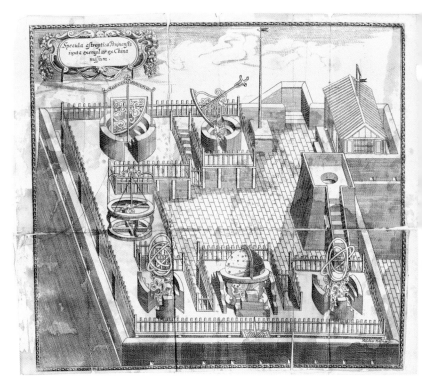

the island of Hven, and its mission was to measure the precise coordinates of Uraniborg. A young Copenhagen astronomer, Olaus Roemer (Ole Rømer), returned with the expedition to become a member of the French Académie.[106] In 1676, precisely one hundred years after the founding of Uraniborg, he became the first astronomer to measure the speed of light.

Across Europe and into far corners of the world, natural philosophy became public and collaborative in the spirit of Tycho Brahe. Professionals and amateurs alike in academies, observatories, universities and at courts took up Tycho's methods of verifiable observation and experimentation and

98 Ferdinand Verbiest, S. J., Beijing Observatory, 1687, engraving.

shaped the results of their research into nature in mathematical hypotheses and laws.

Tycho Brahe's legacy to science resounds to the present, but there was another, more personal side to his legacy, and Baroness Ulrike von Levetzow, the last great love of the German poet Johann Wolfgang von Goethe, played her part in it. She was seventeen and Goethe 72 years old when he caught a glimpse of her at Marienbad in 1821 and was so smitten by her wit, intelligence and aristocratic grace that he sent her a proposal of marriage. Her refusal inspired one of his finest poems, but she was still unmarried a half-century later, when she lived at Château Trieblitz in Bohemia. The château brimmed with the cultural treasures of many generations of aristocratic families. When she inherited it in 1868, it seemed to her that all these precious books, manuscripts and *objets de vertu* and learning were too valuable to be locked away in a private château. They were part of the cultural heritage of the nation – indeed, of the world – and should be in an institution of public trust. She chose the Society of Museums of the Kingdom of Bohemia to be that institution.

In his report to the annual meeting in Prague on 13 June 1868, the Director of the Society announced that Baroness Ulrike von Levetzow's donation had enriched the Society's library by

> 10,000 volumes of books and artistic treasures of extraordinary worth, formerly the property of His Excellency, Imperial *Hofkammerpräsident* Franz Count of Klebelsberg . . . a significant number of incunabula . . . a large number of historical and even more

geographical books and rare old and new travel books
... Numismatic literature, archaeology, and art books,
graphic and plastic arts, and especially architecture
in great richness and splendour ... rare old musical
publications and libretti ... In the manuscript depart-
ment, we emphasize the valuable treasure of *Tycho de
Brahe's* autograph book, which the famous astronomer
gave to his son at the time of his studies in Wittenberg.

The line of descent from Tycho Brahe to Ulrike von Levetzow's
stepfather was reflected in another part of the donation,
'thirty documents concerning the renowned Tengnagel von
Camp family and a Bohemian memoir by the lovable Elizabeth
Ludmila née Tengnagel von Camp, who through her marriage
to Rudolph Adam Baron von Lysau und auf Neu-Stranow
connected the house of Tycho de Brahe with the Counts von
Klebelsberg'.[107]

Thus it was that Baroness Ulrika von Levetzow made her
contribution to preserving the legacy of Tycho Brahe. Her
stepfather, Count Franz von Klebelsberg zu Thumburg, left no
issue but was by no means the last of Tycho Brahe's descendants. In his day and now, the DNA of Tycho Brahe lives in the
heritage of aristocrats scattered across Europe, from princes of
Hanover, Liechtenstein and Hohenlohe to branches of great
noble houses including Ossoliński, Thun-Hohenstein, Fugger,
Esterházy and many others. Alois Lexa von Aehrenthal, the
foreign minister who annexed Bosnia and Herzegovina to the
Austro-Hungarian Empire, was a descendant of Tycho Brahe,
and so is the Italian film director Edoardo Winspeare, as well
as more generals, jurists, ambassadors, government ministers,

men and women of distinction than one can count on both hands – but not a single astronomer.

Tycho Brahe's move to the court of the Holy Roman Emperor was driven in part by his desire to assure the future of his family and in part to assure his legacy in science. In both ways, time has proven that he was eminently successful. His life was not in vain.

REFERENCES

Preface: Denmark and the Renaissance

1 Michael Andersen, Birgitte Bøggild Johannsen and Hugo Johannsen, eds, *Reframing the Danish Renaissance: Problems and Prospects in a European Perspective* (Copenhagen, 2011). Kaufmann's essay is on pp. 33–50, Bøggild Johannsen's on pp. 11–31 and 51–70.

2 Text Carsten Bach-Nielsen et al., eds, *Danmark og renæssancen, 1500–1650* (Copenhagen, 2006), pp. 174–85.

3 Håkan Håkansson, ed., *Att låta själen flyga mellan himlens tinnar – Tycho Brahe och Renässansen* (Stockholm, 2006).

4 Adam Mosley, ibid., p. 195.

5 Poul Grinder-Hansen, ed., *Tycho Brahes Verden – Danmark i Europa, 1550–1600* (Copenhagen, 2006).

6 J. R. Christianson, 'Tycho Brahe in Scandinavian Scholarship', *History of Science*, XXXVI (1998), pp. 467–84.

7 Victor E. Thoren, *The Lord of Uraniborg: A Biography of Tycho Brahe*, with contributions by John R. Christianson (Cambridge, 1990). Peter Zeeberg, *Tycho Brahes 'Urania Titani', et digt om Sophie Brahe* (Copenhagen, 1994).

8 John Robert Christianson, *On Tycho's Island: Tycho Brahe and His Assistants, 1570–1601* (New York and Cambridge, 2000); revised and expanded Danish edition, *Tycho Brahe: Renæssancen på Hven*, trans. Jan Teuber (Copenhagen, 2008).

9 Poul Grinder-Hansen, *Frederik 2., Danmarks Renæssancekonge* (Copenhagen, 2013). Poul Grinder-Hansen, *Kronborg* (Copenhagen, 2018). Eliška Fučiková et al., eds, *Rudolf II and Prague:*

The Imperial Court and Residential City as the Cultural and Spiritual Heart of Central Europe (Prague, London and Milan, 1997).

10 I.L.E. Dreyer, ed., *Tychonis Brahe Dani Opera Omnia*, 15 vols (Copenhagen, 1913–29). Adam Mosley, Nicholas Jardine and Karin Tybjerg, 'Epistolary Culture, Editorial Practices, and the Propriety of Tycho's *Astronomical Letters*', *Journal for the History of Astronomy*, XXXIV (2003), pp. 421–51.

1 Birthright Challenged, 1546–70

1 I.L.E. Dreyer, ed., *Tychonis Brahe Dani Opera Omnia*, 15 vols (Copenhagen, 1913–29), vol. XIV, p. 3. Today, the name is written *Knudstrup* in Danish and *Knutstorp* in Swedish.

2 Albert Fabritius, 'Brahe †', in *Danmarks adels årbog* (Copenhagen, 1950), pt II, p. 15.

3 Tycho Brahe, *Instruments of the Renewed Astronomy (Astronomiæ Instauratæ Mechanica)*, trans. and ed. Alena Hadravová, Petr Hadrava and Jole R. Schackelford (Prague, 1996), p. 117.

4 Ibid.

5 Ibid. Keld Grinder-Hansen, 'Dannelse og uddannelse', in *Tycho Brahes Verden: Danmark i Europa, 1550–1600,* ed. Poul Grinder-Hansen (Copenhagen, 2006), pp. 33–45. Birte Andersen, *Adelig opfostring: Adelsbørns opdragelse i Danmark, 1536–1660* (Copenhagen, 1971), pp. 52–83.

6 Frede P. Jensen, 'Omkring Peder Oxes fald', *Historisk tidsskrift*, LXXIX/2 (1979), pp. 311–37.

7 Victor E. Thoren, with contributions by John R. Christianson, *The Lord of Uraniborg: A Biography of Tycho Brahe* (Cambridge, 1990), pp. 8–12.

8 Thomas Cortsen Wegner, *Exercitium Hominis Christiani . . . S[alig] Velbiurdig Sthen Brahe til Knudstrup Danmarckis Rigis Raad, hans liighs Sørgelig begengelse* (Copenhagen, 1621).

9 In descending order of precedence, *Rigshofmester, Kongens Kansler, Rigsmarsk, Rigsadmiral* and *Rigskansler*.

10 Knud J. V. Jespersen, 'Fra fødselsadel til rangadel: Den danske adel 1600–1800', in *Riget, magten og æren: Den danske adel, 1350–1660,* ed. Per Ingesman and Jens Villiam Jensen (Aarhus, 2001), pp. 604–9.

11 Queen Margarethe II of Denmark (born 1940) and King Harald
    V of Norway (born 1937). Charles, Prince of Wales (born 1948),
    and the exiled King Constantine II of Greece (born 1940) also
    descend in direct male lines from King Christian I.

12 Michael Roberts, *The Early Vasas: A History of Sweden, 1523–1611*
    (Cambridge, 1968), pp. 15–19. King Gustavus Vasa was Tycho's
    second cousin twice removed.

13 J. R. Christianson, 'Terrestrial and Celestial Spaces of the Danish
    Court, 1550–1650', in *The Politics of Space: European Courts ca. 1500–
    1750*, ed. Marcello Fantoni, George Gorse and Malcolm Smuts
    (Rome, 2009), pp. 91–3.

14 Paul Douglas Lockhart, *Denmark, 1513–1660: The Rise and Decline
    of a Renaissance Monarchy* (Oxford, 2007), pp. 12–28.

15 Frede P. Jensen, 'Christian III, Peder Oxe og herredagen i 1557:
    Kongelige udrensninger før et tronskifte', *Historisk tidsskrift,*
    CVIII/2 (2008), p. 344. Jespersen, 'Fra fødselsadel til rangadel',
    pp. 612, 617. Sebastian Olden-Jørgensen, 'Hofkultur, ritual og
    politik i Danmark 1536–1746', in *Ritualernes magt*, ed. Ulrik Langen
    (Roskilde, [1996] 2002), pp. 50–53.

16 Morten Fink-Jensen, *Fornuften under troens lydighed: Naturfilosofi,
    medicin og teologi i Danmark, 1536–1636* (Copenhagen, 2004), pp.
    45–95. Holger Fr. Rørdam, *Kjøbenhavns Universitets Historie*, 4 vols
    (Copenhagen, 1863–74), vol. I, pp. 44–115. Martin Schwarz
    Lausten, *Philipp Melanchthon: Humanist and Luthers reformator i Tyskland
    og Danmark* (Copenhagen, 2010), pp. 74–90, 303–12. Karl
    Hartfelder, *Philipp Melanchthon als Perceptor Germaniae* (Berlin, 1899).

17 Petrus Gassendus, *Tychonis Brahe, Equitis Dani, Astronomorum Coryphæi,
    Vita* (The Hague, 1655), pp. 4–5.

18 Tycho also bought works by Petrus Bayrus and Aemilius Macer:
    see Wilhelm Norlind, *Tycho Brahe: En levnadsteckning med nya bidrag
    belysande hans liv och verk* (Lund, 1970), pp. 339, 350 and 352.

19 *Ioannis de Sacrobusto libellus de sphæra* (Wittenberg, 1549), sig. [A5v]:
    'manifesta Dei uestigia in natura'. Sachiko Kusukawa, ed.,
    Melanchthon: Orations on Philosophy and Education, trans. Christine
    F. Salazar (Cambridge, 1999), pp. 105–12.

20 Sachiko Kusukawa, *The Transformation of Natural Philosophy: The Case
    of Philip Melanchthon* (Cambridge, 1995), pp. 27–74.

21 J. L. Heilbron, *The Sun in the Church: Cathedrals as Solar Observatories* (Cambridge, MA, and London, 1999), pp. 51–62.

22 Peter Apian, *Cosmographia Petri Apiani, per gemmam Frisium apud Louanienses Medicum & Mathematicum insignem* (Paris, 1553). Norlind, *Tycho Brahe*, p. 338.

23 Norlind, *Tycho Brahe*, p. 361.

24 John Robert Christianson, 'Tycho Brahe's Facts of Life', *Fund og forskning i det kongelige biblioteks samlinger*, XVII (1970), pp. 21–8.

25 Lockhart, *Denmark, 1513–1660*, pp. 118–19.

26 Poul Colding, *Studier i Danmarks politiske historie i slutningen af Christian III.s og begyndelsen af Frederick II.s tid* (Copenhagen, 1939), pp. 345–67, 413–56.

27 Brahe, *Instruments*, p. 118; 'mathematics' in this context means astronomy. Tycho called Vedel his *pædagogus*, Dreyer, *Tychonis Opera*, V, p. 106.

28 Claudia Roth Pierpont, 'Angels and Men: The World According to Leonardo da Vinci', *New Yorker*, 16 October 2017, p. 88.

29 Frede P. Jensen, *Danmarks konflikt med Sverige, 1563–1570* (Copenhagen, 1982), pp. 61–72.

30 Margaret Aston, 'The Fiery Trigon Conjunction: An Elizabethan Astrological Prediction', *Isis*, LXI/2 (1970), pp. 159–87, esp. p. 161, n. 9.

31 Brahe, *Instruments*, pp. 118, 119.

32 Adam Gopnik, 'Wired', *New Yorker*, 4 December 2017, p. 75.

33 Dreyer, *Tychonis Opera*, vol. X, pp. 3–4.

34 Vello Helk, *Stambogskikken i det danske monarki indtil 1800* (Odense, 2001).

35 Brahe, *Instruments*, pp. 118–19.

36 Ibid., p. 119. Bartolomæus Scultetus, *Gnomonice de solariis, sive doctrina practica terriae partis astronomiae* (Görlitz, 1572), sign. Bij–[Bijv], described a variant of this method ascribed to Peurbach and Regiomontanus.

37 Dreyer, *Tychonis Opera*, vol. X, p. 5.

38 Brahe, *Instruments*, p. 119.

39 Gianna Pomata, 'Observation Rising: Birth of an Epistemic Genre, 1500–1650', in *Histories of Scientific Observation*, ed. Lorraine Daston and Elizabeth Lunbeck (Chicago, IL, and London, 2011), pp. 46–8.

40 Katharine Park, 'Observation in the Margins, 500–1500', in Daston and Lunbeck, ed., *Histories*, p. 34.

41 Brahe, *Instruments,* pp. 119–20.

42 J.L.E. Dreyer, *Tycho Brahe: A Picture of Scientific Life and Work in the Sixteenth Century* (Edinburgh, 1890), p. 20.

43 Christianson, 'Facts of Life', p. 24.

44 Peder Hansen Resen, *Inscriptiones Haffnienses Latinoe Danicæ et Germanicæ* (Copenhagen, 1668), p. 83.

45 He did note a lunar eclipse on 7 November 1565, see Dreyer, *Tychonis Opera,* vol. X, p. 13.

46 Christianson, 'Facts of Life', pp. 24–5.

47 Dreyer, *Tychonis Opera,* vol. I, pp. 135–6, and vol. X, p. 13.

48 Leo Tandrup, *Mod triumf eller tragedie* (Aarhus, 1979), vol. I, p. 123. Leo Tandrup, 'Manderup Parsberg', in *Dansk biografisk leksikon*, ed. S. Cedergreen Bech, 16 vols (Copenhagen, 1979–84), vol. XI (1982), p. 161.

49 Thoren with Christianson, *Lord of Uraniborg*, pp. 22–3.

50 Gassendus, *Tychonis Brahe*, p. 10.

51 Frede P. Jensen, 'Peder Oxe, 1520–75', in Bech, *Dansk biografisk,* vol. II, pp. 108–9. Poul Colding, 'Danmark-Lothringen 1565–66 og Peder Oxes hjemkomst', *Historisk tidsskrift*, 10th series, VI (1942–4), pp. 637–59.

52 Dreyer, *Tychonis Opera,* vol. X, p. 14.

53 Ibid., vol. VII, p. 3.

54 Ibid., vol. XIV, p. 4.

55 Ibid., vol. XIV, p. 3, dated 14 May 1568.

56 Wegner, *Sthen Brahe,* sig. [Ciijv]–[Ciiij].

57 Brahe, *Instruments,* pp. 104–7. Thoren with Christianson, *Lord of Uraniborg*, pp. 18–19.

58 Dreyer, *Tychonis Opera,* vol. III, p. 157. Robert W. Karrow, Jr, *Mapmakers of the Sixteenth Century and Their Maps: Bio-bibliographies of the Cartographers of Abraham Ortelius, 1570* (Chicago, IL, 1993), pp. 64–7.

59 Norlind, *Tycho Brahe*, p. 24. Vello Helk, *Dansk-norske studierejser fra reformationen til enevælden, 1536–1660* (Copenhagen, 1987), pp. 160, 179, 255, 366, 379.

60 Dreyer, *Tychonis Opera,* vol. II, p. 343, and vol. VII, p. 328.

61 Adam Mosley, *Bearing the Heavens: Tycho Brahe and the Astronomical Community of the Late Sixteenth Century* (Cambridge, 2007), pp. 270–76. Bruce T. Moran, 'Princes, Machines and the Valuation of Precision in the 16th Century', *Sudhoff's Archiv,* LXI/3 (1977), p. 217. Adam Mosley, 'Objects of Knowledge: Mathematics and Models in Sixteenth-century Cosmology and Astronomy', in *Transmitting Knowledge: Words, Images, and Instruments in Early Modern Europe,* ed. Sachiko Kusukawa and Ian Maclean (Oxford, 2006), pp. 199–201. Robert S. Westman, *The Copernican Question: Prognostication, Skepticism, and Celestial Order* (Berkeley and Los Angeles, CA, and London, 2011), p. 37.

62 Günther Oestmann, 'Cyprian Leovitius, der Astronom und Astrolog Ottheinrichs', in *Pfalzgraf Ottheinrich: Politik, Kunst und Wissenschaft im 16. Jahrhundert,* ed. Barbara Zeitelhack (Regensburg, 2002), pp. 348–59.

63 C. Doris Hellman, *The Comet of 1577: Its Place in the History of Astronomy* (New York, 1944), p. 135, n. 37.

64 Krzysztof Pomian, 'Astrology as a Naturalistic Theology of History', in *'Astrologi hallucinati': Stars and the End of the World in Luther's Time,* ed. Paola Zambelli (Berlin and New York, 1986), pp. 29–43. Aston, 'The Fiery Trigon Conjunction', pp. 164–9.

65 Cyprian Leovitius, *De conivnctionibvs magnis insignioribvs svperiiorvm planetarum, Solis defectionibus, & Cometis, in quarta Monarchia, cum eorundem effectuum historica expositione* (Lauingen, 1564), sig. G–[G iiijv].

66 Ibid., sig. [N iiv]–[N iiijv].

67 Dreyer, *Tycho Brahe,* p. 30, speaking of Leovitius: 'It does not seem to have struck him, nor, indeed, any one before Tycho, that the only way to produce correct tables of the motions of the planets was by a prolonged series of observations, and not by taking an odd observation now and then.'

68 Raimund Minderer, *De calcantho sev vitriolo eivsqve qvalitate, virtvte, ac viribvs, nec non Medicinis ex eo parandis disqvisitio iatrochymicai* (Augsburg, 1617), p. 21.

69 Dreyer, *Tychonis Opera,* vol. VIII, p. 234. Hugh Trevor-Roper, 'The Paracelsian Movement', in *Renaissance Essays* (London, [1985] 1986), pp. 149–99. Cf. Jole Shackelford, *A Philosophical Path for Paracelsian Medicine: The Ideas, Intellectual Context, and Influence of Petrus Severinus*

(1540/2–1602) (Copenhagen, 2004), p. 63, and D. P. Walker, *Spiritual and Demonic Magic from Ficino to Campanella* (University Park, PA, [1958] 2000), p. 96.

70 Brahe, *Instruments*, p. 113.

71 Ibid., p. 113. Mosley, *Bearing the Heavens,* pp. 1–30, 217–43 and 16, note 36.

72 Dreyer, *Tychonis Opera*, vol. X, pp. 16–37. Brahe, *Instruments,* p. 120.

73 Dreyer, *Tychonis Opera*, vol. II, pp. 343–4.

74 Cf. Brahe, *Instruments*, p. 97, note 164. The circle is divided into 360 equal degrees, each degree into 60 arcminutes, and each minute into 60 arcseconds.

75 Brahe, *Instruments*, pp. 96–9.

76 Dreyer, *Tychonis Opera*, vol. V, p. 36. Thoren with Christianson, *Lord of Uraniborg*, p. 224 and figure 7.2.

77 Petrus Ramus, *Defensio pro Aristotele adversvs Iacobum Schecium* (Lausanne, 1571), pp. 116–17.

78 Dreyer, *Tychonis Opera,* vol. VI, pp. 88–9. Cf. Peter Barker, 'The Role of Religion in the Lutheran Response to Copernicus', in *Rethinking the Scientific Revolution*, ed. Margaret J. Osler (Cambridge, 2000), pp. 78–9.

79 Dreyer, *Tychonis Opera*, vol. X, pp. 36–7.

2 Cloister into Observatory: The New Star, 1570–73

1 I.L.E. Dreyer, ed., *Tychonis Brahe Dani Opera Omnia*, 15 vols (Copenhagen, 1913–29), vol. XIV, p. 37.

2 Rigsarkivet (Danish National Archives), Copenhagen, 'Brahe, Otte Tygesen', Archive Number 00287, P0121, Archive Series: '1555–1570, Kongelige åbne breve, kongeligt missive, pantebrev, regnskaber'.

3 Dreyer, *Tychonis Opera,* vol. XII, pp. 3–5.

4 Victor E. Thoren, *The Lord of Uraniborg: A Biography of Tycho Brahe,* with contributions by John R. Christianson (Cambridge, 1990), pp. 37–9. Alex Wittendorff, *Tyge Brahe* (Copenhagen, 1994), pp. 66–8.

5 Jens Villiam Jensen, 'Skifte af adeligt jordegods, 1400–1660', in *Riget, magten og æren: Den danske adel 1350–1660,* ed. Per Ingesman and Jens Villiam Jensen (Aarhus, 2001), pp. 451–77. Each son received

two daughter's shares of an inheritance, each daughter one share
plus a dowry and marriage settlement.

6 L. Laursen, ed., *Kancelliets Brevbøger, 1571–1575* (Copenhagen, 1898),
   pp. 36, 406 and 459; Albert Fabritius, 'Brahe †', in *Danmarks adels
   årbog* (1950), pt II, pp. 15–18.

7 Paul Douglas Lockhart, *Denmark, 1513–1660: The Rise and Decline
   of a Renaissance Monarchy* (Oxford, 2007), pp. 53, 107–11. John
   Robert Christianson, 'The Infrastructure of the Royal Hunt:
   King Frederik II of Denmark, 1559–1588', in *Le cacce reali nell'Europa
   dei principi*, ed. Andrea Merlotti (Florence, 2017), pp. 3–20.

8 C. F. Wegener, *Om Anders Sørensen Vedel, kongelig Historiograph*
   (Copenhagen, 1846), pp. 46–50.

9 Frede P. Jensen, *Bidrag til Frederick II's og Erik XIV's historie*
   (Copenhagen, 1978), pp. 13–44.

10 Laursen, ed., *Kancelliets Brevbøger, 1571–1575*, p. 142.

11 Joh. Grundtvig, 'Frederik II dens og Formynderstyrelsens Hof- og
    Regeringspersonale, 1559–1596', *Meddelelser fra Rentekammerarchivet*
    (Copenhagen, 1873–6), p. 158.

12 Holger F. Rørdam, 'Charles de Danzay, fransk Resident ved det
    danske Hof', *Historiske Samlinger og Studier vedrørende danske Forhold og
    Personligheder især i det 17. Aarhundrede*, vol. III (Copenhagen, 1898),
    pp. 319–21. Holger Fr. Rørdam, 'Et dansk Øjenvidnes Beretning
    om Bartholomæusnatten i Paris', *Ny Kirkehistoriske Samlinger*, 5
    (1871), pp. 244–53.

13 Jole Shackelford, *A Philosophical Path for Paracelsian Medicine: The
    Ideas, Intellectual Context, and Influence of Petrus Severinus (1540/2–1602)*
    (Copenhagen, 2004), pp. 100–103, 143–58.

14 Jane Hellstedt, *Slott och borgherrar i Skåne* (Stockholm, 1990), p. 83.

15 Jens Schjerup Hansen, *Bystruktur og havekultur,* ed. Lise Bek
    (Copenhagen, 2008), pp. 104–5.

16 Dreyer, *Tychonis Opera,* vol. IX, p. 173. Wittendorff, *Tyge Brahe*,
    p. 68.

17 John Robert Christianson, 'Adelsmannen, familjemedlemmen,
    läraren och vetenskapsmannen', forthcoming from Tycho Brahe
    Museum, Hven.

18 John Robert Christianson, *Cloister and Observatory: Herrevad Abbey
    and Tycho Brahe's Uraniborg*, University Microfilms (Ann Arbor, MI,

1964), pp. 92–4, 76–101. Rigsarkivet (Danish National
Archives), Copenhagen, Regnskaber 1559–1660, Lensregnskaber,
Helsingborg, B. Jordebøger Skåne 1612–1615, 'Jordbogen
till Herridswad Closter, fraa Philipi Jacobs Dag 1613 Och
till Aarsdagen 1614', fol. 122–33, starting with image 249
at https://www.sa.dk, accessed 30 April 2019.

19 Holger Fr. Rørdam, *Danske Kirkelove*, 3 vols (Copenhagen,
1883–9), vol. I, pp. 122–6, 133, 150–60. Kr. Erslev, *Danmarks
Len og Lensmænd i det sextende Aarhundrede* (Copenhagen, 1879),
p. 146.

20 Christianson, *Cloister and Observatory*, pp. 72–3.

21 Ibid., pp. 40–45.

22 Ibid., p. 63.

23 Iver Iversen Hemmet, *Predicken udi Knud Brahe til Engelstholm,
Liigs nedsættelse udi Weile Kircke d. 18. Febr. 1615* (Copenhagen, 1615),
p. 35.

24 Niels Michelsøn, *En Predicken som skede wdi Erlig og Velbyrdig Mands,
Salige Sten Bildis Begraffuelse i Helsingborrig* (Copenhagen, 1587);
W. Mollerup and Fr. Meidell, *Bille-Ættens Historie*, 2 vols
(Copenhagen, 1887–93), vol. I, p. 764.

25 Henry Bruun, 'Jens Bille' and 'Steen Bille', in *Dansk biografisk leksikon*,
ed. S. Cedergreen Bech, 16 vols (Copenhagen, 1979–84), vol. II,
pp. 108, 113–14.

26 E. Kroman, 'Jens Billes visebog', *Danske Studier* (1923), pp. 170–79.
Hanne Ruus, 'Dansk Folkevisekultur 1550–1700', in *Svøbt i mår:
Dansk Folkevisekultur, 1500–1700*, ed. Flemming Lundgreen-Nielsen
and Hanne Ruus, 4 vols (Copenhagen, 1999–2002), vol. I,
pp. 11–20.

27 Christianson, *Cloister and Observatory*, pp. 96–101.

28 Ove K. Nordstrand, *Danmarks ældste papirmøller og deres vandmærker*
(Copenhagen, 1961), p. [5]; Dreyer, *Tychonis Opera*, vol. I, p. 65;
L. Laursen, *Kancelliets Brevbøger, 1576–79* (Copenhagen, 1900),
p. 6.

29 C. Nyrop, 'Dansk Jern', *Historisk tidsskrift*, 6 (1877–8), pp. 128–33;
C. F. Bricka, ed., *Kancelliets Brevbøger, 1556–60* (Copenhagen, 1888),
pp. 177–8, 315–16, 439–40; L. Laursen, ed., *Kancelliets Brevbøger,
1561–65* (Copenhagen, 1895), pp. 38, 60, 90, 408; L. Laursen, ed.,

Kancelliets Brevbøger, 1566–70 (Copenhagen, 1896), pp. 150, 547–8;
L. Laursen, ed., *Kancelliets Brevbøger, 1576–79* (Copenhagen, 1900),
pp. 318–19, 671.

30 Hiro Hirai, '*Logoi Spermatikoi* and the Concept of Seeds in the
Mineralogy and Cosmogony of Paracelsus', *Histoire des sciences*, LXI
(2008), pp. viii–xvi.

31 Svante Forenius, Annika Willim and Lena Grandin, *Blästbruk
under 1500–1600-tal i Östra Spång. Analysrapport nummer 16-2005*,
Riksantikvarieämbetet, Swedish National Heritage Board,
at http://samla.raa.se, accessed 18 June 2015, see especially
pp. 57–8.

32 Lars T. Schultze, 'Kort berättelse, om myr-ugnar eller såkallade
bläster-wärk, uti Östra och Wästra Dahle-orterne brukelige:
Relation, indgifven til Kongl. Bergskollegium, 1732', *Jernkontorets
Annaler*, XXIX/1 (1845), pp. 1–32 and pls. 1–3.

33 Dreyer, *Tychonis Opera*, vol. II, p. 307.

34 Laursen, ed., *Kancelliets Brevbøger, 1571–1575*, pp. 98–9.

35 Ibid., p. 121. Carl F. Hermelin and Elsebeth Welander-Berggren,
Glasboken: historia, teknik och form: handbok (Stockholm, 1980).

36 Dreyer, *Tychonis Opera*, vol. VII, pp. 7–10; Christianson, *On Tycho's
Island*, p. 323.

37 Dreyer, *Tychonis Opera*, vol. V, pp. 80–83; Tycho Brahe, *Instruments
of the Renewed Astronomy (Astronomiæ Instauratæ Mechanica)*, trans.
and ed. Alena Hadravová, Petr Hadrava and Jole R. Schackelford
(Prague, 1996), pp. 87–90.

38 Brahe, *Instruments*, p. 89; Dreyer, *Tychonis Opera*, vol. V, p. 82, and
vol. II, pp. 330–36; J.L.E. Dreyer, *Tycho Brahe: A Picture of Scientific Life
and Work in the Sixteenth Century* (Edinburgh, 1890), p. 40.

39 Dreyer, *Tychonis Opera*, vol. I, p. 16, cf. vol. II, p. 308.

40 Tycho's observations of the new star are his only observations that
have not survived: see Thoren with Christianson, *Lord of Uraniborg*,
p. 55.

41 Dreyer, *Tychonis Opera*, vol. I, p. 21, cf. vol. II, p. 336 for revised
figures.

42 Dreyer, *Tychonis Opera*, vol. V, pp. 80–87. Brahe, *Instruments*,
pp. 87–95.

43 Rørdam, 'Danzay', p. 294.

44 Dreyer, *Tychonis Opera*, vol. III, pp. 93–4.

45 Peter Zeeberg, *Heinrich Rantzau: A Bibliography* (Copenhagen, 2004), pp. 13–16.

46 Dreyer, *Tycho Brahe*, pp. 57–69.

47 Michael Dupont and Jens Vellev, 'Tycho Brahes salg af hovedgården Knutstorp i Skåne 1594–98: Fra skøde og dombrev til låsebrev', *Danske Magazin*, 51 (2010), pp. 3–32.

48 Wegner, *Sthen Brahe*, sig. [Ciiijv]; Pernille Arenfeldt, 'Frederick II's hof: Husholdning og centraladministration', in *Svøbt i mår: Danske folkevisekultur 1550–1700*, ed. Flemming Lundgreen-Nielsen and Hanne Ruus, 4 vols (Copenhagen, 1999–2002), vol. I, pp. 358–9, 364.

49 Lauritz Nielsen, *Boghistoriske studier til dansk bibliografi, 1550–1600* (Copenhagen, 1923), pp. 11–17, 63–71, 149–54.

50 Robert S. Westman, *The Copernican Question: Prognostication, Skepticism, and Celestial Order* (Berkeley and Los Angeles, CA, and London, 2011), pp. 84–7, summarizes Pico's attack on astrology.

51 Dreyer, *Tycho Brahe*, pp. 53–5, summarized the section on the lunar eclipse.

52 Dreyer, *Tychonis Opera*, vol. I, pp. 65–70. Peter Zeeberg, 'Tycho Brahes Uraniaelegi: Nyoversættelse, tekst og kommentar', *Renæssanceforum: Tidsskrift for renæssanceforskning*, 3 (2007), www.renaessanceforum.dk.

53 Sachiko Kusukawa, *The Transformation of Natural Philosophy: The Case of Philip Melanchthon* (Cambridge, 1995), pp. 27–74, 110–14, 160–67, 201–2.

3 Finding a New Life, 1573–6

1 I.L.E. Dreyer, ed., *Tychonis Brahe Dani Opera Omnia*, 15 vols (Copenhagen, 1913–29), vol. V, pp. 12–15; Tycho Brahe, *Instruments of the Renewed Astronomy (Astronomiæ Instauratæ Mechanica)*, trans. and ed. Alena Hadravová, Petr Hadrava and Jole R. Schackelford (Prague, 1996), pp. 11–15.

2 Dreyer, *Tychonis Opera*, vol. V, p. 30, and VII, pp. 10–12; Brahe, *Instruments*, p. 33; John Robert Christianson, *On Tycho's Island: Tycho Brahe and His Assistants, 1570–1601* (Cambridge, 2000), p. 265.

3 Stéphane Toussaint, 'Ficino, Archimedes and the Celestial Arts', in *Marsilio Ficino: His Theology, His Philosophy, His Legacy*, ed. Michael J. B. Allen and Valery Rees (Leiden, 2001), pp. 307–26.

4 Dreyer, *Tychonis Opera*, vol. X, pp. 38–9.

5 Ibid., pp. 40–41.

6 Hugues Daussy, 'Un diplomat protestant au service d'un roi catholique: Charles de Danzay, ambassadeur de France au Danemark (1515–1589)', in *Élites et notables de l'Ouest, XVIe–XXe siècle: Entre conservatisme et modernité*, ed. Frédérique Pitou (Rennes, 2004), pp. 277–94.

7 Jens Glebe-Møller, 'Niels Hemmingsen', in *Dansk biografisk leksikon*, ed. S. Cedergreen Bech, 16 vols (Copenhagen, 1979–84), vol. VI, pp. 247–9. Holger Fr. Rørdam, *Kjøbenhavns Universitets Historie*, 4 vols (Copenhagen, 1863–74), vol. II, p. 384.

8 Phillip Melanchthon, 'Preface to *On the Sphere* (1531)', in *Melanchthon: Orations on Philosophy and Education*, ed. Sachiko Kusukawa, trans. Christine F. Salazar (Cambridge, 1999), pp. 92–3.

9 'Tycho Brahe's 1574 oration', trans. Jeremiah Reedy (manuscript, 1966).

10 Niels Hemmingsen, *Historia Domini Ihesv Christi dei et hominis, Regis cœli et terræ . . . ex principio Euangelij Iohannis* (Copenhagen, 1562), pp. 97–112; Torben Brink, 'Niels Hemmingsens forståelse af troldom – en nyvurdering', *Fortid og nutid* (1993), pt 2, pp. 119–33.

11 Trans. Reedy (1966).

12 Dreyer, *Tychonis Opera*, vol. I, pp. 171–2, and vol. VII, p. 41.

13 Alex Wittendorff, 'Niels Hemmingsen, Tyge Brahe og virkeligheden', in *Niels Hemmingsen, Om Naturens Lov 1562, 3. del*, trans. and ed. Richard Mott (Virum, 1993), pp. i–xiv.

14 Dreyer, *Tychonis Opera*, vol. I, p. 172.

15 Kristian Peder Moesgaard, 'Copernican Influence on Tycho Brahe', in *The Reception of Copernicus' Heliocentric Theory*, ed. Jerzy Dobrzycki (Dordrecht and Boston, MA, 1972), p. 32.

16 John Robert Christianson, 'Tycho Brahe's Facts of Life', *Fund og forskning i det kongelige biblioteks samlinger,* 17 (1970), pp. 24–5.

17 Peter Zeeberg, 'Peder Flemløses lærde hyrder', in *Danmark og renæssancen, 1500–1650*, ed. Carsten Bach-Nielsen et al. (Copenhagen, 2006), pp. 206–15.

18 Joh. Grundtvig, 'Frederick II dens og Formynderstyrelsens
    Hof- og Regeringspensonale 1558–96', *Meddelelser fra
    Rentekammerarkivet* (Copenhagen, 1876), pp. 158–60.

19 Brahe, *Instruments*, p. 83, mentions taking the sextant.

20 Karsten Gaulke, 'Scrutinising a Legend: A New Look at the
    Mathematical Instruments and Clocks of William IV of Hesse-
    Kassel and the "Wissenschaftskammer"', in *Who Needs Scientific
    Instruments? Conference on Scientific Instruments and Their Users*, ed. Bart
    Grob and Hans Hooijmaijers (Leiden, 2005), p. 38.

21 Karsten Gaulke, '"The First European Observatory of the
    Sixteenth Century, as Founded by Landgrave Wilhelm IV
    of Hesse-Kassel": A Serious Historiographic Category or a
    Misleading Marketing Device?', in *European Collections of Scientific
    Instruments, 1550–1750,* ed. Giorgio Strano, Stephen Johnston, Mara
    Miniati and Alison Morrison-Low (Leiden, 2009), pp. 87–8.

22 Bruce T. Moran, 'Princes, Machines and the Valuation of Precision
    in the 16th Century', *Sudhoffs Archiv,* LXI/3 (1977), pp. 209–28.

23 Dreyer, *Tychonis Opera,* vol. III, p. 131.

24 'S 2. Le petit globe de Baldewein réalisé pour le landgrave
    Guillaume IV de Hesse-Cassel en 1574', *Sphères, l'art des mécaniques
    célestes,* Galerie Kugel, Paris, www.galeriekugel.com/expo_
    spheres/c/s3_en.htm, accessed 1 May 2019.

25 Manfred H. Grieb, ed., *Nürnberger Künstlerlexikon,* vol. I (Munich,
    2007), p. 875.

26 Paul Adolf Kirchvogel, 'Tycho Brahe als astronomischer Freund
    des Landgrafen William IV. von Hessen-Kassel', *Sudhoffs Archiv,* 61,
    pt 2 (1977), p. 166. 'Dukes of Brabant and Landgraves of Hesse 7',
    http://genealogy.euweb.cz/brabant/brabant7.html, accessed 1 May
    2019.

27 Dreyer, *Tychonis Opera,* vol. I, p. 234. Peter Zeeberg, 'Tycho Brahe's
    Uraniborg, Research Centre and Aristocratic Residence', in *On
    Renaissance Academies,* ed. Marianne Pade (Rome, 2011), p. 157.

28 Norlind, *Tycho Brahe,* pp. 67–8 and 177; Alessandro Minelli, ed.,
    The Botanical Garden of Padua, 1545–1995 (Venice, 1995), pp. 59–62;
    British Library, 'Database of Italian Academies', www.bl.uk, 19
    September 2018.

29 Brahe, *Instruments*, p. 113; Dreyer, *Tychonis Opera,* vol. VII, p. 20.

30 Dreyer, *Tychonis Opera*, vol. VII, p. 38. Hanne Honnens de
    Lichtenberg, *Johan Gregor van der Schardt: Bildhauer bei Kaiser Maximilian
    II., am dänischen Hof und bei Tycho Brahe,* trans. from Danish by Georg
    Albrecht Mai (Copenhagen, 1991), pp. 15–20; Robert S. Westman,
    The Copernican Question: Prognostication, Skepticism, and Celestial Order
    (Berkeley and Los Angeles, CA, and London, 2011), pp. 236–42.

31 Hagecius may have gotten it from Paul Wittich: see Jerzy
    Dobrzycki and Lech Szczucki, 'On the Transmission of
    Copernicus' *Commentariolus* in the Sixteenth Century', *Journal for the
    History of Astronomy*, XX (1989), pp. 25–8.

32 Victor E. Thoren with contributions by John R. Christianson,
    The Lord of Uraniborg: A Biography of Tycho Brahe (Cambridge, 1990),
    pp. 99–100.

33 John Robert Christianson, 'Crypto-Calvinism and Lutheran
    Concord at the Court of Denmark, 1559–1596', in *La Corte en
    Europa: Política y Religión (Siglos XVI–XVIII)*, ed. José Martínez Millán,
    Manuel Rivero Rodríguez and Gijs Versteegen, 3 vols (Madrid,
    2012), vol. II, pp. 831–2; J. R. Christianson, 'Tycho Brahe's
    German Treatise on the Comet of 1577: A Study in Science and
    Politics', *Isis*, LXX (1970), pp. 114–15.

34 Rørdam, *Kjøbenhavns Universitets*, vol. II, pp. 135–6.

35 H. F. Rørdam, 'Bidrag til de filippistiske Bevægelser og til D. Niels
    Hemmingsens Historie', *Kirkehistoriske Samlinger,* 6 (Copenhagen,
    1867–8), pp. 299–300.

36 Dreyer, *Tychonis Opera*, vol. VII, p. 25.

37 Ibid., pp. 25–6.

38 Thoren with Christianson, *Lord of Uraniborg*, p. 152; Victor Thoren,
    'New Light on Tycho's Instruments', *Journal for the History of
    Astronomy*, IV (1973), pp. 27–9.

39 Brahe, *Instruments*, pp. 16–20.

40 Dreyer, *Tychonis Opera,* vol. VII, pp. 26–7.

41 Ibid., vol. VI, p. 11.

42 Ibid., vol. VII, pp. 30–31.

43 Ibid., vol. XIV, pp. 4–5.

44 Ibid., pp. 5–6.

45 L. Laursen, *Kancelliets Brevbøger, 1576–79* (Copenhagen, 1900),
    pp. 58–9.

4 Treasures of the Sea King: Kronborg and Uraniborg, 1576–82

1 Andrea Palladio, *The Architecture of A. Palladio in Four Books*, ed. Giacomo Leoni (London, 1715), Book Two, pp. 17–18; James S. Akerman, *The Villa: Form and Ideology of Country Houses* (Princeton, NJ, 1985), pp. 35–42, 62–109.

2 Gadi Algazi, 'Scholars in Households: Refiguring the Learned Habitus, 1480–1660', *Science in Context*, XVI (2003), pp. 9–42; Alistair Kwan, 'Tycho's Talisman: Astrological Magic in the Design of Uraniborg', *Early Science and Medicine*, XVI (2011), pp. 95–119.

3 Peter Zeeberg, 'Tycho Brahe's Uraniborg, Research Centre and Aristocratic Residence', in *On Renaissance Academies*, ed. Marianne Pade (Rome, 2011), p. 158; Peter Zeeberg, 'Den latinske Tycho', in *Tycho Brahes Verden: Danmark i Europa, 1550–1600,* ed. Poul Grinder-Hansen (Copenhagen, 2006), p. 92.

4 Vitruvius, *The Ten Books of Architecture,* trans. Morris Hicky Morgan (Cambridge, MA, 1914), pp. 72–3; Kwan, 'Tycho's Talisman', pp. 101–2.

5 Hugo Johannsen, 'Arkitektur på papir – og Tychos huse', in *Tycho Brahes Verden: Danmark i Europa, 1550–1600,* ed. Poul Grinder-Hansen (Copenhagen, 2006), pp. 95–108; Carl Henrik Jern, *Uraniborg: Herresäte och himlaborg* (Lund, 1976), pp. 70–75; Francis Beckett, *Uraniborg og Stjærneborg* (Copenhagen and London, 1921), pp. 2–5.

6 Tito M. Tonietti, *And Yet It Is Heard: Musical, Multilingual and Multicultural History of the Mathematical Sciences*, vol. I (Basel, 2014), p. 10.

7 Birgitte Bøggild Johannsen and Hugo Johannsen, 'Adelsvælde og renæssance', in *Herregården: Menneske, samfund, landskab, bygninger*, ed. John Erichsen and Mikkel Venborg Pedersen, 4 vols (Copenhagen, 2004–6), vol. II, p. 91; Cf. Rudolf Wittkower, *Architectural Principles in the Age of Humanism* [1949] (London, 1952), p. 62.

8 I.L.E. Dreyer, ed., *Tychonis Brahe Dani Opera Omnia*, 15 vols (Copenhagen, 1913–29), vol. XIV, pp. 5–6; John Robert Christianson, *On Tycho's Island: Tycho Brahe and His Assistants, 1570–1601* (Cambridge, 2000), pp. 28–33.

9 Jern, *Uraniborg*, pp. 20, 40–42.

10 Hanne Honnens de Lichtenberg, 'Hans Floris', *Kunstindeks Danmark and Weilbachs Kunstnerleksikon* (1994), www.kulturarv.dk, accessed 25 February 2016.

11 Tycho Brahe, *Instruments of the Renewed Astronomy (Astronomiæ Instauratæ Mechanica)*, trans. and ed. Alena Hadravová, Petr Hadrava and Jole R. Schackelford (Prague, 1996), pp. 147–8; Dreyer, *Tychonis Opera*, vol. V, p. 143; Peder Hansen Resen, *Inscriptiones Haffnienses Latinæ Danicæ et Germanicæ* (Copenhagen, 1668), pp. 103, 107–8.

12 Dreyer, *Tychonis Opera*, vol. IX, pp. 174–7.

13 Ibid., vol. X, p. 42.

14 Kristian Peder Moesgaard, 'Astronomi', in *Københavns universitet, 1479–1979*, vol. XII, ed. Mogens Pihl (Copenhagen, 1983), pp. 259–61.

15 Dreyer, *Tychonis Opera*, vol. IV, pp. 368–77 and vol. V, pp. 153–4; Brahe, *Instruments*, pp. 161–3; Bernard R. Goldstein, 'Levi ben Gerson: On Instrumental Errors and the Transversal Scale', *Journal for the History of Astronomy*, VIII (1977), pp. 102–12.

16 Victor E. Thoren, *The Lord of Uraniborg: A Biography of Tycho Brahe*, with contributions by John R. Christianson (Cambridge, 1990), p. 123.

17 Dreyer, *Tychonis Opera*, vol. XV, p. 3.

18 Ibid., vol. I, pp. 179–208; Tycho Brahe, 'Horoscopus Regis Christiani IV', MS. GKS 1821 kvart, The Royal Library, Copenhagen; Laursen, *Kancelliets Brevbøger, 1576–79*, pp. 167–8, 183–4.

19 Dreyer, *Tychonis Opera*, vol. VII, pp. 45–6; Holger Fr. Rørdam, *Kjøbenhavns Universitets Historie*, 4 vols (Copenhagen, 1863–74), vol. II, pp. 174–5, 369–72; J. R. Christianson, 'Crypto-Calvinism and Lutheran Concord at the Court of Denmark, 1559–1596', in *La Corte en Europa: Política y Religión (Siglos XVI–XVIII)*, ed. José Martinez Millán, Manuel Rivero Rodriguez and Gijs Versteegen, 3 vols (Madrid, 2012), vol. II, pp. 815–40.

20 Dreyer, *Tychonis Opera*, vol. XIV, pp. 6–7; V. A. Secher, 'Det danske fyrvæsens historie 1560–1660', *Samlinger til jydsk historie og topografi*, 3rd series, 2 (1900), pp. 329–400.

21 F. R. Friis, *Samlinger til Dansk Bygnings- og Kunsthistorie* (Copenhagen, 1878), p. 314.

22 Christianson, *On Tycho's Island*, pp. 177–80, 336–7.

23 Dreyer, *Tychonis Opera*, vol. IV, p. 5.

24 Ibid., p. 33; Tycho Brahe, 'Observationes septem Cometarum ab anno 1577 ad 1596 Uraniburgi', MS. GKS 1826 kvart, The Royal Library, Copenhagen.

25 Dreyer, *Tychonis Opera*, vol. VII, p. 47, although Tycho must have written from Hven, not Copenhagen, cf. *Nye Samlinger til Dansk Historie*, III (1794), p. 131.

26 Jørgen Christoffersen Dybvad, *En nyttig Vnderuissning, om den COMET, som dette Aar 1577, in Nouembrj, først haffuer ladet sig see* (Copenhagen, 1578), sign. D. Rørdam, *Kjøbenhavns Universitets Historie*, vol. II, pp. 182–3, 563–7.

27 Dreyer, *Tychonis Opera*, vol. IV, p. 235 and vol. XIII, pp. 288–304; Brahe, *Instruments*, p. 19; Thoren with Christianson, *Lord of Uraniborg*, pp. 123–33.

28 Dreyer, *Tychonis Opera*, vol. XIII, p. 303; Miguel A. Granada, Adam Mosley and Nicholas Jardine, *Christoph Rothmann's Discourse on the Comet of 1585* (Leiden and Boston, MA, 2014), pp. 326–39.

29 Dreyer, *Tychonis Opera*, vol. IV, pp. 381–96; J. R. Christianson, 'Tycho Brahe's German Treatise on the Comet of 1577: A Study in Science and Politics', *Isis*, LXX/1 (1979), pp. 120–40.

30 Christianson, 'German Treatise', p. 133; Dreyer, *Tychonis Opera*, vol. IV, pp. 382–3.

31 Dreyer, *Tychonis Opera*, vol. IV, p. 387.

32 Ibid., p. 387.

33 Ibid., pp. 383–4.

34 Jasper Hopkins, *Nicholas of Cusa on Learned Ignorance: A Translation and an Appraisal of De Docta Ignorantia* [1981] (Minneapolis, MN, 1990); James A. Weisheipl, O. P., 'The Nature, Scope, and Classification of the Sciences', in *Science in the Middle Ages*, ed. David C. Lindberg (Chicago, IL, 1978), pp. 461–82.

35 Dreyer, *Tychonis Opera*, vol. IV, p. 386.

36 Christianson, 'German Treatise', pp. 128–9; Dreyer, *Tychonis Opera*, vol. IV, p. 388.

37 Dreyer, *Tychonis Opera*, vol. IV, p. 393. Part of this prognostication was inadvertently omitted in Christianson, 'German Treatise', pp. 138–9.

38 Dreyer, *Tychonis Opera*, vol. IV, pp. 394–5; Håkan Håkansson,
'Tycho the Apocalyptic: History, Prophecy and the Meaning
of Natural Phenomena', in *Science in Contact at the Beginning of the
Scientific Revolution*, ed. Jitka Zamrzlová (Prague, 2004),
pp. 211–36; Håkan Håkansson, 'Profeten Tycho Brahe: Astrologi
och apokalyps i 1500-talets naturvetenskap', *[Svensk] Historisk
tidskrift*, CXXV/4 (2005), pp. 683–709.

39 Hugues Daussy, 'Duplessis-Mornay, Languet et Danzay en guerre
contre les théologiens', *Siècles*, XVIII (2003), pp. 93–103.

40 Dreyer, *Tychonis Opera*, vol. XIV, pp. 6–9; Siegward Petersen and
Otto Gregers Lundh, *Norske Rigs-Registranter, Andet Bind 1572–1588*
(Oslo, 1863), pp. 371, 278–9; Jacob Aaland, 'Nordfjords lensherrer
og fogder', *Skrifter udgivne af Bergens Historiske Forening*, IV (1898),
p. 12.

41 On 22 May 1578, see A. Heise, 'Bidrag til Familien Rosenkrantz's
Historie i det 16. Aarhundredes sidste Halvdel', *Historisk Tidsskrift*,
5th series, VI (1886–7), pp. 621–2.

42 'Väsby kyrka', sv.wikipedia.org/wiki/Väsby_kyrka, accessed
28 November 2017.

43 [Niels Kaas, ed.] *Den rette Judske Lowbog* (Copenhagen, 1590),
Book One, Chapter XXVII; J. Nellemann, 'Retshistoriske
Bemærkninger om kirkelig Vielse som Betingelse for lovligt
Ægteskab i Danmark', *Historisk Tidsskrift*, 5th series, I (1879),
pp. 370–76, 422–8.

44 J.L.A. Kolderup-Rosenvinge, ed., 'Kong Frederik den Andens
Gaardsret', *Samling af gamle danske Love, Femte Deel* (Copenhagen,
1827), pp. 37–46.

45 Dreyer, *Tychonis Opera*, vol. VII, pp. 48–53.

46 Ibid., vol. X, pp. 72–3, 79, 90–91.

47 Ibid., vol. X, pp. 67–72

48 Jern, *Uraniborg*, p. 94, noted that 'rolling planning' was common,
whereby a master builder worked out solutions to construction
problems as they emerged.

49 Dreyer, *Tychonis Opera*, vol. VII, p. 347, see also vol. V, p. 31; Jern,
Uraniborg, pp. 93–6; Christianson, *On Tycho's Island*, pp. 362–3.

50 Dreyer, *Tychonis Opera*, vol. V, pp. 19 and 151; vol. VII, p. 273; Brahe,
Instruments, pp. 20, 157–8.

51 Ernst Zinner, *Regiomontanus*, trans. E. Brown [1968] (Amsterdam, 1990), pp. 26–7, 99.

52 Moesgaard, 'Astronomi,' pp. 262–3.

53 Frances A. Yates, *Giordano Bruno and the Hermetic Tradition* [1964] (New York, 1969), p. 4.

54 For example, Dreyer, *Tychonis Opera*, vol. X, pp. 55–6.

55 Ibid., pp. 55–8.

56 Ibid., vol. I, pp. 209–50, omits the German version.

57 Ibid., vol. VII, pp. 56–7; A. Thiset, 'Christen Holcks Stambog', *Personalhistorisk Tidsskrift*, 5th series, II (1905), pp. 13–16; Vello Helk, *Dansk-norske studierejser fra reformationen til enevælden, 1536–1660* (Odense, 1987), p. 178.

58 Laursen, *Kancelliets Brevbøger, 1580–83*, p. 123; Dreyer, *Tychonis Opera*, vol. XIV, pp. 9–15; Petersen and Lundh, *Registranter, 1572–1588*, pp. 340, 343, 391–2.

59 Rørdam, *Kjøbenhavns Universitets Historie*, vol. II, pp. 165–8.

60 Paul Douglas Lockhart, *Frederik II and the Protestant Cause: Denmark's Role in the Wars of Religion, 1559–1596* (Leiden and Boston, MA, 2004), pp. 171–2.

61 Dreyer, *Tychonis Opera*, vol. XIV, pp. 16–17, 19; Christianson, *On Tycho's Island*, pp. 92–3; Zeeberg, 'Tycho Brahe's Uraniborg', p. 158.

62 Hugo Johannsen, 'Stonemasons in Denmark from the Reigns of Frederik II (1559–1588) and Christian IV (1588–1648)', *Masters, Meanings and Models: Studies in the Art and Architecture of the Renaissance in Denmark* (Copenhagen, 2010), pp. 168–71; Chr. Axel Jensen, *Danske adelige Gravsten fra Sengotikens og Renaissancens Tid*, 2 vols and 114 tables (Copenhagen, 1953), vol. II, pp. 13–32; Cf. Hanne Honnens de Lichtenberg, *Tro, håb and forfængelighed: Kunstneriske udtryksformer i 1500-tallets Danmark* (Copenhagen, 1989), pp. 106–13.

63 Dreyer, *Tychonis Opera*, vol. X, pp. 80–83.

64 Peder Hansøn Resen, *Kong Frederichs den Andens Krønicke* (Copenhagen, 1680), pp. 321–4.

65 Holger Fr. Rørdam, *Danske Kirkelove*, 3 vols (Copenhagen, 1883–9), vol. II (Copenhagen, 1886), pp. 310–12.

66 Christianson, 'Crypto-Calvinism and Lutheran Concord', pp. 820–36.

67 Rørdam, *Danske Kirkelove*, vol. II, pp. 322–3.
68 Thoren with Christianson, *Lord of Uraniborg*, p. 248;
    Owen Gingerich and Robert S. Westman, *The Wittich
    Connection: Conflict and Priority in Late Sixteenth-century Cosmology*
    (Philadelphia, PA, 1988), pp. 8–17; Robert Goulding,
    'Henry Savile and the Tychonic World-system',
    Journal of the Warburg and Courtauld Institutes, LVIII (1995),
    pp. 152–79.
69 Heinz Scheible, *Aufsätze zu Melanchthon* (Tübingen, 2010),
    pp. 360–61; Edward Rosen, *Three Copernican Treatises*,
    2nd edition [1939] (New York, 1959), pp. 1–90.
70 Gingerich and Westman, *Wittich Connection*, pp. 2, 5–8, 27–31.
71 Thoren with Christianson, *Lord of Uraniborg*, pp. 238–47.
72 Ibid., pp. 236–7; Gingerich and Westman, *Wittich Connection*,
    pp. 42–50, 77–140; Westman, *Copernican Question*, pp. 248–50,
    281–6.
73 Goulding, 'Henry Savile', pp. 157–9.
74 Dreyer, *Tychonis Opera*, vol. XIII, pp. 305–6.
75 Thoren with Christianson, *Lord of Uraniborg*, p. 236.
76 Dreyer, *Tychonis Opera*, vol. XIII, p. 309.
77 Ibid., pp. 313–17.
78 Victor E. Thoren, 'Prosthaphaeresis Revisited', *Historia Mathematica*,
    XV (1988), pp. 32–9; Anton Edler von Braunmühl, *Vorlesungen
    über Geschichte der Trigonometrie*, vol. I (Leipzig, 1900), pp. 193–
    203; Klaus Kuehn and Jerry McCarthy, 'Prosthaphaeresis and
    Johannes Werner' (Nuremberg, 2009), www.oughtred.org,
    accessed 20 May 2016.
79 Thoren with Christianson, *Lord of Uraniborg*, pp. 237–8; J.L.E.
    Dreyer, 'Tycho Brahe's Manual of Trigonometry', *The Observatory*,
    39 (1916), pp. 127–31.
80 Wilhelm Norlind, *Tycho Brahe: En levnadsteckning med nya bidrag
    belysande hans liv och verk* (Lund, 1970), pp. 337–8 (20 florins
    at 3.5 gof gold each); Christianson, *On Tycho's Island*, pp. 25
    and 45; Marcel Mauss, *The Gift*, trans. Ian Cunnison [1925]
    (London, 1966).
81 Dreyer, *Tychonis Opera*, vol. VII, pp. 58–60.
82 Goulding, 'Henry Savile', p. 175.

83 Ibid., pp. 175–7.

84 Dreyer, *Tychonis Opera*, vol. X, p. 88 and vol. V, pp. 102–5; Brahe, *Instruments*, pp. 112–16; Thoren with Christianson, *Lord of Uraniborg*, p. 160.

85 Brahe, *Instruments*, pp. 21, 73.

86 Ibid., pp. 163–5.

87 Thoren with Christianson, *Lord of Uraniborg*, pp. 162–3; Dreyer, *Tychonis Opera*, vol. V, pp. 36–9, 92–3 and vol. X, pp. 85–9, 92; Brahe, *Instruments*, pp. 40–43, 100–102.

88 Dreyer, *Tychonis Opera*, vol. XIV, pp. 17–19; Christianson, *On Tycho's Island*, pp. 40–43.

89 Dreyer, *Tychonis Opera*, vol. XIV, pp. 19–22; Petersen and Lundh, *Registranter 1572–1588*, p. 400.

90 *Danmarks Adels Aarbog* (1900), p. 432.

91 Bue Kaae, *Familielivet på 'Liljebjerget' i Ribe omkring 1600* (Esbjerg, 1983), p. 10.

92 Dreyer, *Tychonis Opera*, vol. X, pp. 124–9, 'pinnacidia Sextantis', 'Sextantem nouum non admittentem parallaxim', 'nouum Sextantem Biformem', and by 22 January 1582, p. 130, 'Sext. Trig,' (Sextans Trigonicus); Cf. Thoren with Christianson, *Lord of Uraniborg*, pp. 165–8.

93 Dreyer, *Tychonis Opera*, vol. V, pp. 24–7 and vol. X, p. 130; Brahe, *Instruments*, pp. 26–9;

94 Tycho also received an astrolabe and 'astronomical rings' (a simplified armillary sphere) by Joachim Sterck van Ringelbergh; Dreyer, *Tychonis Opera*, vol. VII, pp. 15–20.

95 Dreyer, *Tychonis Opera*, vol. V, pp. 53, 57 and vol. VII, p. 45; Brahe, *Instruments*, pp. 57–61.

96 Dreyer, *Tychonis Opera*, vol. V, pp. 52–5 and vol. X, pp. 100–102, 104, 125–6, 138–9; Brahe, *Instruments*, pp. 57–61.

97 Dreyer, *Tychonis Opera*, vol. X, pp. 92–129 and vol. XIII, p. 334, '*magister* Johannes'.

98 Christianson, *On Tycho's Island*, pp. 351–3 and 373–4; Dreyer, *Tychonis Opera*, vol. X, pp. 121 and 156.

99 Christianson, *On Tycho's Island*, pp. 363–5; see also John Christianson, 'Tycho Brahe's Facts of Life', *Fund og Forskning*, 17 (1970), pp. 21–8; and Ole Kongsted, 'Tyge Brahe og Musikken',

in *Tycho Brahes Verden: Danmark i Europa, 1550–1600*, ed. Poul Grinder-Hansen (Copenhagen, 2006), pp. 123–31.

100 Dreyer, *Tychonis Opera*, vol. XIV, pp. 22–3.

101 Ibid., vol. X, p. 124.

102 Ibid., pp. 131–2.

103 Thoren with Christianson, *Lord of Uraniborg*, pp. 287–8.

104 Dreyer, *Tychonis Opera*, vol. X, pp. 138–224.

105 Moesgaard, 'Astronomi', p. 263; Dreyer, *Tychonis Opera*, vol. X, p. 183.

106 Brahe, *Instruments*, p. 31, n. 55; Thoren with Christianson, *Lord of Uraniborg*, pp. 163–4.

107 Dreyer, *Tychonis Opera*, vol. V, pp. 28–31; Brahe, *Instruments*, pp. 30–35.

108 Walter G. Wesley, 'The Accuracy of Tycho Brahe's Instruments', *Journal for the History of Astronomy*, IX (1978), pp. 42–53; Walter G. Wesley, 'Tycho Brahe's Solar Observations', *Journal for the History of Astronomy*, X (1979), pp. 96–101; Moesgaard, 'Astronomi', pp. 259–65; Yas Maeyama, 'Tycho Brahe's Stellar Observations: An Accuracy Test', in *Tycho Brahe and Prague: Crossroads of European Science*, ed. J. R. Christianson, Alena Hadravová, Petr Hadrava and Martin Šolc (Frankfurt am Main, 2002), pp. 113–19.

109 Dreyer, *Tychonis Opera*, vol. X, pp. 133–5.

110 Rørdam, *Danske Kirkelove*, vol. II, pp. 337–9.

111 Henning Matzen, 'Adelen', *Forelæsninger over Den danske Retshistorie, Offentlig Ret I.* (Copenhagen, 1893), p. 57.

112 Laursen, *Kancelliets Brevbøger, 1580–83*, pp. 378–9.

113 Ibid., pp. 520–21.

114 Ibid., pp. 523–4, 545; Resen, *Kong Frederichs Den Andens Krønicke*, p. 334; Harald Ilsøe, 'Gesandtskaber som kulturformidlende faktor: Forbindelser mellem Danmark og England-Skotland o. 1580–1607', *Historisk Tidsskrift*, 11th series, 6 (1960), pp. 574–600, English summary pp. 598–600; C. Molbech, 'Bidrag til Historien af det Gesandtskab, som Dronning Elisabeth 1582 sendte til Danmark, for at bringe Kong Frederik II. den engelske Hosebaandsorden', *Nye Danske Magazin*, 4 (1823), pp. 255–67.

115 Harald Langberg, *Dansesalen på Kronborg* (Copenhagen, 1985); John Robert Christianson, 'Terrestrial and Celestial Spaces of the Danish Court, 1550–1650', in *The Politics of Court Space: European Courts ca. 1500–1750*, ed. Marcello Fantoni, George

Gorse and Malcolm Smuts (Rome, 2009), p. 101, n. 28. Ulrik
Reindel, *Kronbergtapeterne: Pragt & propaganda på Frederick II's Kronborg*
(Copenhagen, 2009).

116 Thomas Moffet, *Health's Improvement* (London, 1746), p. 396;
Jole Shackelford, *A Philosophical Path for Paracelsian Medicine: The
Ideas, Intellectual Context, and Influence of Petrus Severinus (1540/2–1602)*
(Copenhagen, 2004), pp. 253–7.

5 Star Castle: Going Down to See Up, 1582–8

1 Owen Gingerich and James R. Voelkel, 'Tycho Brahe's Copernican
   Campaign', *Journal for the History of Astronomy*, XXIX (1998), pp. 1–34;
   J. L. Heilbron, *The Sun in the Church: Cathedrals as Solar Observatories*
   (Cambridge, MA, 1999), pp. 120–43.

2 Kristian Peder Moesgaard, 'Astronomi', in *Københavns universitet,
   1479–1979*, vol. XII, ed. Mogens Pihl (Copenhagen, 1983),
   pp. 248–50, 262–7.

3 I.L.E. Dreyer, ed., *Tychonis Brahe Dani Opera Omnia*, 15 vols
   (Copenhagen, 1913–29), vol. IX, p. 6 and vol. X, pp. 174–5, 176–8,
   196–203, 243–9, 283–8; Gingerich and Voelkel, 'Copernican
   Campaign', pp. 5–9.

4 Gingerich and Voelkel, 'Copernican Campaign', pp. 1–34; Owen
   Gingerich and James R. Voelkel, 'Tycho and Kepler: Solid Myth
   versus Subtle Truth', *Social Research*, LXXII/2 (2005), pp. 77–81;
   Victor E. Thoren, *The Lord of Uraniborg: A Biography of Tycho Brahe*,
   with contributions by John R. Christianson (Cambridge, 1990),
   pp. 249–61.

5 John Robert Christianson, *On Tycho's Island: Tycho Brahe and His
   Assistants, 1570–1601* (Cambridge, 2000), pp. 323–5.

6 Dreyer, *Tychonis Opera*, vol. X, pp. 130, 231–3.

7 Moesgaard, 'Astronomi', pp. 259–65, esp. p. 261.

8 Thoren with Christianson, *The Lord of Uraniborg*, pp. 222–3.

9 Ibid., p. 171, n. 49: *arcum astronomicum* or *Arcvs Bipartitvs*; Dreyer, *Tychonis
   Opera*, vol. V, pp. 58, 68–75, vol. II, pp. 247–50 and vol. X, pp. 246,
   275; Tycho Brahe, *Instruments of the Renewed Astronomy (Astronomiæ
   Instauratæ Mechanica)*, trans. and ed. Alena Hadravová, Petr Hadrava
   and Jole R. Schackelford (Prague, 1996), pp. 64–5, 75–82.

10 Tycho Brahe, 'Prins Hans' Nativitet (1583)', e-manuskripter,
    Det Kongelige Bibliotek, Copenhagen, www.kb.dk, accessed
    3 March 2017.

11 Christianson, *On Tycho's Island,* pp. 307–8.

12 Dreyer, *Tychonis Opera*, vol. IX, p. 11 and vol. X, pp. 250–52.

13 Ibid., vol. X, pp. 250–64.

14 Thoren with Christianson, *The Lord of Uraniborg*, p. 171; Dreyer,
    Tychonis Opera, vol. II, p. 153; vol. V, pp. 48–51 and vol. X, pp. 236,
    243; Brahe, *Instruments*, pp. 53–6.

15 Dreyer, *Tychonis Opera*, vol. XIV, pp. 25–6; John Robert
    Christianson, 'Addenda to Tychonis Brahe Opera Omnia tomus
    XIV', *Centaurus*, XVI (1972), pp. 231–3.

16 L. Laursen, *Kancelliets Brevbøger, 1584–88* (Copenhagen, 1906),
    pp. 20, 34.

17 Peder Hansøn Resen, *Kong Frederichs Den Andens Krønicke*
    (Copenhagen, 1680), pp. 340–41.

18 Sachiko Kusukawa, *Picturing the Book of Nature* (Chicago, IL, 2012),
    pp. 94, 26–97; Owen Gingerich, *The Book Nobody Read: Chasing the
    Revolutions of Nicolaus Copernicus* (New York and London, 2004),
    pp. 121–9.

19 Christianson, *On Tycho's Island*, pp. 296–7; Lauritz Nielsen, *Tycho
    Brahes Bogtrykkeri* (Copenhagen, 1946), pp. 11–12; Dreyer, *Tychonis
    Opera*, vol. VII, pp. 77, 81–2.

20 Moesgaard, 'Astronomi', pp. 262–5; Thoren with Christianson,
    The Lord of Uraniborg, p. 226.

21 Kr. Peder Moesgaard, 'Copernicus og Tycho Brahe', in *Tycho
    Brahes Verden: Danmark i Europa, 1550–1600,* ed. Poul Grinder-Hansen
    (Copenhagen, 2006), p. 160.

22 Thoren with Christianson, *Lord of Uraniborg,* pp. 194–6, 220–35;
    Moesgaard, 'Astronomi', pp. 259–62.

23 Laursen, *Kancelliets Brevbøger, 1584–88*, p. 69; Dreyer, *Tychonis Opera*,
    vol. IX, pp. 25–8.

24 Dreyer, *Tychonis Opera*, vol. X, pp. 345–8.

25 Ibid., vol. VI, pp. 103–4, vol. IX, pp. 27–8, and vol. X, pp. 345–6,
    347–8.

26 Dreyer, *Tychonis Opera*, vol. VI, pp. 265–7 and II, pp. 31–2; Thoren
    with Christianson, *Lord of Uraniborg,* pp. 194–6.

27 Ann Blair, 'Tycho Brahe's Critique of Copernicus and the
    Copernican System', *Journal of the History of Ideas*, LI/3 (1990),
    pp. 355–77.
28 Dreyer, *Tychonis Opera*, vol. V, pp. 44–7; Brahe, *Instruments,*
    pp. 48–52, 128.
29 Christianson, *On Tycho's Island*, pp. 269–71, 362–3.
30 Dreyer, *Tychonis Opera*, vol. XIV, pp. 26–7; Christianson, *On Tycho's
    Island*, p. 127.
31 Christianson, *On Tycho's Island*; Victor E. Thoren, 'Tycho Brahe as
    the Dean of a Renaissance Research Institute', in *Religion, Science,
    and Worldview*, ed. Margret J. Osler and Paul Lawrence Farber
    (Cambridge, 1985), pp. 275–95; Peter Zeeberg, 'Tycho Brahe's
    Uraniborg, Research Centre and Aristocratic Residence', in *On
    Renaissance Academies*, ed. Marianne Pade (Rome, 2011), pp. 155–60;
    Peter Galison and Bruce Hevly, eds, *Big Science: The Growth of Large-
    scale Research* (Stanford, CA, 1992).
32 Thomas Lyngby, *Måder at bo på: Indretning, liv, stemninger og
    bevidsthedsformer i danske overklasseboliger i byen 1570–1870* (Hillerød,
    2015), pp. 56–60, 93–6, 102–6.
33 Ole Kongsted, 'Tyge Brahe og Musikken', in *Tycho Brahes Verden*,
    ed. Grinder-Hansen, pp. 123–31.
34 Paula Findlen, 'Anatomy Theaters, Botanical Gardens, and
    Natural History Collections', in *The Cambridge History of Science*,
    vol. III: *Early Modern Science*, ed. Kathrine Park and Lorraine Daston
    (Cambridge, 2006), pp. 272–89.
35 Cf. Bruce T. Moran, *Chemical Pharmacy Enters the University* (Madison,
    WI, 1991), p. 5.
36 Gemma Frisius had considered these coordinates in 1534, see
    Thoren with Christianson, *Lord of Uraniborg*, p. 174; Cf. Dreyer,
    Tychonis Opera, vol. IV, p. 381, and Joseph Needham, *Science and
    Civilisation in China*, vol. III: *Mathematics and the Sciences of the Heavens and
    the Earth* (Cambridge, 1959), pp. 229–30, 266, 377–9.
37 Dreyer, *Tychonis Opera*, vol. X, p. 318; Cf. Thoren with Christianson,
    Lord of Uraniborg, p. 165.
38 Holger Fr. Rørdam, 'Et dansk Øjenvidnes Beretning om
    Bartholomæusnatten i Paris', *Ny Kirkehistoriske Samlinger*, V
    (Copenhagen, 1869–71), pp. 244–53.

39 Dreyer, *Tychonis Opera*, vol. IX, p. 29 and vol. X, pp. 295–6, 305, 307, 318–19; Nicolaus Reymers, *Godæsia Ranzoviana: LandtRechnen vnd Feldmessen* (Leipzig, 1583).

40 Peter Zeeberg, *Urania Titani: Et digt om Sophie Brahe* (Copenhagen, 1994), pp. 254–7; cf. Dreyer, *Tychonis Opera*, vol. VII, pp. 321–2, 387–8.

41 Nicolai Raimari Vrsi Dithmarsi, *De Astronomicis Hypothesibvs, Sev Systemate Mvndano* (Prague, 1597), sign. [Aiiijv].

42 Edward Rosen, *Three Imperial Mathematicians: Kepler Trapped Between Tycho Brahe and Ursus* (New York, 1981), pp. 251–2.

43 Peter Zeeberg, 'Amor på Hven: Tycho Brahes digt til Erik Lange', in *Renæssancen: Dansk – Europæisk – Globalt,* ed. Marianne Pade and Minne Skafte Jensen (Copenhagen, 1988), pp. 151–81; Christianson, *On Tycho's Island*, pp. 44–52, 91–2.

44 Dreyer, *Tychonis Opera*, vol. IX, pp. 179–80; Resen, *Kong Frederichs,* pp. 398–436.

45 Dreyer, *Tychonis Opera*, vol. VII, pp. 81–2, 85–6.

46 Ibid., vol. X, p. 302; Lauritz Nielsen, *Boghistoriske studier til dansk bibliografi, 1550–1600* (Copenhagen, 1923), pp. 94–6; Lauritz Nielsen, *Tycho Brahes Bogtrykkeri*, pp. 12–20.

47 Peter Zeeberg, 'Science versus Secular Life: A Central Theme in the Latin Poems of Tycho Brahe', in *Acta Conventus Neo-Latini Torontonensis*, ed. Alexander Dalzell, Charles Fantazi and Richard J. Schoeck (Binghamton, NY, 1991), pp. 831–8; Peter Zeeberg, *Den praktiske muse*, pp. 14–37.

48 Dreyer, *Tychonis Opera*, vol. VII, pp. 90–91, 106; Nielsen, *Tycho Brahes Bogtrykkeri,* p. 12.

49 Brahe, *Instruments*, p. 69; Dreyer, *Tychonis Opera*, vol. V, pp. 60–63 and vol. X, pp. 297, 336–8; Gingerich and Voelkel, 'Copernican Campaign', pp. 9–16; Thoren with Christianson, *Lord of Uraniborg*, pp. 227–9.

50 Moesgaard, 'Copernicus og Tycho', p. 157; Ann Blair, 'Tycho Brahe's Critique of Copernicus and the Copernican System', *Journal of the History of Ideas*, LI (1990), pp. 355–77.

51 Dreyer, *Tychonis Opera*, vol. XIV, p. 42; Laursen, *Kancelliets Brevbøger, 1584–88*, pp. 211–2.

52 Christianson, 'Tycho Brahe's Cosmology from the *Astrología* of 1591', *Isis*, LIX/3 (1968), pp. 312–18.

53 Dreyer, *Tychonis Opera*, vol. VII, pp. 89–90, 93–4.

54 Christianson, *On Tycho's Island*, pp. 254, 266–7, 269–71, 277–80, 287, 323–5, 351–2; Dreyer, *Tychonis Opera*, vol. XIII, pp. 336–71.

55 Thoren with Christianson, *Lord of Uraniborg*, pp. 190–91.

56 Elias Olai Cimbrum [Morsing], *Diarivm Astrologicvm et Metheorologicvm Anni a Nato Christo 1586* (Uraniborg, 1586); Dreyer, *Tychonis Opera*, vol. IV, pp. 399–407, 512–13; Miguel A. Granada, Adam Mosley and Nicholas Jardine, *Christoph Rothmann's Discourse on the Comet of 1585* (Leiden, 2014), pp. 252–7.

57 Wilhelm Norlind, *Tycho Brahe* (Lund, 1970), pp. 96, 181, 353–5; Nielsen, *Tycho Brahes Bogtrykkeri*, pp. 23–6; F. R. Friis, *Elias Olsen Morsing og Hans Observationer* (Copenhagen, 1880), pp. 3–4.

58 Dreyer, *Tychonis Opera*, vol. VI, pp. 255–62, 271–88, described the portal as 'schwartzen Tutzstein' on p. 256, and 'saxum Porphyrius' on p. 272.

59 Dreyer, *Tychonis Opera*, vol. VI, pp. 64–7 and vol. X, p. 302; Thoren with Christianson, *Lord of Uraniborg*, pp. 172–6.

60 Dreyer, *Tychonis Opera*, vol. X, pp. 351–6.

61 Ibid., vol. VI, p. 259, 'starck vnd stieff'.

62 Ibid., pp. 29–33; Karsten Gaulke, 'The First European Observatory of the Sixteenth Century, as Founded by Landgrave Wilhelm IV of Hesse-Kassel', in *European Collections of Scientific Instruments, 1559–1750*, ed. Giorgio Strano et al. (Leiden and Boston, MA, 2009), pp. 87–99; Granada, Mosley and Jardine, *Rothmann's Discourse*, pp. 19–23, 246–9; Adam Mosley, *Bearing the Heavens: Tycho Brahe and the Astronomical Community of the Late Sixteenth Century* (Cambridge, 2007), pp. 39–50.

63 Dreyer, *Tychonis Opera*, vol. VI, pp. 33–40, 41–8.

64 Robert S. Westman, *The Copernican Question: Prognostication, Skepticism, and Celestial Order* (Berkeley and Los Angeles, CA, and London, 2011), pp. 224–6, see also 281–306.

65 Poul Grinder-Hansen, *Frederik 2., Danmarks Renæssancekonge* (Copenhagen, 2013), pp. 178–97; Paul Douglas Lockhart, *Frederik II and the Protestant Cause: Denmark's Role in the Wars of Religion, 1559–1596*

(Leiden and Boston, MA, 2004); Hugues Daussy, 'Duplessis-Mornay, Languet et Danzay en guerre contre les théologiens', *Siècles*, XVIII (2003), pp. 93–103.

66 Laursen, *Kancelliets Brevbøger, 1584–88*, pp. 547–73.

67 Carsten Neumann, 'Kunst, Kultur und Wissenschaft', in *Renaissance in Mecklenburg*, ed. Michael Bischoff and Hillert Ibbeken (Berlin, 2011), pp. 49–62.

68 Lyngby, *Måder at bo på*, pp. 54–60; John Robert Christianson, 'Tycho and Sophie Brahe: Gender and Science in the Late Sixteenth Century', in *Tycho Brahe and Prague: Crossroads of European Science*, ed. J. R. Christianson et al. (Frankfurt am Main, 2002), pp. 30–45.

69 Karen Thuesen, ed., *Anders Sørensen Vedels Hundredvisebog* (Copenhagen, 1993), pp. 26–7.

70 Ibid., pp. 69–77; 'Grimhild's Vengeance', trans. G. H. Borrow, www.odins-gift.com, accessed 29 June 2017.

71 Ellen Jørgensen and Johanne Skovgaard, 'Sofie', in *Danske Dronninger* (Copenhagen, 1910), p. 121, see also pp. 115–40.

72 Dreyer, *Tychonis Opera*, vol. IX, pp. 45–6.

73 Lockhart, *Protestant Cause*, pp. 252–64.

74 Dreyer, *Tychonis Opera*, vol. VI, p. 266; vol. VII, p. 110; vol. IX, p. 47.

75 Grinder-Hansen, *Frederik II*, p. 301.

76 Lockhart, *Protestant Cause*, pp. 259–60; Laursen, *Kancelliets Brevbøger, 1584–88,* pp. 526, 536, 565–6, 571, 574, 578–81; Poul Grinder-Hansen, '"Im Grünen": The Types of Informal Space and their Use in Private, Political and Diplomatic Activities of Frederik II, King of Denmark', in *Beyond Scylla and Charybdis: European Courts and Court Residences outside Habsburg and Valois/Bourbon Territories 1500–1700*, ed. Birgitte Bøggild Johannsen and Konrad Ottenheym (Copenhagen, 2015), pp. 179–80.

77 Dreyer, *Tychonis Opera*, vol. VI, p. 12; Cf. Christianson, *On Tycho's Island*, pp. 376–7.

78 Dreyer, *Tychonis Opera*, vol. VI, pp. 48–58, 75–80; Granada, Mosley and Jardine, *Rothmann's Discourse,* pp. 29, 78–145; Cf. Mosley, *Bearing the Heavens*, p. 62. Gaulke, 'The First European Observatory', pp. 87–8.

79 Dreyer, *Tychonis Opera*, vol. VI, pp. 59–63.

80 Thoren with Christianson, *Lord of Uraniborg*, pp. 280–83.

81 Dreyer, *Tychonis Opera*, vol. VI, pp. 63–75, 85–104.

82 Mosley, *Bearing the Heavens*, p. 44.

83 Granada, Mosley and Jardine, *Rothmann's Discourse*; Mosley, *Bearing the Heavens*; Miguel A. Granada, Jürgen Hamel and Ludolf von Mackensen, *Christoph Rothmanns Handbuch der Astronomie von 1589* (Frankfurt am Main, 2003).

84 Mosley, *Bearing the Heavens*, pp. 31–125; Nicholas Jardine and Alain-Philippe Segonds, *La Guerre des Astronomes*, vol. I (Paris, 2008).

85 Robert S. Westman, 'The Melanchthon Circle, Rheticus, and the Wittenberg Interpretation of the Copernican Theory', *Isis*, LXVI (1975), pp. 164–93; Westman, *The Copernican Question*, pp. 141–70, 288–300.

86 Granada, Mosley and Jardine, *Rothmann's Discourse*, pp. 1–30; Miguel A. Granada, 'Did Tycho Eliminate the Celestial Spheres Before 1586', *Journal for the History of Astronomy*, XXXVII (2006), pp. 130–32.

87 Peter Barker, 'Stoic Alternatives to Aristotelian Cosmology: Pena, Rothmann and Brahe', *Revue d'histoire des sciences*, LXI (2008), pp. 265–86.

88 The annual orbit of the Earth around the Sun would cause an apparent shift called annual parallax unless the stars were much farther away than most astronomers believed. Blair, 'Tycho Brahe's Critique'; Miguel A. Granada, 'Tycho Brahe, Caspar Peucer, Christoph Rothmann on Cosmology and the Bible', in *Nature and Scripture in the Abrahamic Religions*, ed. J. M. van der Meer and S. Mandelbrote, vol. II (Leiden, 2008), pp. 563–83; Christopher M. Graney, 'Regarding How Tycho Brahe Noted the Absurdity of the Copernican Theory regarding the Bigness of Stars, while the Copernicans appealed to God to Answer that Absurdity' (2012), www.arxiv.org, accessed 13 January 2018.

89 Translated in Kristian P. Moesgaard, 'Copernican Influence on Tycho Brahe', in *The Reception of Copernicus' Heliocentric Theory*, ed. Jerzy Dobrzycki (Dordrecht and Boston, MA, 1972), p. 50. Dreyer, *Tychonis Opera*, vol. VI, p. 178.

90 Dreyer, *Tychonis Opera*, vol. XIV, pp. 32, 34–8; Petersen and Lundh, *Registranter 1572–1588*, pp. 640–41, 654–6.

91 Brahe, *Instruments*, pp. 32–3; Dreyer, *Tychonis Opera*, vol. V, p. 30; Grinder-Hansen, *Tycho Brahes Verden*, pp. 40, 60.

92 P.B.C. Westergaard, *Danske Portræter i Kobberstik, Litografi og Træsnit*,
    2 vols (Copenhagen, 1930–34), vol. I, p. 198, n. 1376.

93 Dreyer, *Tychonis Opera*, vol. V, pp. 32–5, vol. X, p. 427 and
    vol. XI, pp. 1–5; Thoren with Christianson, *Lord of Uraniborg*,
    pp. 176–7.

94 Laursen, *Kancelliets Brevbøger, 1584–88*, pp. 667–8.

95 Otto Carøe, Kong Frederik II's Kalenderoptegnelser for Aarene
    1583, 1584 og 1587', *Historisk Tidsskrift*, 4th series, 3 (1872), p. 570.

96 Michael Roberts, *The Early Vasas: A History of Sweden, 1523–1611*
    (Cambridge, 1968), pp. 269–70; Paul Douglas Lockhart,
    Frederik II and the Protestant Cause: Denmark's Role in the Wars of Religion,
    1559–1596 (Leiden and Boston, MA, 2004), pp. 264–5.

97 Dreyer, *Tychonis Opera*, vol. VII, p. 166; Christianson, *On Tycho's*
    Island, pp. 218, 223, 314, 381; Owen Gingerich and Robert S.
    Westman, *The Wittich Connection: Conflict and Priority in Late Sixteenth-*
    century Cosmology (Philadelphia, PA, 1988), pp. 20–23; Adam
    Morawiec, 'In Defense of Paul Wittich: † 9 January 1587', *Sudhoffs*
    Archiv, XCIX/2 (2015), pp. 235–9.

98 Dreyer, *Tychonis Opera*, vol. VII, p. 110.

99 Ibid., vol. XIV, p. 27. Rørdam, *Kjøbenhavns Universitets Historie*, vol.
    II, pp. 83–5, 294, 694–5, on Gellius and the *stipendium regium*.
    Christianson, *On Tycho's Island*, pp. 17, 72, 132, 351.

100 Christianson, *On Tycho's Island*, pp. 266–7, 289–90, 313, 340–44,
    350–53.

101 John Robert Christianson, *Tycho Brahe: Renæssancen på Hven*
    (Copenhagen, 2008), pp. 306–8; James Orchard Holliwell, ed.,
    The Private Diary of Dr John Dee (London, 1842), pp. 28, 30, 31.

102 Dreyer, *Tychonis Opera*, vol. XI, p. 137.

103 Ibid., vol. IX, p. 64.

104 Ibid. and vol. IV, pp. 1–378; Max Caspar, ed., *Johannes Kepler*
    Gesammelte Werke, Band XIV. Briefe 1599–1603 (Munich, 1949),
    pp. 101–2; Thoren with Christianson, *Lord of Uraniborg*, pp. 135–7,
    249–64; Norlind, *Tycho Brahe*, pp. 101–27; Nielsen, *Bogtrykkeri*,
    pp. 27–31, 40, 67–8.

105 Brahe, *Instruments*, pp. 21, 73.

106 Dreyer, *Tychonis Opera*, vol. V, pp. 36–9.

107 Ibid., vol. VI, pp. 250–62, 271–88, 293–4.

108 Ibid., vol. XIV, p. 37; Laursen, *Kancelliets Brevbøger, 1584–88*, p. 824;
     Carøe, 'Kalenderoptegnelser', pp. 575–7.
109 Dreyer, *Tychonis Opera*, vol. XIV, pp. 38–9.
110 Ibid., vol. VII, pp. 116–19.
111 Cf. Gábor Almási, 'Tycho Brahe and the Separation of
     Astronomy from Astrology: The Making of a New Scientific
     Discourse', *Science in Context*, XXVI/I (2013), pp. 3–30; and Morten
     Fink-Jensen, 'Astronomien, astrologien og bibelen hos Tycho
     Brahe', in Grinder-Hansen, *Tycho Brahes Verden,* pp. 165–74.
112 Grinder-Hansen, *Frederik II*, pp. 300–307; Resen, *Kong Frederichs*,
     pp. 356–7.

6 On the Move, 1588–99

  1 Steffen Heiberg, *Christian 4: en europæisk statsmand* (Copenhagen,
     2009), pp. 26, 38.
  2 I.L.E. Dreyer, ed., *Tychonis Brahe Dani Opera Omnia*, 15 vols
     (Copenhagen, 1913–29), vol. IX, p. 64 and vol. XIV, pp. 39–52;
     J. R. Christianson, 'Addenda to Tychonis Brahe Opera Omnia
     tomus XIV', *Centaurus*, XVI (1972), pp. 236–7; Laursen, *Kancelliets
     Brevbøger, 1588–1592*, pp. 70, 404.
  3 Victor E. Thoren, *The Lord of Uraniborg: A Biography of Tycho Brahe,*
     with contributions by John R. Christianson (Cambridge, 1990),
     pp. 273–4; Wilhelm Norlind, *Tycho Brahe: En levnadsteckning med nya
     bidrag belysande hans liv och verk* (Lund, 1970), pp. 122–7.
  4 Dreyer, *Tychonis Opera*, vol. V, pp. 119–24; vol. VII, p. 324 and
     vol. XIV, pp. 32–4.
  5 Ibid., pp. 324–5.
  6 John Robert Christianson, *On Tycho's Island: Tycho Brahe and His
     Assistants, 1570–1601* (Cambridge, 2000), pp. 167–8, 252–3, 290–91,
     313–19.
  7 Ibid., pp. 251–2, 254–6, 290–91, 308–11, 340–43.
  8 Ibid., pp. 151–7, 280–81.
  9 Charles Whitney, 'Francis Bacon's Instauratio: Dominion
     of and over Humanity', *Journal of the History of Ideas*, L/3 (1989),
     pp. 371–90.
 10 Dreyer, *Tychonis Opera*, vol. VII, pp. 131–3.

11 Ibid., vol. VII, pp. 386–7; Christianson, *On Tycho's Island*, pp. 94–8;
    Cf. Jens Schjerup Hansen, *Bystruktur og havekultur mellem Senmiddelalder
    og Renæssance*, ed. Lise Bek (Copenhagen 2008), pp. 9–46.

12 Geoffrey Parker, *Success Is Never Final: Empire, War, and Faith in Early
    Modern Europe* (New York, 2002), pp. 97–121; Christianson,
    On Tycho's Island, pp. 132–4.

13 Michael Jones, 'Tycho Brahe', in *Geographers: Biobibliographical
    Studies*, ed. Hayden Lorimer and Charles W. J. Withers, vol. XXVII
    (London and New York, 2008), pp. 1–27; N. D. Haasbroek,
    Gemma Frisius, Tycho Brahe and Snellius and their Triangulations (Delft,
    1968), pp. 10–14, 29–36.

14 William R. Mead, 'Scandinavian Renaissance Cartography',
    in *The History of Cartography*, vol. III: *Cartography in the European
    Renaissance*, ed. David Woodward (Chicago, IL, 2007),
    pp. 1788–92.

15 Jones, 'Tycho Brahe', pp. 11, 15–17; Dreyer, *Tychonis Opera*, vol. V,
    pp. 301–4, 309, 342; vol. XII, p. 219 and vol. IX, pp. 73–4, 78.

16 Christianson, *On Tycho's Island*, pp. 294–5.

17 Dreyer, *Tychonis Opera*, vol. VI, p. 198; vol. IX, pp. 74, 89 and vol.
    XIV, pp. 60–61; Bjørn Westerbeek Dahl, 'Valentin "den gamle
    graver"', *Personalhistorisk tidsskrift* (2007), pp. 1–15; Jens Vellev,
    'Tycho Brahes papermølle på Hven – og om N. A. Møller
    Nicolaisens udgravninger 1933–34', *Grafiana: Årbog for Danmarks
    Grafiske Museum, Danmarks Pressemuseum* (Odense, 2000), pp. 27–37.

18 F. R. Friis, *Sofie Brahe Ottesdatter, En biografisk Skildring* (Copenhagen,
    1905), pp. 9–10; F. R. Friis, 'Nogle Meddelelser om Erik Lange
    den yngre til Engelsholm', *Samlinger til jydsk Historie og Topografi*, 3rd
    ser., 2 (1899–1900), pp. 497–9, 502–4.

19 Dreyer, *Tychonis Opera*, vol. IX, p. 82.

20 Peter Zeeberg, 'The Inscriptions at Tycho Brahe's Uraniborg',
    in *A History of Nordic Neo-Latin Literature*, ed. Minna Skafte Jensen
    (Odense, 1995), pp. 264–5.

21 Christianson, *On Tycho's Island*, pp. 77–8.

22 Dreyer, *Tychonis Opera*, vol. II, p. 12.

23 Ibid., vol. VI, pp. 261, 287 and vol. IX, p. 84.

24 Petrus Gassendus, *Tychonis Brahei, Equitis Dani, Astronomorum Coryphæi,
    Vita* (The Hague, 1655), pp. 119–20, 196, citing Willem Jansz. Blaeu.

25 Dreyer, *Tychonis Opera*, vol. IX, pp. 88, 119.

26 Ibid., vol. VI, p. 234.

27 Christianson, *On Tycho's Island*, p. 377; Lauritz Nielsen, *Tycho Brahes Bogtrykkeri: En bibliografisk-boghistorisk Undersøgelse* (Copenhagen, 1946), p. 33; Dreyer, *Tychonis Opera*, vol. IX, pp. 89–91.

28 Zeeberg, *Urania Titani*, pp. 13–18, 257; John Robert Christianson, 'Tycho and Sophie Brahe: Gender and Science in the Late Sixteenth Century', in *Tycho Brahe and Prague: Crossroads of European Science*, ed. J. R. Christianson, Alena Hadravová, Petr Hadrava and Martin Šolc (Frankfurt am Main, 2002), pp. 30–45.

29 Dreyer, *Tychonis Opera*, vol. IX, pp. 89–91 and vol. XII, pp. 32, 89.

30 P.B.C. Westergaard, *Danske Portræter i Kobberstik, Litografi og Træsnit*, 2 vols (Copenhagen, 1930–34), vol. I, p. 199, n. 1377; Dreyer, *Tychonis Opera*, vol. VII, p. 300.

31 Dreyer, *Tychonis Opera*, vol. IX, pp. 72, 99–100; see also Volker R. Remmert, 'The Art of Garden and Landscape Design and the Mathematical Sciences in the Early Modern Period', in *Gardens, Knowledge and the Sciences in the Early Modern Period*, ed. Hubert Fischer, V. R. Remmert and J. Wolschke-Bulmahn (Basel, 2016), pp. 9–28.

32 Peder Jacobsøn Flemløse, *En Elementisch og Jordisch* Astrologia *Om Luften forendring* (Uraniborg, 1591), sign. Aij - [Aiiijv]; John [Robert] Christianson, 'Tycho Brahe's Cosmology from the *Astrologia* of 1591', *Isis*, LIX/3 (1968), pp. 312–18; F. R. Friis, ed., *Peder Jacobsen Flemløses elementiske og jordiske Astrologie om Luftens Forandring* (Copenhagen, 1865); Nielsen, *Bogtrykkeri*, pp. 33–7.

33 John Robert Christianson, *Tycho Brahe: Renæssancen på Hven*, trans. Jan Teuber (Copenhagen, 2008), pp. 356–8, 379–80; Christianson, *On Tycho's Island*, pp. 333–5.

34 Dreyer, *Tychonis Opera*, vol. XIV, p. 60.

35 F. R. Friis, *Tyge Brahe: En historisk Fremstilling efter trykte og utrykte Kilder* (Copenhagen, 1871), p. 362, n. 112.

36 Kresten Andresen and Klara Sørensen, *Engelsholms Historie* (Jelling, 1993), pp. 12–20, 61–8.

37 Thoren with Christianson, *Lord of Uraniborg*, pp. 287–300.

38 Brahe, *Instruments of the Renewed Astronomy*, p. 33. Dreyer, *Tychonis Opera*, vol. V, p. 30.

39 Friis, *Tyge Brahe* (Copenhagen, 1871), pp. 201–2; Chr. Gorm
    Tortzen, *Liber Compositionum: Christian IV's latinske brevstile, 1591–1593*
    (Herning, 1988), pp. 96–7, 118–19.

40 Dreyer, *Tychonis Opera*, vol. XIV, pp. 6–7, 12–15, 21–6, 28–9 and
    49–50, 69–71; Christianson, 'Addenda', pp. 231–5; Christianson,
    On Tycho's Island, pp. 334–6; Hugo Johannsen, 'Dignity and Dynasty:
    On the History and Meaning of the Royal Funeral Monuments
    for Christian III, Frederik II and Christian IV in the Cathedral of
    Roskilde', *Masters, Meanings and Models: Studies in the Art and Architecture
    of the Renaissance in Denmark* (Copenhagen, 2010), pp. 116–49.

41 Dreyer, *Tychonis Opera*, vol. XIV, p. 66.

42 Ibid., vol. XIV, pp. 60, 66, 68–9, 106; Christianson, 'Addenda',
    pp. 240–41.

43 Christianson, 'Addenda', pp. 238–9.

44 Michael Dupont and Jens Vellev, 'Tycho Brahes salg af
    hovedgården Knutstorp i Skåne 1594–98: Fra skøde og dombrev
    til låsebrev', *Danske Magazin*, LI (2010), pp. 3–32; Christianson,
    On Tycho's Island, pp. 210–11.

45 Marcel Mauss, *The Gift: Forms and Functions of Exchange in Archaic
    Societies*, trans. Ian Cunnison (London, 1966).

46 Dreyer, *Tychonis Opera*, vol. IX, pp. 193–207, 323–7; Zeeberg, *Urania
    Titani*; Oluf Friis, *Den danske Litteraturs Historie, I: Fra Oldtiden indtil
    Renæssancen* (Copenhagen, 1945), pp. 448–50.

47 Dreyer, *Tychonis Opera*, vol. VI, pp. 231–49, 303–4.

48 Thoren with Christianson, *Lord of Uraniborg*, pp. 316–27. Victor
    Thoren, 'Tycho Brahe's Discovery of the Variation', *Centaurus*, XII
    (1967), pp. 151–66.

49 Thoren with Christianson, *Lord of Uraniborg*, pp. 327–30.

50 Victor E. Thoren, 'An Early Instance of Deductive Discovery:
    Tycho Brahe's Lunar Theory', *Isis*, LVIII/1 (1967), pp. 19–36.

51 Thoren with Christianson, *Lord of Uraniborg*, p. 333.

52 Christianson, *On Tycho's Island,* pp. 330–32.

53 Adam Mosley, 'Tycho Brahe and John Craig: The Dynamic of a
    Dispute', in Christianson et al., *Tycho Brahe and Prague*, pp. 70–83.

54 Edward Rosen, *Three Imperial Mathematicians: Kepler Trapped between
    Tycho Brahe and Ursus* (New York, 1986); Nicholas Jardine, *The
    Birth of History and Philosophy of Science: Kepler's A Defence of Tycho against*

Ursus, with Essays on its Provenance and Significance (Cambridge, 1984);
Nicholas Jardine et al., 'Tycho v. Ursus: The Build-up to a Trial,
Parts 1. & 2.', *Journal for the History of Astronomy*, XXXVI (2005),
pp. 81–106, 125–65. Nicholas Jardine and Alain-Philippe Segonds,
*La Guerre des Astronomes: La querelle au sujet de l'origine du système géo-
héliocentrique à la fin du XVIe siècle*, 2 vols (Paris, 2008).

55 Christianson, *On Tycho's Island*, pp. 171–93.

56 Holger Fr. Rørdam, *Kjøbenhavns Universitets Historie fra 1537 til 1621*,
vol. III (Copenhagen, 1877), pp. 25–47. With Gellius: Thomas
Fincke, Hans Resen, Peter Winstrup, and Jørgen Dybvad; and
with Tycho: Anders Christensen, Anders Krag and Niels Krag.

57 Christianson, *On Tycho's Island*, pp. 171–94; Dreyer, *Tychonis Opera*,
vol. XIV, pp. 71–97. [Jacob Langebek], ed., 'En Skue-Penge, med
endeel mest utrykte Efterretninger, om Tyge Brahe', *Danske
Magazin*, vol. II (Copenhagen, 1746), pp. 284–8, 290–307.

58 Augustus Erich, *Klarlige oc Visse Beskriffuelse, Om den Stormectige,
Høybaarne Førstes oc Herris, Herr Christians den Fierdis, Danmarckis, Norgis,
Vendis oc Gottis Konnings: Hertugs vdi Slesuig, Holsten, Stormarn oc Ditmersken:
Græffuis vdi Oldenborg oc Delmenhorst: Kongelige Kroning, som lycksaligen bleff
holden vdi Kiøbenhaffn, den 29. Augusti, Anno 1596* (Copenhagen, 1598),
sign. [Mv]-Mij. Dreyer, *Tychonis Opera*, vol. IX, p. 142.

59 Heiberg, *Christian 4*, p. 124.

60 Otto Gr. Lundh and I. E. Sars, eds., *Norske Rigs-Registranter, Tredie
Bind, 1588–1602* (Oslo, 1865), p. 440; Eiler Nystrøm, 'Tyge Brahes
Brud med Fædrelandet', in *Festskrift til Kristian Erslev*, ed. Poul
Nørlund (Copenhagen, 1927), pp. 300–301.

61 Adam Mosley, Nicholas Jardine and Karin Tybjerg, 'Epistolary
Culture, Editorial Practices, and the Propriety of Tycho's
Astronomical Letters', *Journal for the History of Astronomy*, XXXIV (2003),
pp. 421–51; Adam Mosley, 'Korrespondenten', in *Att låta själen flyga
mellan himlens tinnar: Tycho Brahe och Renässansen*, ed. Håkan Håkansson
(Stockholm, 2006), pp. 169–95; Norlind, *Tycho Brahe*, pp. 172–210.

62 Gábor Almási, 'Humanistic Letter-writing', in *European History
Online* (EGO), 2010, http://ieg-ego.eu/en, accessed 2 April 2018.

63 Westergaard, *Danske Portraeter*, vol. I, pp. 201–2, n. 1394.

64 Dreyer, *Tychonis Opera,* vol. XIV, pp. 98–101.

65 Ibid., pp. 101–2.

66 Ibid., vol. VII, p. 380.

67 Christianson, *On Tycho's Island*, pp. 139–40; O. Nielsen, *Kjøbenhavn i Aarene, 1536–1660* (Copenhagen, 1881), pp. 361–4, 438–9.

68 Dreyer, *Tychonis Opera*, vol. VIII, p. 176 and vol. XIII, pp. 98–100; Thoren with Christianson, *Lord of Uraniborg*, pp. 364–5.

69 Alex Wittendorff, 'Tyge Brahes brud med Danmark', in *Tycho Brahes Verden: Danmark i Europa, 1550–1600*, ed. Poul Grinder-Hansen (Copenhagen, 2006), pp. 201–15.

70 Ibid., vol. VII, p. 380.

71 Dreyer, *Tychonis Opera*, vol. XIII, pp. 79, 81–2 and 94–5.

72 Ibid., vol. XIV, p. 102.

73 Ibid., pp. 102–3; Christianson, *On Tycho's Island*, pp. 202–3.

74 Dreyer, *Tychonis Opera*, vol. IX, p. 146; Christianson, *On Tycho's Island*, pp. 332–3.

75 Christianson, *On Tycho's Island*, pp. 203–4, 377–9.

76 Dreyer, *Tychonis Opera*, vol. VII, p. 384; Nystrøm, 'Tyge Brahes Brud', pp. 307, 309.

77 Dreyer, *Tychonis Opera*, vol. XIV, p. 105; Rørdam, *Kjøbenhavns Universitets Historie*, vol. III, pp. 542–62 and vol. IV (1874), p. 430.

78 Christianson, *On Tycho's Island*, p. 205; Nystrøm, 'Tyge Brahes Brud', p. 308.

79 Dreyer, *Tychonis Opera*, vol. XIV, p. 106; Christianson, 'Addenda', pp. 240–41; Nystrøm, 'Tyge Brahes Brud', p. 309.

80 Dreyer, *Tychonis Opera*, vol. XIV, pp. 108–11; Nystrøm, 'Tyge Brahes Brud', pp. 309–11, noted that the original no longer exists; Frede P. Jensen, *Bidrag til Frederik II's og Erik XIV's historie* (Copenhagen, 1978), pp. 22–4.

81 Dreyer, *Tychonis Opera*, vol. VIII, pp. 5, 14, 111–14.

82 Ibid., vol. XIV, pp. 114–18; Christianson, *On Tycho's Island*, pp. 210–11.

83 Dreyer, *Tychonis Opera*, vol. VIII, pp. 5–6, vol. XIV, pp. 142–5; Christianson, *On Tycho's Island*, pp. 213–14.

84 Dreyer, *Tychonis Opera*, vol. XIV, pp. 121–3.

85 Ibid., vol. XIII, pp. 102–4.

86 Ibid., vol. XIII, pp. 104, 106, 109, 113.

87 Hanne Honnens de Lichtenberg, *Tro, håb & forfængelighed: Kunstneriske udtryksformer i 1500-tallets Danmark* (Copenhagen, 1989), pp. 362–3; Vinlandicus, *Kunstværket* (Copenhagen, 2010), pp. 93–6.

88 Christianson, *On Tycho's Island*, pp. 328–9; Nielsen, *Bogtrykkeri*, pp. 57–60.

89 Heiberg, *Christian 4*, p. 104.

90 Dreyer, *Tychonis Opera*, vol. XIV, pp. 126–30.

91 Joachim Frederick was still a Margrave at the wedding but became Elector on 8 January 1598 and wrote to Denmark soon after. Ibid., vol. XIV, pp. 131–3.

92 Ibid., XIV, p. 135; Christianson, *On Tycho's Island*, pp. 220–22 and 326–8.

93 Dreyer, *Tychonis Opera*, vol. VIII, pp. 14–15, 44.

94 Christianson, *On Tycho's Island*, p. 223.

95 Dreyer, *Tychonis Opera*, vol. VIII, p. 9.

96 Christianson, *On Tycho's Island*, p. 225.

97 Dreyer, *Tychonis Opera*, vol. VIII, pp. 26–7, 49 and 60.

98 Ibid., p. 88.

99 Ibid., vol. XIV, pp. 157–9, 177–82.

100 Ibid., vol. V, pp. 119–24, vol. VII, pp. 262–3.

101 J.L.E. Dreyer, *Tycho Brahe: A Picture of Scientific Life and Work in the Sixteenth Century* (Edinburgh, 1890), pp. 265–6.

102 Dreyer, *Tychonis Opera*, vol. XIV, pp. 309–11.

103 Ibid., vol. VIII, pp. 80–83 and vol. XIV, pp. 140–42.

104 Ibid., vol. V, pp. 1–162; Hans Ræder, Elis Strömgren and Bengt Strömgren, trans. and eds, *Tycho Brahe's Description of His Instruments and Scientific Work as given in Astronomiae Instauratae Mechanica (Wandesburgi 1598)* (Copenhagen, 1946); Tycho Brahe, *Instruments of the Renewed Astronomy*, trans. Raeder et al. (Copenhagen, 1946), rev. and ed. Alena Hadravová, Petr Hadrava and Jole R. Shackelford (Prague, 1996).

105 Thoren with Christianson, *Lord of Uraniborg*, pp. 402–3.

106 Norlind, *Tycho Brahe*, p. 288.

107 Christianson, *On Tycho's Island*, pp. 227–8.

108 László Ruttkay, 'Jessenius als Professor in Wittenberg – zum 350. Todesjahr von Jessenius', *Orvostöteneti Közlemények: Communicationes de Historia Artis Medicinae*, LXII–LXIII (1971), pp. 13–55.

109 Christianson, *On Tycho's Island*, p. 255.

110 Victor E. Thoren, 'An "Unpublished" Version of Tycho Brahe's Lunar Theory', *Centaurus*, XVI (1972), pp. 203–30.

III Thoren with Christianson, *Lord of Uraniborg*, pp. 404–9;
     Christianson, *On Tycho's Island*, pp. 230–31, 272–3, 297–8.

II2 Štambuch Tychona Brahe, http://v2.manuscriptorium.com,
     accessed 12 November 2016.

7 The Emperor's Astrologer and his Legacy, 1599–1687

1 John Robert Christianson, *On Tycho's Island: Tycho Brahe and His
   Assistants, 1570–1601* (Cambridge and New York, 2000), p. 232;
   Jiři Pešek, 'Prague between 1550 and 1650', in *Rudolf II and Prague:
   The Imperial Court and Residential City as the Cultural and Spiritual Heart
   of Central Europe*, ed. Eliška Fučiková et al. (Prague, London and
   Milan, 1997), pp. 252–69.

2 J.L.E. Dreyer, ed., *Tychonis Brahe Dani Opera Omnia*, 15 vols
   (Copenhagen, 1913–29), vol. XIV, p. 190.

3 Felix Stieve, 'Rudolf II., deutscher Kaiser', in *Abhandlunge, Vorträge
   und Reden* (Leipzig, 1900), p. 97, see also pp. 93–124; R.J.W. Evans,
   Rudolf II and His World: A Study in Intellectual History (Oxford, 1973),
   pp. 47, 48–9.

4 Beket Bukovinská, 'The *Kunstkammer* of Rudolf II'; Paula Findlen,
   'Cabinets, Collecting and Natural Philosophy', and Penelope
   Gouk, 'Natural Philosophy and Natural Magic', in *Rudolf II and
   Prague*, ed. Fučiková et al., pp. 199–208, 209–18, 231–7; Thomas
   DaCosta Kaufmann, *The Mastery of Nature: Aspects of Art, Science, and
   Humanism in the Renaissance* (Princeton, NJ, 1993), pp. 174–94.

5 Victor E. Thoren with contributions by John Robert Christianson,
   The Lord of Uraniborg: A Biography of Tycho Brahe (New York and
   Cambridge, 1990), pp. 410–13.

6 Dreyer, *Tychonis Opera*, vol. VIII, pp. 163–71.

7 Sacha Kacki et al., 'Rich Table but Short Life: Diffuse Idiopathic
   Skeletal Hyperostosis in Danish Astronomer Tycho Brahe (1546–
   1601) and its Possible Consequences', *PLOS One*, 19 April 2018,
   www.journals.plos.org, accessed 8 June 2018.

8 Eliška Fučiková, 'Prague Castle under Rudolf II, His Predecessors
   and Successors', in *Rudolf II and Prague*, ed. Fučiková et al., p. 4.

9 Christianson, *On Tycho's Island*, pp. 234–6.

10 Thoren with Christianson, *Lord of Uraniborg*, pp. 409–10.

11 Tycho Brahe, *Instruments of the Renewed Astronomy*, English trans. rev.
    and ed. Alena Hadravová, Petr Hadrava and Jole R. Shackelford
    (Prague, 1996), pp. 3–4; Dreyer, *Tychonis Opera*, vol. V, p. 5.

12 Brahe, *Instruments of the Renewed Astronomy*, pp. 6–7; Dreyer, *Tychonis
    Opera*, vol. V, pp. 6–7.

13 Dreyer, *Tychonis Opera*, vol. XIII, pp. 160–61, 186–7.

14 Ibid., vol. VIII, pp. 177–8.

15 Kirsten Bendixen, *Denmark's Money* (Copenhagen, 1967),
    pp. 71–3.

16 Heinz Noflatscher, 'Rudolf II', in *Handbuch Höfe und Residenzen im
    spätmittelalterlichen Reich, I: Dynastich-topographisches Handbuch der fürstlichen
    Höfe und Residenzen*, vol. XV (2012), p. 393; Anton Gindely, *Rudolf II
    und seine Zeit, 1600–1612*, 2nd edn (Prague, 1863), vol. I, pp. 32–3.

17 Dreyer, *Tychonis Opera*, vol. VIII, pp. 158–9.

18 Ibid., vol. XIV, pp. 175–6 and vol. IX, pp. 167–9; Thoren with
    Christianson, *Lord of Uraniborg*, p. 507.

19 Thoren with Christianson, *Lord of Uraniborg*, pp. 416–19.

20 Dreyer, *Tychonis Opera*, vol. XIII, pp. 161–2.

21 Christianson, *On Tycho's Island*, p. 277; Johannes Sinapius, *Des
    Schlesischen Adels Anderer Theil* (Leipzig and Breslau, 1728), p. 621;
    David Kaclik et al., 'A Biographical Sketch of Johannes Jessenius',
    Clinical Anatomy, XXV/2 (2012), p. 151.

22 Dreyer, *Tychonis Opera*, vol. XIV, p. 190.

23 Ibid., vol. VIII, p. 232 and vol. XIV, p. 179; Thoren with
    Christianson, *Lord of Uraniborg*, pp. 508–9.

24 Dreyer, *Tychonis Opera*, vol. VIII, pp. 246–8.

25 Christianson, *On Tycho's Island*, pp. 298, 329.

26 Nicholas Jardine and Alain Segonds, 'The Formal Refutation of
    Ursus's *Demonstratio* by Johannes Müller, briefed by Tycho Brahe',
    Journal for the History of Astronomy, XXXVI (2005), pp. 137–48;
    Nicholas Jardine and Alain-Philippe Segonds, *La Guerre des
    Astronomes: La querelle au sujet de l'origine du système géo-héliocentrique à la fin
    du XVIe siècle*, 2 vols (Paris, 2008), vol. I, pp. 181–9.

27 Thoren with Christianson, *Lord of Uraniborg*, pp. 429–30;
    Christianson, *On Tycho's Island*, pp. 281–2; Dreyer, *Tychonis Opera*,
    vol. XIV, pp. 168, 179.

28 Dreyer, *Tychonis Opera*, vol. XIII, pp. 193–241.

29 Johannes Kepler, *Gesammelte Werke*, ed. Walther von Dyck, Max
    Caspar et al., 27 vols to date (Munich, 1938–), vol. XIII, p. 292.

30 Kepler to Tycho, 5 April 1600, in Dreyer, *Tychonis Opera*, vol. VIII,
    p. 296.

31 James R. Voelkel, *The Composition of Kepler's Astronomia Nova*
    (Princeton, NJ, and Oxford, 2001), pp. 100–102.

32 Quoted ibid., p. 113.

33 Thoren with Christianson, *Lord of Uraniborg*, pp. 432–42; Max
    Caspar, *Kepler*, trans. and ed. C. Doris Hellman, intro. Owen
    Gingerich [1939] (New York, 1993), pp. 103–4.

34 Nicolas Jardine, *The Birth of History and Philosophy of Science: Kepler's
    A Defense of Tycho Against Ursus with Essays on Its Provenance and Significance*
    (Cambridge and New York, 1984), pp. 59–65.

35 Ibid., pp. 67–71; Jardine and Segonds, *La Guerre*, vol. I, pp. 243–4
    and vol. II, pp. 24–39.

36 Dreyer, *Tychonis Opera*, vol. XIV, pp. 296–9, 305–7; Caspar, *Kepler*,
    pp. 104–7.

37 Dreyer, *Tychonis Opera*, vol. VIII, pp. 307–9, 319; Caspar, *Kepler*, p. 108.

38 Dreyer, *Tychonis Opera*, vol. XIV, pp. 201–3.

39 H. R. Hiort-Lorenzen and A. Thiset, eds, *Danmarks Adels Aarbog*,
    vol. XIII (Copenhagen, 1896), pp. 428–9, 439.

40 László Ruttkay, 'Jessenius als Professor in Wittenberg – zum 350.
    Todesjahr von Jessenius', *Orvostörteneti Közlemények: Communicationes
    de Historia Artis Medicinae*, LXII–LXIII (1971), pp. 42–5, 53–4.

41 Thoren with Christianson, *Lord of Uraniborg*, p. 442.

42 Josef von Hasner, *Tycho Brahe und J. Kepler in Prag* (Prague, 1872), p. 10.

43 Dreyer, *Tychonis Opera*, vol. XIV, pp. 222–3.

44 Ibid., vol. VIII, pp. 340–41 and vol. XIII, p. 200.

45 Ibid., vol. XIII, pp. 200, 366; Thoren with Christianson,
    Lord of Uraniborg, pp. 443, 466–8.

46 Christianson, *On Tycho's Island*, pp. 297–8, 329, 356–61.

47 Dreyer, *Tychonis Opera*, vol. VIII, pp. 381–2; Stieve, 'Rudolf II',
    p. 100. Manfred Staudinger, *Documenta Rudolphina*, http://
    documenta.rudolphina.org, accessed 16 May 2018.

48 Peder Hansen Resen, *Inscriptiones haffnienses Latinæ danicæ et Germanicæ
    unà cum inscriptionibus amagriensibus Uraniburgicis et Stellæburgicis*
    (Copenhagen, 1668), p. 351.

49 Nicholas Jardine, *The Birth of History and Philosophy of Science: Kepler's
    A Defense of Tycho Against Ursus with Essays on Its Provenance and Significance*
    (Cambridge and New York, 1984), pp. 20–28; Edward Rosen,
    'Kepler's Defense of Tycho against Ursus', *Popular Astronomy*, LIV
    (1946), pp. 405–12; Edward Rosen, *Three Imperial Mathematicians:
    Kepler Trapped Between Tycho Brahe and Ursus* (New York, 1981);
    Nicholas Jardine et al., 'Tycho v. Ursus: The Build-up to a Trial,
    Parts 1 & 2', *Journal for the History of Astronomy*, XXXVI (2005),
    pp. 81–106 and 125–65; Jardine and Segonds, *La Guerre
    des Astronomes*; Thoren with Christianson, *Lord of Uraniborg*,
    pp. 459–61.

50 Juan D. Serrano, 'Trying Ursus: A Reappraisal of the Tycho-Ursus
    Priority Dispute', *Journal for the History of Astronomy*, XLIV (2013),
    pp. 17–46.

51 Jardine, *The Birth*, p. 144.

52 Ibid.; Robert S. Westman, *The Copernican Question: Prognostication,
    Skepticism, and Celestial Order* (Berkeley and Los Angeles, CA, and
    London, 2011), pp. 305–35.

53 Jardine, *The Birth*, p. 146.

54 Ibid., pp. 206–7.

55 Christianson, *On Tycho's Island*, p. 367.

56 Dreyer, *Tychonis Opera*, vol. XIV, p. 217; F. R. Friis, *Nogle Efterretninger
    om Tyge Brahe og hans Familie* (Copenhagen, 1902), pp. 21–2.

57 Dreyer, *Tychonis Opera*, vol. VIII, pp. 398–9; Wilhelm Norlind,
    Tycho Brahe, mannen och verket, efter Gassendi översatt med kommentar
    (Lund, 1951), pp. 334–5.

58 Christianson, *On Tycho's Island*, pp. 268, 273–6, 319–21, 339–40,
    356–7.

59 Dreyer, *Tychonis Opera*, vol. XIII, pp. 200, 253–82; Cf. Thoren with
    Christianson, *Lord of Uraniborg*, pp. 446–7.

60 Dreyer, *Tychonis Opera*, vol. XIV, p. 218, 221; Thoren with
    Christianson, *Lord of Uraniborg*, p. 517.

61 Dreyer, *Tychonis Opera*, vol. XIV, pp. 218–32; Thoren with
    Christianson, *Lord of Uraniborg*, p. 512.

62 Wilhelm Norlind, *Tycho Brahe: En levnadsteckning med nya bidrag belysande
    hans liv och verk* (Lund, 1970), pp. 311–13.

63 Caspar, *Kepler*, p. 121.

64 Thoren with Christianson, *Lord of Uraniborg*, p. 451.

65 Thoren with Christianson, *Lord of Uraniborg*, pp. 453–5.

66 Petrus Gassendus, *Tychonis Brahe, Equitis Dani, Astronomorum Coryphæi, Vita* (The Hague, 1655), p. 177.

67 Aleš Stejskal, 'At the Court Table of Petr Svamberg: Renaissance Banquet Regulations', trans. Kathleen Hay, *Cour d'honneur: Castles, Palaces, Stately Homes*, 3 (Prague, 1999), pp. 29–31.

68 Johannes Kepler, *Tychonis Brahei Dani Hyperaspistes, adversvs Scipionis Claramontii* (Frankfurt am Main, 1625): 'honoris causa nominandum mihi video, Illustrem & Generosum D. Ericum Brahe Suecum . . . cuius in vlnis; aspectante me, summus vir expirauit'.

69 Dreyer, *Tychonis Opera*, vol. XIII, p. 283; Thoren with Christianson, *Lord of Uraniborg*, p. 468–9.

70 Caspar, *Kepler*, pp. 122–3.

71 Martha List, *Der handschriftliche Nachlaß der Astronomen Johannes Kepler und Tycho Brahe* (Munich, 1961), p. 8.

72 The undocumented assertion that Tycho was poisoned has been refuted by pathological evidence from the 2010 exhumation of his remains, see Kacki et al., 'Rich table'; Cf. Edv. Gotfredsen, 'Tycho Brahes sidste sygdom og død', *Fund og Forskning*, 2 (1955), pp. 33–8; Dreyer, *Tychonis Opera*, vol. XIV, pp. 233–41, cf. 243–5.

73 Gassendus, *Tychonis Brahe*, pp. 235–42; Hans Wieland, trans. and ed., *Keplers Elegie In obitum Tychonis Brahe*, Nova Kepleriana, Neue Folge, Heft 8 (Munich, 1992).

74 J. R. Christianson, 'Tycho Brahe's Personality', manuscript presented to a seminar on the island of Hven, 2–5 March 2003.

75 Sinapius, *Des Schlesischen Adels*, p. 621; Štambuch Tychona Braha ml., http://v2.manuscriptorium.com, accessed 12 June 2018, fol. 28r, 118r, 142r, 145r; Martin Ruland, *De Morbo Vngarico recte cognoscendo et foeliciter curando* (Leipzig, 1610), pp. 697–8.

76 Christianson, *On Tycho's Island*, pp. 263–4, 311–12; Peter Zeeberg, *Tycho Brahes Urania Titani* (Copenhagen, 1994), pp. 281–96.

77 Lauritz Nielsen, *Tycho Brahes Bogtrykkeri* (Copenhagen, 1946), pp. 68–9.

78 Kepler, *Gesammelte Werke*, vol. X, p. 18*; Voelkel, *The Composition*, p. 145.

79 Dreyer, *Tychonis Opera*, vol. III, pp. 300–323.

80 Ibid., vol. XIV, pp. 251–2, 254–5, 265; Friis, *Efterretninger,* p. 22. August von Doerr, *Der Adel der böhmischen Kronländer* (Prague, 1900), pp. 72–3, does not list them as granted Bohemian nobility in 1603.

81 Kepler, *Gesammelte Werke*, vol. XIX, pp. 50–51; Documents in Prague Castle Archives, Dvorská komora, Karton 5, Nr. 664, and Vienna, Austrian State Archives, Alte Hofkammer, Hoffinanz, Band 573-R, 567-E, 571-R, cited in www.documenta.rudolphina.org, accessed 16 June 2018.

82 Dreyer, *Tychonis Opera*, vol. XIV, pp. 247–54; Anton Schimon, *Der Adel von Böhmen, Mähren und Schlesien* (Česká Lipá, 1859), p. 14.

83 Dreyer, *Tychonis Opera*, vol. XIV, pp. 256–7; List, *Der handschriftliche Nachlaß*, p. 9.

84 Voelkel, *The Composition*; List, *Der handschriftliche Nachlaß*, p. 9.

85 Wilson, *Thirty Years War*, pp. 269–308, 347–61; Anton Chroust, *Vom Einfall des Passauer Kriegsvolks bis zum Nürnberg Kurfürstentag* (Munich, 1903), pp. 606, 670; Kachlik et al., 'Jesensky', pp. 159–61.

86 Adrien Baillet, *La vie de Monsieur Descartes*, vol. I (Paris, 1691), pp. 73–6.

87 Anton von Braunmühl, *Christoph Scheiner als Mathematiker, Physiker und Astronom* (Bamberg, 1891), pp. 38, 53–6; Heinrich Schreiber, *Geschichte der Albert-Ludwigs-Universität zu Freiburg im Breisgau, II. Theil* (Freiburg, 1859), pp. 263–5.

88 List, *Der handschriftliche Nachlaß*, pp. 11–13.

89 Braunmühl, *Scheiner*, pp. 53–6, 74–5.

90 Petr Bilek, *Komentovaná bibliografie časopisu Genealogické a heraldické listy v letech 1969–1981,* BA thesis, University of Hradec Králové (Prague, 2014), p. 5, https://theses.cz, accessed 5 July 2018.

91 Friis, *Efterretninger,* p. 27; Dreyer, *Tychonis Opera*, vol. XIV, pp. 189–91, 296.

92 Štambuch Tychona Brahe ml., fol. 3.

93 Michael Spark, *Learned Tico Brahae his Astronomicall Coniecture of the new and much Admired ⋆ Which Appered in the year 1572* (London, 1632).

94 Holger Rørdam, 'Hertug Ulrik, Kong Christian IV's Søn', *Historiske Samlinger og Studier,* II (Copenhagen, 1896), pp. 67–73; C. F. Wegener, ed., 'Brev fra Hertug Ulrik til hans Fader Kong Christian IV, hvorved han oversender denne Tyge Brahes Himmelglobus',

Aarsberetninger fra Det kongelige Geheimearchiv, vol. VI (Copenhagen, 1882), Tillæg, pp. 23–4.

95 Bilek, *Komentovaná bibliografie*, p. 5; Wilson, *Thirty Years War*, pp. 614–15.

96 Dreyer, *Tychonis Opera*, vol. XIV, pp. 307–8; Štambuch Tychona Brahe ml., fol. 3.

97 Dreyer, *Tychonis Opera*, vol. XIV, pp. 298–300; Friis, *Efterretninger*, pp. 31–2, 37–9. Roman Freiherr von Procházka, *Genealogisches Handbuch erloschener böhmischer Herrenstandsfamilien* (Neustadt an der Aisch, 1973), pp. 41–5.

98 Lucius Barettus [Albert Curtius], *Historia Coelestis ex libris commentariis manuscriptis observationum vicennalium viri generosi Tichonis Brahe Dani* (Augsburg, 1666).

99 List, *Der handschriftliche Nachlaß*, p. 23; Dreyer, *Tycho*, pp. 371–4.

100 Holger Fr. Rørdam, *Kjøbenhavns Universitets Historie*, 4 vols (Copenhagen, 1863–74), vol. III, p. 146.

101 Oskar Garstein, *Cort Aslakssøn: Studier over dansk-norsk universitets- og lærdomshistorie omkring år 1600* (Oslo, 1953)

102 Morten Fink-Jensen, *Fornuften under troens lydighed: Naturfilosofi, medicin og teologi i Danmark, 1536–1636* (Copenhagen, 2004).

103 N. D. Haasbroek, *Gemma Frisius, Tycho Brahe and Snellius and their Triangulations* (Delft, 1968), pp. 21–3; Christian Longomontanus, *Introductio in Theatrum Astronomicum* (Copenhagen, 1639), fol. [A3v]-[B4r]; Kristian Peder Moesgaard, 'Astronomi', in *Københavns universitet, 1479–1979*, vol. XII, ed. Mogens Pihl (Copenhagen, 1983), pp. 275–7; Christianson, *On Tycho's Island*, pp. 254–6, 358–61.

104 Villads Villadsen, 'Universitets bygninger', in *Københavns universitet, 1479–1979*, vol. IV, ed. Svend Ellehøj and Leif Grane (Copenhagen, 1980), p. 164.

105 Hugo Johannsen and Claus M. Schmidt, *Danmarks arkitektur: Kirkens huse* (Copenhagen, 1985), p. 135.

106 Jean Picard, *Voyage d'Uranibourg; ou, Observations Astronomiques faites en Dannemarck* (Paris, 1680).

107 [Václav Vladivoj Tomek], *Vortrage des Geschäftsleiters in der General-Versammlung der Gesellschaft des Museums des Königreiches Böhmen am 13. Juni 1868* (Prague, 1868), pp. 4–7.

FURTHER READING

Andersen, Michael, Birgitte Bøggild Johannsen and Hugo Johannsen,
    eds, *Reframing the Danish Renaissance: Problems and Prospects in a European
    Perspective* (Copenhagen, 2011)
Beckett, Francis, and Charles Christensen, *Uraniborg og Stjærneborg*
    (Copenhagen and London, 1921)
Brahe, Tycho, *Instruments of the Renewed Astronomy (Astronomiae Instauratae
    Mechanica)*, ed. and trans. Alena Hadravová, Petr Hadrava and Jole
    R. Schackelford (Prague, 1996)
Christianson, John Robert, *On Tycho's Island: Tycho Brahe and His Assistants,
    1570–1601* (Cambridge and New York, 2000)
—, Alena Hadravová, Petr Hadrava and Martin Šolc, eds,
    Tycho Brahe and Prague: Crossroads of European Science (Frankfurt
    am Main, 2002)
Dobrzycki, Jerzy, ed., *The Reception of Copernicus' Heliocentric Theory*
    (Dordrecht and Boston, MA, 1972)
Dreyer, J.L.E., ed., *Tychonis Brahe Dani Opera Omnia*, 15 vols
    (Copenhagen, 1913–29)
Gingerich, Owen, and Robert S. Westman, *The Wittich Connection:
    Conflict and Priority in Late Sixteenth-century Cosmology* (Philadelphia,
    PA, 1988)
Granada, Miguel A., Adam Mosley and Nicholas Jardine, *Christoph
    Rothmann's Discourse on the Comet of 1585* (Leiden and Boston, MA, 2014)
Grinder-Hansen, Poul, ed., *Tycho Brahes verden: Danmark i Europa 1550–1600*
—, *The World of Tycho Brahe* (Copenhagen, 2006)
Haasbroek, N. D., *Gemma Frisius, Tycho Brahe and Snellius and their
    Triangulations* (Delft, 1968)

Jardine, Nicholas, *The Birth of History and Philosophy of Science: Kepler's
    A defence of Tycho against Ursus, with Essays on its Provenance and Significance*
    (Cambridge, 1984)
—, and Alain-Philippe Segonds, *La guerre des astronomes: La querelle au sujet de
    l'origin du système géo-héliocentrique à la fin du XVIe siècle*, 2 vols (Paris, 2008)
Jern, Carl Henrik, *Uraniborg: Herresäte och himlaborg* (Lund, 1976)
Kusukawa, Sachiko, *The Transformation of Natural Philosophy: The Case
    of Philip Melanchthon* (Cambridge, 1995)
List, Martha, *Der handschriftliche Nachlaß der Astronomen Johannes Kepler
    und Tycho Brahe* (Munich, 1961)
Lockhart, Paul Douglas, *Frederik II and the Protestant Cause:
    Denmark's Role in the Wars of Religion, 1559–1596* (Leiden and
    Boston, MA, 2004)
Lorimer, Hayden, and Charles W. J. Withers, eds, *Geographers:
    Biobibliographical Studies*, vol. XXVII (London and New York, 2008)
Mosley, Adam, *Bearing the Heavens: Tycho Brahe and the Astronomical
    Community of the Late Sixteenth Century* (Cambridge, 2007)
Norlind, Wilhelm, *Tycho Brahe: En levnadsteckning med nya bidrag belysande
    hans liv och verk* (Lund, 1970)
North, John, *Cosmos: An Illustrated History of Astronomy and Cosmology*
    (Chicago, IL, and London, 2008)
Pade, Marianne, ed., *On Renaissance Academies* (Rome, 2011)
Park, Katharine, and Lorraine Daston, eds, *The Cambridge History
    of Science,* vol. III (Cambridge, 2006)
Rosen, Edward, *Three Imperial Mathematicians: Kepler Trapped between
    Tycho Brahe and Ursus* (New York, 1986)
Shackelford, Jole, *A Philosophical Path for Paracelsian Medicine: The Ideas,
    Intellectual Context, and Influence of Petrus Severinus (1540/42–1602)*
    (Copenhagen, 2004)
Thoren, Victor E., with contributions by John Robert Christianson,
    The Lord of Uraniborg: A Biography of Tycho Brahe (Cambridge, 1990)
Voelkel, James R., *The Composition of Kepler's Astronomia Nova* (Princeton,
    NJ, and Oxford, 2001)
Westman, Robert S., *The Copernican Question: Prognostication, Skepticism,
    and Celestial Order* (Berkeley and Los Angeles, CA, and London, 2011)
Zeeberg, Peter, *Tycho Brahes 'Urania Titani', et digt om Sophie Brahe*
    (Copenhagen, 1994)

ACKNOWLEDGEMENTS

A grant by Nationalbanken, the Danish National Bank, allowed me to live in an apartment at Nyhavn 18 in 2016–17, in order to work at the Royal Library and other cultural institutions in and around Copenhagen.

Uffe Gråe Jørgensen of the Niels Bohr Institute, Copenhagen, and Paul Christianson of Queens University, Kingston, Ontario, kindly read the entire manuscript and offered many valuable suggestions.

My work was encouraged and supported in various ways by colleagues including Almási Gábor, Birgitte Bøggild Johannsen, Karsten Gaulke, Christopher M. Graney, Poul Grinder-Hansen, Peter Hvilshøj Andersen-Vinilandicus, Steffen Heiberg, Alan Macdonald, Adam Mosely, Göran Nyström, Ove von Spaeth, Claus Thykier, Chr. Gorm Tortzen, Jens Vellev, Mara Wade, Peter Zeeberg, Mattias Larsson with Stine Nordahn Frederiksen and Nina Petersson at the Tycho Brahe Museum on Hven, and the staffs of the Royal Library (Det Kongelige Bibliotek) in Copenhagen, the Austrian National Library (Österreichische Nationalbibliothek) in Vienna, the Wilson Library and Walter Library at the University of Minnesota, and the Hennepin County Main Library in Minneapolis. This book would not have been possible without Birgitte Christianson, who read the manuscript at several stages, discussed it frequently, offered many wise suggestions, shared all her days with me, and has supported my life, work and well-being in countless ways since 1962.

PHOTO ACKNOWLEDGEMENTS

The author and publishers wish to express their thanks to the below sources of illustrative material and/or permission to reproduce it. Some locations of artworks are also given below, in the interests of brevity:

From Peter Apian, *Cosmographia* (Antwerp, 1564), courtesy John Carter Brown Library, Providence, RI: 9; from Tycho Brahe, *Astronomiæ instavratæ mechanica* (Wandsburg, 1598): 12, 20, 21, 23, 31, 39, 43, 45, 48, 49, 50, 51, 52, 54, 55, 58, 61, 62, 65, 69, 71, 72, 96; from Tycho Brahe, *Astronomiae instavratæ progymnasmata* (Prague, 1602), courtesy Library of Congress, Washington, DC: 16, 17; from Tycho Brahe, *De mundi ætherei recentioribus phænomenis* (Prague, 1603), courtesy Library of Congress, Washington, DC: 25, 38; from Tycho Brahe, *De Nova Stella* [facsimile reprint of the 1573 edition] (Copenhagen, 1901), courtesy Gerstein Library, University of Toronto: 18; from Tycho Brahe and Albert Curtz, ed., *Historia Coelestis*, vol. I (Augsburg, 1666): 93; from Georg Braun and Franz Hogenberg, *Civitates Orbis Terrarum*, vol. IV (Cologne, 1588): 1, 2, 32, 74, 75; John Robert Christianson: 4, 19, 22, 28, 53, 81, 82, 83, 95; collection of the author: 59, 68, 88; from Johann Gabriel Doppelmayr, *Historische Nachricht von den Nurnbergischen Mathematicis und Kunstler* (Nuremberg, 1730), courtesy Universitätsbibliothek Heidelberg: 56; from John Louis Emil Dreyer, *Tychonis Brahe Dani Opera Omnia* (Copenhagen, 1913–29), courtesy Robarts Library, University of Toronto: 34, 35, 47, 66 [vol. VI], 42 [vol. X], 70 [vol. IV]; from Gaspar Ens Lorchensis, *Rerum Danicarum Friderico II* (Frankfurt, 1593), courtesy Österreichischen Nationalbibliothek, Vienna: 46; from Abraham Fischer, *Prospecter af åtskillige märkvärdige Byggnader, Säterier och Herre-Gårdar uti Skåne* (Stockholm, 1756) courtesy Universitetsbiblioteket,

Lund: 14; Galerie J. Kugel, Paris: 24; Gallerie dell'Accademia, Venice: 33; from Henry Green, ed., *Andreae Alciati Emblematum Fontes Quatuor* [with photo-lith facsimiles of the 1531, 1534 and 1546 editions] (Manchester and London, 1870), courtesy Harold B. Lee Library, Brigham Young University, Provo, UT: 30; Det Kongelige Bibliotek, Copenhagen (GKS 1824 4°): 8; Kunsthistorisches Museum, Vienna: 89; from Peter Lindeberg, *Hypotyposis Arcivm, Palatiorum, Librorum, Pyramidum, Obeliscorum, Cipporum, Molarum, Fontium, Monumentorum & Epitaphiorum* (Hamburg, 1591), courtesy Getty Research Institute: 86; from Michael Maier, *Atalanta fugiens, hoc est, Emblemata nova de secretis naturae chymica* (Oppenheim, 1618), courtesy Getty Research Institute: 5; Mathematisch-Physikalischer Salon, Staatliche Kunstsammlungen Dresden/photo John Robert Christianson: 26; from Frederik Vilhelm Berg Meidell, *Bille—Ætten Historie, Anden Del, Første Afsnit* (Copenhagen, 1887): 15; Metropolitan Museum of Art, New York: 7; from Joachim Meyer, *Gründtliche Beschreibung der freyen ritterlichen unnd adelichen Kunst des Fechtens* (Strasbourg, 1570), courtesy Metropolitan Museum of Art, New York: 10; Det Nationalhistoriske Museum på Frederiksborg, Hillerød (inv. nr. A1277): 3; Nationalmuseet, Copenhagen: 63, 76, 85 (photo John Lee); Österreichischen Nationalbibliothek, Vienna: 36, 60, 67; from Andrea Palladio, *I quattro libri dell'architettura* (Venice, 1570), courtesy Metropolitan Museum of Art, New York: 29; from Gregor Reisch, *Margarita philosophica nova* (Strasbourg, 1508), courtesy Boston Public Library: 11; from Johann Adolf Repsold, *Zur Geschichte der astronomischen Messwerkzeuge* (Leipzig, 1908): 27; from Peder Hansen Resen, *Inscriptiones Haffnienses* (Copenhagen, 1668): 97; Rijksmuseum, Amsterdam: 37, 77, 84; Rosenborg Slot, Copenhagen: 13, 64; from Johannes de Sacrobosco, *Libellvs de sphæra* (Wittenberg, 1543), courtesy John Carter Brown Library, Providence, RI: 6; Skokloster Slott, Håbo Municipality (inv. nr. 11593): 87; Statens Museum for Kunst, Copenhagen (inv. nr. KKSGB 5009): 73; Sternwarte Kremsmünster/photo P. Amand Kraml: 91; from Anders Thiset, 'Christen Holcks Stambog', in *Personalhistorisk Tidsskrift*, series 5, vol. 11 (Copenhagen, 1905): 44; Tycho Brahe Museet på Hven: 40, 41; from Ferdinand Verbiest, *Astronomia Europæa, sub Imperatore Tartaro Sinico Cám Hý* (Dillingen, 1687): 98.

Holger Weinandt, the copyright holder of image 57, has published it online under conditions imposed by a Creative Commons Attribution–Share Alike 3.0 Germany license. Zdeněk Fiedler, the copyright holder of image 94; Øyvind Holmstad, the copyright holder of image 92; and Horak Vlado, the copyright holder of image 90, have published them online under conditions imposed by a Creative Commons Attribution–Share Alike 3.0 Unported license.

Readers are free to:

Share – copy and redistribute the material in any medium or format
Adapt – remix, transform, and build upon the material for any purpose, even commercially.

Under the following conditions:

Attribution – You must give appropriate credit, provide a link to the license, and indicate if changes were made. You may do so in any reasonable manner, but not in any way that suggests the licensor endorses you or your use.

Share Alike – If you remix, transform, or build upon the material, you must distribute your contributions under the same license as the original.

INDEX

Illustration numbers are indicated by *italics*.